SIXTY YEARS
A RED
...AND COUNTING!

SIXTY YEARS
A RED
...AND COUNTING!
A Lifetime's Passion

BRIAN BARWICK OBE

Foreword by Jamie Carragher

First published by Pitch Publishing, 2021

Pitch Publishing
A2 Yeoman Gate
Yeoman Way
Worthing
Sussex
BN13 3QZ
www.pitchpublishing.co.uk
info@pitchpublishing.co.uk

ISBN 978 1 78531 980 8

Typesetting and origination by Pitch Publishing
Printed and bound in Great Britain by TJ Books Ltd, Padstow

Contents

Acknowledgements   11

Foreword by Jamie Carragher   13

1961/62 … It Is in the Blood   15

1962/63 – Last-Gasp Glory   21

1963/64 – Panorama and The Kop   25

1964/65 – Ice and Fire   30

1965/66 – Life in the Big League   37

1966/67 – A Hunt for the Biggest Prize   42

1967/68 – Going for a Song   47

1968/69 – The Blonde Bombshell   51

1969/70 – Change Is in the Air   55

1970/71 – Shankly's New Army   60

1971/72 – A Star Is Born   65

1972/73 – Get the Silver Polish Out!   69

1973/74 – Shankly's Own Wembley Wizards   74

1974/75 – Shock Waves and Still Waters   80

1975/76 – A Modest Success   85

1976/77 – European Glory   91

1977/78 – The Scottish Spine   97

1978/79 – Another Trophy in Another Haul   103

1979/80 – Departures and a Dream Job   108

1980/81 – Winners and Wine Gums 113

1981/82 – The Changing of the Guard 119

1982/83 – Cups and Caps 125

1983/84 – Smokin' Joe and a Roman Holiday 130

1984/85 – Heysel 135

1985/86 – At the Double 140

1986/87 – Not in a Rush 146

1987/88 – Liverpool's Five-Star B & B 151

1988/89 – Hillsborough 157

1989/90 – Kop That! And Cop That! 163

1990/91 – King Kenny Steps Out 168

1991/92 – A Silver Lining 173

1992/93 – Form Dips and Royal VIPs 178

1993/94 – The Kop's Last Stand 185

1994/95 – The Young Ones 190

1995/96 – Armani's White Army 194

1996/97 – The Magnificent Seven 200

1997/98 – The Macca and Mo Show 206

1998/99 – Bienvenue Gérard, Adieu Roy 212

1999/2000 – Out with Old, in with the New 217

2000/01 – Time for a Treble! 222

2001/02 – A Sense of Perspective 230

2002/03 – The French Connection 236

2003/04 – Gérard and Gerrard 241

2004/05 – Lift Off! 246

2005/06 – Football Royalty 254

2006/07 – The Wild West 261

2007/08 – Liverpool's Number Nine! 267

2008/09 – Oh, Not Chelsea Again!?! 273

2009/10 – All Hat, No Cattle 279

2010/11 – High Noon and Hi Kenny! 284

2011/12 – The Flawed Little Genius 290

2012/13 – Ambitions Realised! 297

2013/14 – Many a Slip 303

2014/15 – One of a Kind 310

2015/16 – The Perfect Fit 315

2016/17 – This is Anfield 321

2017/18 – Second Is Nowhere 325

2018/19 – A Season of the Extraordinary 332

2019/20 – Champions!!!! 339

2020/21 – Alisson in Wonderland 345

One for the Road 351

To Gerry, Jack and Joe – my very own Firmino, Mané and Salah.

ACKNOWLEDGEMENTS

FIRSTLY, CAN I thank Jamie Carragher for so generously providing the foreword for the book. I am so pleased his brilliant career at Liverpool FC has subsequently been followed up with an outstanding new professional life as an informed and respected football pundit across the breadth of modern media.

I would also like to thank football statisticians, Dave Ball and Ged Rea for their sterling fact-checking work on each season's contents. Their knowledge of the subject matter is quite extraordinary, and slightly unnerving. And it has kept me on my toes!

My much-valued colleague, Michelle Gibson, has been a huge source of encouragement and support – and she has also helped me stick to the publisher's guidelines and tidied up my occasional offbeat English grammar.

Paul and Jane Camillin of Pitch are both delightful people to deal with, and have given me regular positive thumbs ups during the writing of the book. Thank you for giving me the opportunity to time-travel with my favourite football club.

And thanks also to Duncan Olner for his work on designing the book's front and back covers, which give a real sense of what lies on the pages between them.

I have a collection of thousands of programmes and around 200 books on or about Liverpool FC, and the personalities who've been the living, breathing history of this world-famous football club, and I have dipped into many of them to remind me of 'what happened when' – and have also used some of the modern dedicated websites to do some more of the 'memory refreshing' needed to write a book of this nature. So, thank you.

Of course, it would be remiss of me not to thank all the managers, players, figureheads and senior executives from Liverpool Football Club who have passed through my professional and personal life over many years, and that have given me the confidence, knowledge and first-hand experience of this world-famous sporting institution to write a book of this kind.

Finally, much love and thanks go to my wife, Gerry, for her love, encouragement and patience! We first met when I was producing short films for BBC TV's *Football Focus* in the early 1980s. She was a BBC film editor. We have now been married for nearly four decades – but this book will help her catch up on the adventures of my favourite club in the two decades before I met her!

And, finally, thank you to the readers, for taking the trouble to spend some time with me through the pages that lie before you. Much appreciated.

Brian Barwick OBE
(July 2021)

FOREWORD BY
JAMIE CARRAGHER

IT IS quite a sobering thought that I scored my first goal in my first league start for Liverpool over 24 years ago.

Brian Barwick was at that match, and had already been watching his beloved Reds for 36 years by then – and that's a sobering thought for him!

Brian has been in and around the Anfield scene all his life. He grew up a Red, and as a schoolboy had his own regular spec in the Paddock before moving on to the Kop in his teens. Like many Liverpool fans, he was in awe of Bill Shankly, and grew up cheering on heroes like Roger Hunt, Ian St John and Ron Yeats. He followed Bob Paisley's hugely successful side and was there to see Emlyn Hughes lift the European Cup in Rome. And he has been at every European final since.

His working life at BBC TV Sport, ITV Sport and the Football Association has given him a privileged insight into how the football and broadcasting industries work, but his book also explains the delicate balance he has had to play in those roles in terms of professional objectivity and his personal passion for the Reds.

Now heading for a well-earned retirement, he does point out that when he was at the FA, Liverpool did win the UEFA

Champions League, the UEFA Super Cup, the FA Cup, the FA Community Shield and the FA Youth Cup – twice!

Brian has been a trusted and respected figure in broadcasting and sport for over 40 years, and recently received an OBE in the 2021 New Year Honours list. This book reflects 60 years of following the fortunes of his favourite team – the highs and lows. As well as tracking the club's progress from the Second Division to European glory, he gives his own take on the players, the teams, the managers, the matches, the rivals in an absorbing way.

When I retired from football and started my new career in broadcasting, Brian kindly contacted me and gave me a few tips – one of which was 'Don't hit every ball for six!' I stuck to that maxim until the idea of the European Super League was dropped on us!

Brian is a Red through and through. What I didn't know was that he also gave a certain Mr Gary Neville his first break in TV too!

Enjoy this fascinating and unique journey of a Liverpool fan who celebrates six decades of following his favourite football team.

1961/62 ... IT IS IN THE BLOOD

THERE ARE many ways in which the strength, quality and depth of devotion to your favourite football club can be measured. It has always been the stuff of a good pub debate or playground argument. Who is the better supporter? And why?

One person's undying loyalty to their team is another person's casual pastime. One person's 'never miss a match' is another person's 'never miss them when they're on the telly'. One fan's connection to their team is seminal to their well-being; another uses it as a convenient icebreaker at a party.

Some follow their team to the ends of the earth; others follow their progress from the comfort of their favourite armchair. Some live and breathe their heroes from cradle to grave; others knock it on the head with a dismissive 'they're all paid too much money these days anyway'.

Some fans would sell their car to get a ticket for a big game, whilst others would sell their ticket to get the car! There are those who would never be seen *not* wearing their team's colours – while some others wouldn't be seen dead in them.

There are no rules, nor do there need to be. Some people proudly say they know where they fit on the club loyalty 'chart'. Others have long stopped caring. Some only sing 'when they're winning'; others don't even know the words to the songs. And, of course, the ways to follow your chosen team have expanded over the years, with the likes of cheap air travel, global broadcasting and social media adding greater opportunities and choices to the ways you can express that all-important support for your club.

It is no longer about cutting your fixture list out of the newspaper and working out how many games you will get to see – it may be more about how many sports channels you can afford to subscribe to.

One thing is for certain: you cannot start following your team until you are born! Then the slow burn to becoming a passionate or a 'part-time' supporter begins. Or the preset propaganda plugs in exceedingly early. The decision may be made for you – generations of your family will expect you to follow where they have already been.

And that's how it was for me, born 21 June 1954, in a city almost defined by its love of the beautiful game – Liverpool. A city with an unquenchable appetite for football, with clubs who have ruled the roost at special times in their illustrious histories, with famous players, legendary managers, unforgettable matches and special stadiums – all part of a wonderful tapestry woven over the last 130 years or so.

I popped up after the end of the 1953/54 season – a unique one, with Liverpool being relegated to the Second Division and Everton promoted to the First Division. Not a very auspicious start for what turned out to be a lifetime's passion.

Overall, the 1950s was a decade of underachievement for Liverpool – starting with an FA Cup Final defeat against Arsenal, then some embarrassing FA Cup losses against lower opposition, including non-league Worcester City, a perennial failure to be promoted back to the First Division season after season, a record defeat and a record post-war low home league attendance of only 11,976.

Having been relegated as the bottom team in the First Division, the club's fortunes continued to slide in the 1954/55 season – beaten 9-1 by Birmingham City, they ended the campaign with a 6-1 hammering at Rotherham, finishing a club-record low 11th in the Second Division.

Over the next six seasons, with a lack of crucial investment in the team, and a playing staff that boasted bloated quantity over real quality, promotion remained tantalisingly out of reach – third, third, fourth, fourth, third and third in an era when only the first two teams went up.

During this decade, Liverpool did have a hero – Scotsman Billy Liddell, a magnificent one-club man who was also at times a one-man forward line. 'Liddellpool', as the Reds would often be dubbed. Mild-mannered Liddell would combine learning accountancy with adding to his goal tally week by week, his fearsome shooting prowess being one of his standout abilities.

Billy would play 534 games for Liverpool and score 228 goals. He was one of the club's special players – somebody who could comfortably sit alongside Sir Kenny Dalglish and Steven Gerrard as all-time Liverpool greats.

I only ever saw him play once in a testimonial match at South Liverpool in 1967. Mind you, it was a proper contest – Hungary and Real Madrid's Ferenc Puskás captained the opposition.

If Billy Liddell was Liverpool's immediate post-war star man, it was a fellow Scotsman who joined the club in December 1959 that sent the club into orbit.

His name was Bill Shankly. His name will be threaded like a golden ribbon throughout this book but his contribution to Liverpool Football Club's change of status cannot be matched.

His forceful, energetic, engaging, persuasive style took the club and its directors, players and supporters on a remarkable journey in his 15-year reign as manager. And 'reign' is probably the right description for this humble son of Glenbuck, Ayrshire. He made a tight-fisted Liverpool board that lacked ambition back his judgement in buying players, had those players run through brick walls for him, and had supporters who hung on his every word.

As Liddell stepped out of the limelight, Shankly stepped into it. The Scotsman's first full season, 1960/61, ended with the Reds finishing third – again. But at the end of that season and during the close-season break, Shankly's persistence in wanting to improve the quality of his squad saw him land two fellow Scotsmen, Ian St John from Motherwell and Ron Yeats from Dundee United.

Expensive but essential, St John and Yeats became pivotal figures in helping move Liverpool – the club and the team – from the mundane to the magnificent. Star man Shankly had set Liverpool on a path to promotion and beyond.

The 1961/62 season finally delivered the Reds that vital step back into the big time in English football. They won ten of their first 11 league games, scoring 31 goals and conceding only four in the process. They were scoring goals for fun – Roger Hunt would end the season with 41 league goals, and a trip to the 1962 World Cup in Chile. The Reds ended the season having notched 99 league goals and 105 in total.

This was the season I made my first matchday trips to Anfield as a seven-year-old schoolboy.

My dad was a keen Liverpudlian but his work in the Merseyside police force often meant he was working at the matches rather than watching from the terraces.

Anyway, there was an obvious yet important choice to make first. Liverpool or Everton? Red or Blue? Two teams in the city – which was to be mine? I'm not completely sure why I ended up a Red. My dad followed them but not with a huge passion. I do have faint memories of wearing a sleeveless, V-necked, red football shirt as a young infant.

Perhaps the dye was cast. I now speak as somebody who always buys red toothbrushes, drives a red car and, in my early 20s, was the proud owner of a pair of bright red shoes, until my boss told me to dress more appropriately in the office.

Moving on. I do not think anybody can be sure when they saw their first match. Especially, if it was when you were still in short trousers, your bedtime was eight o'clock and your favourite TV programme was *Four Feather Falls*, but everything points to 28 October – Liverpool v Leyton Orient – being my first visit to Anfield to see the Reds play for real. I still have the programme from the game, along with thousands of others now, and scrawled on its front cover is the final score – 3-3.

I now know it is sacrilege to write on the front of a football programme – 'sof' (score on front) as avid collectors disapprovingly describe it. Anyway, 3-3 it was, and two goals by Roger Hunt and a late equaliser from Tommy Leishman secured a point against the London side, who would finish runners-up behind Liverpool in the table.

After the game, my dad and I dropped in for some tea at my auntie's house which was situated on the junction of Anfield Road and Priory Road – just a long throw-in from the stadium itself.

Before the end of the season, I went to Anfield again to see Liverpool play Preston North End. Despite having Ian St John (and Preston defender Tony Singleton) sent off, it turned out a 4-1 win for the Reds, over a team they had played five times during the season, including a three-match FA Cup saga which the Lancastrian side ultimately won.

Starring for Preston in those games was a young winger called Peter Thompson. Shankly had seen enough of the tricky flank man in that series of matches to sign him ahead of the

1963/64 campaign. Peter Thompson would be a special talent for Liverpool over the next nine seasons – and become one of my favourite players. St John's suspension meant he was not on duty when Liverpool secured their place back in the First Division with a 2-0 win over Southampton at a sodden Anfield in April. Two first-half goals from the Scotsman's replacement, Kevin Lewis, sent Liverpool up on a day when the heavens opened above Anfield.

It rained and rained and rained. But whilst the day was grey and dismal, and the crowd figure of 40,410 seriously affected by the atrocious weather, the after-match scenes of celebration were memorable. Literally singing in the rain.

Liverpool were back in the big time – and I was about to go on a lifetime's journey with them.

It would involve huge highs, the odd devastating low; a bus ride, a train journey or an overseas flight – a vast number of passport stamps, scrapbooks, programmes, tickets and autographs. It would take me up the road and around the world. I would meet many of my heroes and rarely be disappointed.

For a spell, my professional life would give me an 'access all areas' to life at Anfield and yet I never lost some of a real fan's wonderment. And it was a journey that still is ongoing – a constant pleasure in what's been a fast-moving life. Millions of memories spread over 60 years. Red toothbrushes, red cars, red shoes – and a red scarf and bobble hat to get it all started.

Off we go.

Kop That – *Bill Shankly saw only three of his fellow countrymen capped in his time at Anfield: Tommy Lawrence, Ron Yeats and Ian St John were the spine of his team, but they amassed just 19 caps whilst on Merseyside.*

1962/63 – LAST-GASP GLORY

ON SATURDAY, 22 September 1962, Merseyside came to a complete standstill. After 11 barren seasons when one or the other was out of the top division, Liverpool and Everton were finally locking horns again in a league derby match.

FA Cup and local cup competitions had kept the flame flickering as the city's fervent fans craved for the return of the seasonal double-header with their nearest rivals.

When Liverpool were promoted back into the big league in 1961/62, it was 'game on' again.

And so a massive crowd of over 73,000 crammed into Goodison Park on a sunny September afternoon to witness Ron Yeats and Roy Vernon, the two teams' respective captains, defying established convention by running out alongside each other with their fired-up team-mates behind them. It was an occasion to savour.

Everton had the ball in the Liverpool net within the very first minute when Roy Vernon took advantage of a nervous mistake by Jim Furnell in the Liverpool goal, and slid the ball home. This effort was controversially disallowed for a foul on the Reds keeper. Lucky Liverpool.

The Toffees did take the lead though, this time referee Kevin Howley adjudging full-back Gerry Byrne to have handled in the penalty area, and Vernon coolly slotted the ball home from the spot. Liverpool hit back as Kevin Lewis, a scorer of important goals and a late replacement for the injured Ian St John, neatly converted an Ian Callaghan cross. Into the second half and Everton were back in front when Johnny Morrissey, the recent subject of a rare transfer between the clubs, joyously scored despite Ronnie Moran's best efforts to clear it off the line. No goal-line technology back then.

Everton seemed destined to take the honours, and, with it, the local bragging rights in this much-anticipated renewal of a very private, keenly fought sporting rivalry. However, there was one more late twist, as in the final minute A'Court and Lewis combined to give Roger Hunt a chance to dramatically square things up for the Reds. He duly obliged.

For those unable to get a ticket, or gathered outside the stadium following the pitch-and-toss of the game by the respective roars of the crowd, salvation came by the way of a short set of edited highlights on BBC TV's *Saturday Sport*, a forerunner of the iconic *Match of the Day*.

Even the programme slot in the schedules, 10.15pm, had a ring of familiarity about it, but it was on too late for this eight-year-old. And there were no recordings or repeats in those days. Bah!

Mind you, I had enjoyed my own first slice of Merseyside derby action that afternoon as one of the 4,142 fans who went to Anfield to watch Liverpool Reserves play Everton Reserves in the mini-derby, as it was then coined.

Part of the experience of becoming a senior Liverpool player was a healthy stint in the club's reserve team for many young hopefuls – and so it was for young supporters as well. You served your time both as a player and a fan. The odd first-team match but a steady run of reserve games under your belt. And so it was Anfield, not Goodison Park, for me and my dad on that particular September afternoon.

The official programme, a single sheet, cost one old penny, and the two team line-ups gave a hint of things to come. Interestingly too, Kevin Lewis, one of the Liverpool heroes over Stanley Park in the big game, was down in the original line-up to play for the reserves that afternoon.

Tommy Lawrence was in goal for Liverpool Reserves and a young Chris Lawler played at centre-half. Both would go on to enjoy long careers in the senior team, whilst Everton's selection included Derek Temple, who would famously score the winning goal for the Blues in their 1966 FA Cup Final win over Sheffield Wednesday. On the day, Liverpool Reserves came out on top 2-0 with goals from Alf Arrowsmith and George Scott.

The 1962/63 season was best remembered for falling victim to an unprecedented harsh winter. Football, and life in general, came to a complete halt. There was snow, snow and more snow. Liverpool played Blackburn Rovers on 22 December and didn't play again in the league until 13 February, some six weeks later.

They had managed to play two FA Cup ties in January, first beating Wrexham in the third round in front of nearly 30,000 football-starved fans at the Racecourse Ground. Then the Reds were drawn away to Burnley, who were the previous year's beaten finalists, and who had subsequently avenged that defeat by Tottenham Hotspur with a third-round win on an ice rink of a pitch at White Hart Lane. The first match between the two Lancashire sides was a 1-1 draw with Kevin Lewis once again on target for the Reds.

The replay at Anfield fell victim to a frozen pitch on its scheduled date, much to Bill Shankly's annoyance, but when the match was eventually staged, some 25 days after the original contest, a massive 57,906 crowd at Anfield watched a pulsating match, eventually won in the final minute of extra time by a penalty taken by Ronnie Moran. It was a massive goal, scored in a massive game in front of a massive crowd. A very quiet crowd.

Moran later reflected that he sensed that Anfield had suddenly fallen completely silent as he placed the ball on the penalty spot in front of a packed Kop. He took aim and his spot kick narrowly passed the outstretched right arm of the Burnley goalkeeper, Adam Blacklaw. 2-1. The crowd went from silent to full blast. A famous winning goal, earning the headline in the *Liverpool Echo* 'The Thrill of a Lifetime', complete with a very rare colour photo of the memorable last-gasp moment.

The Reds would go on to reach the semi-final of the FA Cup that season before losing to bogey team, Leicester City, 1-0. It was a tight game and Leicester's England goalkeeper, Gordon Banks, produced save after save.

A post-match photograph seeming to frame Banks, and some of his victorious Leicester team-mates, laughing at a distraught Ian St John was later recognised as a 'trick of the camera shot'. As years passed, Banks would ultimately be treated as one of the Reds' most worthy opponents and treated with a hero's welcome by the knowledgeable Liverpool crowd.

The 1962/63 season would end with Everton as league champions and their arch-rivals across Stanley Park ready to make their next big step towards major success.

Kop That *– Liverpool's scorers in that derby, Kevin Lewis and Roger Hunt, were the only players to top the club's scorers lists in the 60s: Lewis on one occasion, whilst Hunt's nine occasions included a club-record eight in succession.*

1963/64 – PANORAMA
AND THE KOP

BACK IN 1987 I set about making a full-length film documentary on the history of Liverpool Football Club. Having worked for a nearly a decade in BBC TV Sport I knew just how much great material existed on the famous football club – some very familiar to fans, and some not. Some regularly broadcast, some gathering dust in rusting film cans or on countless shelves of old video tapes.

Part of producing *The Official History of Liverpool FC* was unearthing the odd gem – and certainly the BBC archive gave us every chance of doing just that. And that is how we hit on that marvellous excerpt from a BBC TV *Panorama* programme screened in April 1964. That week's edition was called 'Liverpool – The Most Talked-About City in Europe'.

The much-acclaimed current affairs show, still running today, sent reporter, John Morgan, and a BBC film crew, to capture the Kop in full voice on the day the Reds were destined to clinch their first title since 1946/47. It was Liverpool's last home match of the season – and beating visitors Arsenal would secure that much sought-after league championship win.

Merseyside was absolutely flying. Around two million people had watched reigning league champions Everton and would-be successors Liverpool that season in their two famous grounds separated by Stanley Park.

But it wasn't just on the football field that the city was absolutely on fire. The Mersey Sound led by the incomparable Fab Four, The Beatles, was a smash hit the world over – and, as well as John, Paul, George and Ringo creating hit after hit, many of the city's other bands and singers were also having huge chart success week in, week out in this extraordinary period of pop-music history. And Liverpool comedians like the maestro, Ken Dodd, and a young Jimmy Tarbuck were also playing to sold-out theatres nationwide and making their name on peak-time television. It was an incredibly good time to be a Scouser.

In that context *Panorama* was there on Merseyside to capture some of the added euphoria from a potential title-winning occasion at Anfield that Saturday afternoon. Indeed, the short feature turned out to be as much about the Kop as the match itself:

'The gladiators enter the arena – the field of praise – Saturday's weather perfect for an historic Scouse occasion.'

'An anthropologist studying this Kop crowd would be introduced into as rich and mystifying popular culture as any South Sea island.'

'Their rhythmic swaying is an elaborate and organised ritual.'

Such colourful prose flowed from John Morgan, a seasoned BBC reporter more akin to describing political intrigue or from overseas war zones, and the Kop put on a memorable virtuoso performance from its growing 'playlist' to accompany the Reds' 5-0, five-star, performance over Arsenal. The title secured on the pitch and captured thankfully on film, but undoubtedly the feature's real stars were the 28,000 faces and voices on the world's most famous terrace.

Their prematch renditions of the likes of Cilla Black's 'Anyone Who Had A Heart' and The Beatles' 'She Loves

You' carried the extra flourish and intensity of respecting the music of 'one of their own'. Of course, the song that became an anthem for the club, and still follows them majestically wherever they go, 'You'll Never Walk Alone', would have also been part of the 'ritual'. That special song began its life in a Rodgers and Hammerstein Broadway musical, *Carousel*, which later became a much-loved film.

And, at the height of the popularity of the Merseybeat revolution, one of the Cavern's other favourite groups, Gerry and the Pacemakers, turned the big emotional number into their third straight chart-topper in 1963. Played as part of a prematch 'Top Ten' countdown on the new public address system at Anfield, it struck a chord with the legions on the Kop – and has become part of the club's DNA ever since.

The BBC *Panorama* feature was one of the highlights in the *Official History* documentary, originally released on VHS, and I have seen excerpts of the BBC film used many, many times since, when subsequent TV and film-makers used its footage to illustrate some of the features that make Liverpool, the club, special, and the Anfield crowd something unique.

The Kop, with its remarkable ability to drive its heroes forward with an atmosphere conceived and conjured up on its own, would go on to also unnerve many a famous opponent in the future.

Liverpool had won the 1963/64 league title with three matches to spare – and that despite inexplicably losing their first three home matches of the season. But it was another three matches, played in four days over the Easter period, that helped set up Bill Shankly and his team's triumphant title win. These days, team managers would go absolutely apoplectic if asked to play two games on successive days, never mind a third two days later, and with roughly the same set of 11 players – no vast first-team squad or substitutes in those days remember.

But these were different days. And clubs just got on and dealt with it. And so did the fans.

I remember at Easter 1968 going to Anfield to watch the Reds play Sheffield United on Good Friday and Sunderland on the following day. Interestingly, 50,000 watched the first game, and 10,000 less the following day.

Back in March 1964, Liverpool's three Easter fixtures looked formidable – Tottenham Hotspur away on Good Friday, bogey team Leicester City at Filbert Street the following day and the reverse fixture with Spurs at Anfield on Easter Monday. The previous season's Easter fixtures between the Reds and Spurs had resulted in a goal fest, Liverpool 5-2 winners at Anfield on Good Friday, the London side retaliating with a 7-2 win at White Hart Lane on Easter Monday.

This time it was Liverpool who took the honours at the Londoners' ground on Good Friday – Roger Hunt scoring a hat-trick in a 3-1 win. He was on target again the following day when he opened the scoring against Leicester City in a game that ultimately finished 2-0 to the Reds.

On Easter Monday, Spurs were put to the sword, 3-1 again, a St John double helping the Reds to a maximum return from their crowded Easter programme.

It helped haul themselves to the top of the First Division, and in doing, knocking Everton off the top spot. And those three wins had only involved using 12 players, Chris Lawler deputising for captain Ron Yeats at Spurs and Leicester. Just for good measure, five days later the Reds beat fellow title challengers Manchester United 3-0 to firm up their place at the top of the table. Their win over Arsenal on that sunny April Saturday afternoon completed a run of seven wins on the trot – it was championship-winning form.

After the match, the Liverpool players did a lap of honour in front of a delirious Anfield crowd and then gathered at the front of the directors' box to receive further acclaim from the fans. Only one thing was missing – the actual league championship trophy itself. Instead, Ron Yeats held aloft a papier mâché replica given to him by a supporter. It remains a much-loved element of that famous day.

It was an occasion without the live multimedia coverage of the modern era, but captured for posterity by a BBC film crew, and narrated by a spellbound reporter, John Morgan, standing directly in front of the Kop as they sang their heads off and cascaded in waves down the terraces towards him.

'Before the Battle of Waterloo, the Duke of Wellington said of his own troops, I don't know what they do to the enemy but by God they frighten me!'

Morgan's next assignment for BBC's *Panorama* had a lot to live up to.

Kop That – *Four of the 17 players utilised in that season's league campaign made only 11 appearances in total, with goalkeeper Jim Furnell retuning to Anfield with new club Arsenal, where he conceded five goals in the title clincher.*

1964/65 – ICE AND FIRE

FROM VAST volcanoes spitting lava and flames into the cool arctic air, to a Latin cauldron sending flares and fireworks into a red-hot Italian sky. Those were the two eye-catching bookends to one of the most important seasons in the rich and vibrant history of Liverpool Football Club.

The 1964/65 campaign remains iconic. The Reds finally won the FA Cup for the very first time, a much overdue achievement, igniting wild celebrations on Merseyside. A long and frustrating wait was over. In a season of firsts, champions Liverpool's opening home league game with Arsenal was chosen to launch a new BBC TV Saturday evening football show – the first-ever *Match of the Day*.

Screened at 6.30pm on shiny new BBC Two, the programme could only be seen in London, and there were twice as many people in Anfield that afternoon as watched this landmark programme go to air.

In the same month, Liverpool made their debut in the European Cup – an adventure that included one of Shankly's men's most famous wins and one of their most controversial defeats. Liverpool had been drawn against minnows, Iceland's Reykjavík, in the first round of the European Cup. The journey to the first leg started with a Sunday flight to London and then on to Prestwick Airport in Scotland, then via Renfrew Airport onwards to the Icelandic capital. As the plane carrying the Liverpool party neared Iceland the pilot took a short aerial detour over an active volcano, which was dramatically spitting out lava and flames from its deep cavernous foundations.

If that was a unique experience for the recently crowned English champions, so was the 24-hour daylight. The football match itself proved to be routine stuff. Gordon Wallace scored the Reds' first-ever goal in European competition after just three minutes in a 5-0 romp. The same player had scored the opener in the previous Saturday's Charity Shield game against West Ham and would score two goals in *Match of the Day*'s premiere the following weekend.

If Liverpool's first leg in the European Cup was straightforward, the second leg proved even easier – 6-1 the final score. The biggest cheer from the Kop that night came when Reykjavík scored a consolation goal, the Liverpool fans playfully booing their Anfield heroes throughout the second half.

Next up Anderlecht – the Belgian champions and a much sterner test. For the first leg at Anfield, Shankly made one major sartorial change. Liverpool played in an all-red kit for the first time.

Shankly chose his captain, Ron Yeats, to model the potential new kit and decided his 'Colossus' looked even more powerful than in his established outfit. The Liverpool boss gave the new look the thumbs up. The Reds put on a stylish performance beating the respected Belgian champions 3-0. A last-minute Roger Hunt goal in the away leg completed an impressive job.

As has now become the norm, European competition went into hibernation over the winter months, while domestically Liverpool set off on their FA Cup trek.

They squeezed home at West Brom in the third round, and then scrambled a 1-1 draw at Anfield in the fourth round against the team then lying in 92nd place in English football, bottom-of-the-pile Stockport County. Bill Shankly, away overseas on a scouting mission in Cologne, must have nearly choked on his schnapps when he heard the result, but the Reds put things right in the replay 2-0.

Back in European Cup quarter-final first leg action, Liverpool shared a 0-0 away draw with FC Köln and, in the FA Cup, beat both Bolton Wanderers and then Leicester City, after a replay, before the return leg with the German side was played. Controversially, the original staging of the second leg at a snowbound Anfield was called off shortly before the kick-off with over 50,000 fans already in the stadium. The Germans were very unhappy – they had already warmed up on the pitch, and felt Bill Shankly must have influenced the Danish referee, Frede Hansen, to make the big call. When the match was eventually played a fortnight later, it too ended goalless, mainly thanks to a wonderful goalkeeping display from Köln's Toni Schumacher.

And so to a third match, held in Rotterdam a week later. This time there were goals – two apiece. Extra time could not split the sides, and so the tie was eventually, and famously, settled by the toss of a coin. Can you imagine that now! There was drama even in that simple action as the first time the referee tossed the disc, red on one side, white on the other, it landed upright in the mud – and the toss had to be repeated. No VAR then.

As the disc landed the second time it was the sight of big Ron Yeats jumping up in the air that clearly indicated this time the coin had landed flat, crucially with the red side showing up. Liverpool were in the semi-finals of the European Cup at their first attempt, but had little time to enjoy it – three days after the drama in Rotterdam, they had an FA Cup semi-final against Chelsea to try and win. Villa Park the venue, and the Londoners must have felt they had a real chance, given Liverpool's midweek exertions.

But such was the spirit in Shankly's team, and their determination to put behind them the misery of their semi-final defeat two years earlier, that the Reds pulled off a wonderful 2-0 win.

Liverpool were off to Wembley to play in the FA Cup Final – back then the biggest game in English football, and an event broadcast the world over.

It is probably hard for younger readers to understand the significance of the FA Cup Final back in those days. In recent times the occasion has been somewhat overshadowed by the glitzy appeal of the Premier League and the Champions League. In truth the FA Cup has lost a little of its lustre and its importance in the domestic calendar. But for many decades it was *the* football event of the season – not least because it was the only domestic club game broadcast live on TV, and by far the biggest.

People put their whole day aside to watch the day's events on TV – from the players having their breakfast in the teams' hotels to the winners traditionally supping milk (and later champagne no doubt) from the most famous piece of silverware in football.

And the Barwick family were no different. This was a red-letter day. I nabbed one of the armchairs early, curtains were drawn to keep the daylight out, and we settled in for the long haul. Nobody would budge until it was all over. David Coleman introduced BBC's *Cup Final Grandstand* from the pitchside at Wembley with all his normal assured mixture of urgency and expectation. The build-up to the match housed the usual ingredients of this annual TV ritual played out in glorious black and white.

'Meet the Teams', 'How They Got There', 'Meet the Managers', prematch pitchside interviews, famous fans, the community singing – the ingredients rarely changed, but the teams involved invariably did.

It was always a big day – but this time it was 'our big day', 'our team', 'our final', 'our chance'. Liverpool v Leeds United. 1 May 1965. The game was no classic, but the result was – three goals in extra time, with Roger Hunt opening the scoring for the Reds, Billy Bremner equalising for Leeds and then Ian St John writing his own personal page in Liverpool's history with the winning goal, an acrobatic diving header. Liverpool had finally won the FA Cup – and Ron Yeats collected the beautiful trophy from the Queen, who just happened to be dressed in red that afternoon.

Liverpool's supporters at Wembley went mad, as did all us fans watching it back home on Merseyside. The city partied long into the night, and then prepared for the return of the Wembley heroes the following day. The team would arrive at Lime Street and parade around the city centre before reaching the Town Hall. From the balcony the cup would be lifted by the players and speeches made.

And I was there – just. My dad was working on crowd control that afternoon, so my mum volunteered to take me and my brother to watch the open-top bus, filled with team and trophy, go past.

The problem was another 250,000 people had the same idea, and so the traffic heading into the city was simply dreadful. And this was Mum's first solo drive, having just passed her test that week (at the fourth time of asking!). She was, shall we say, a little nervous. I have been on gentler journeys, but we got as near as we could, then abandoned the car and walked the last half mile or so. People were five deep at the roadside, but we managed to push our way to the front and witnessed the bus, the players and the cup go past. It all took just a few seconds but 'we were there'. Thanks Mum.

The city was absolutely buzzing with excitement – and there was still more to come. Reigning European and World Club champions Inter Milan were in town to compete in their European Cup semi-final first leg just three days after the FA Cup Final. It would prove to be one of Anfield's greatest nights.

Just before the match, injured players Gordon Milne and Gerry Byrne walked around the jam-packed stadium holding aloft the newly won FA Cup – and the crowd went crazy. It was a shrewd move by Bill Shankly.

Liverpool scored early, Roger Hunt crashing home a wonderful shot. Inter equalised, but the Reds went on to score two more goals through Ian Callaghan and Ian St John. And it could have been more: full-back Chris Lawler, who had actually got married on the previous day, had a seemingly good goal ruled out for offside. On the night, Inter's famous coach Helenio Herrera and his all-conquering side were well and truly put to the sword. At the end of the epic Liverpool performance the Kop adapted the famous Italian refrain 'Santa Lucia' with a chorus of 'Oh Inter, one, two, three ... go back to Italy'.

Eight days later, back in Italy, the second leg took place amid a fiery partisan atmosphere in the San Siro stadium – flares and fireworks were set off at regular intervals. An off-field hate campaign, the vicious atmosphere created by the home fans and some highly controversial decisions by Spanish referee, Ortiz de Mendíbil, contrived to turn fortunes against the Reds. They had arrived with a 3-1 lead in the tie, but left defeated, 3-0 on the night and 4-3 on aggregate. Two of Inter's three goals were dubious at best. The Reds felt they had been cheated out of the game.

It was a situation that left Bill Shankly fuming. And for many years to come. But the Liverpool boss knew that his team, in their first taste of European Cup football, had taken the Italians, who retained the trophy, to the very edge.

'Make no mistake, Inter were a really great side when they came to Anfield. And yet we ran them off their feet. They hadn't met a team like Liverpool.'

Kop That – *Bill Shankly became only the fourth man to win the FA Cup as a player for Preston in 1938 and then as a manager, something which Kenny Dalglish would do with the Reds.*

1965/66 – LIFE IN THE BIG LEAGUE

WHEN JÜRGEN Klopp and his marvellous players finally erased 30 years of hurt by being crowned Premier League champions in 2020, Liverpool fans celebrated the world over.

In a season that had been rudely interrupted by a pitch invader that nobody had seen coming – Covid-19 – the Reds finally clinched that much-awaited title on 25 June. Chelsea's victory over Manchester City guaranteed the Anfield men top spot as the season was resumed post lockdown and was wrapped up behind closed doors. The club were finally able to lift the elegant trophy at the end of their last home match – an entertaining 5-3 win over Chelsea.

Although there were no supporters in the stadium, the moment when captain Jordan Henderson did his familiar jig before thrusting the silver bauble high above his head was still incredibly special. It was undoubtedly the strangest of Liverpool's 19 league title-clinching moments, but also probably the most welcome since the club first claimed that honour back in 1901. In all, 24 players made appearances for Klopp's title-winning side, with only three, Virgil van Dijk, Trent Alexander-Arnold and Roberto Firmino, playing in every game. Of course, this is the era of large squads, rotation in selection and multiple substitutions.

By sharp contrast, back in the 1965/66 season, Bill Shankly's men won their second league title in three years whilst using only 14 players, with two of them, Alf Arrowsmith and Bobby Graham, only making four starts between them in the 42 league games played. Around this time, when the press asked about that forthcoming weekend's team selection, Shankly would quip, 'The same as last season, boys!'

The Reds also played another 11 games across the 1965/66 campaign in various competitions with only a single appearance by Phil Chisnall adding to those numbers. Liverpool clinched the 1965/66 title in their final home game of the season against Chelsea – a Roger Hunt double doing the business for them.

This was a red-letter day for Bill Shankly's men, and a fitting end to a red-letter season for yours truly. Instead of continuing to enjoy an established mixture of first-team, reserve and youth-team football, I had now become a regular watching the 'big heads', as Ronnie Moran later coined the first team. Liverpool's hosting of perennial First Division strugglers Fulham in early September 1965 marked my elevation to a new fortnightly place in the Paddock.

Starting at my new secondary school earlier that month had given me the basis for an argument that it was time to be allowed to go and watch the Reds in all their first-team glory week in, week out. And I won the argument! And so, my matchday routine started to fall into place. Two corporation bus rides, including catching the 'Football Special' from the Old Swan, a short walk up Priory Road, jam-packed with excited and expectant fans, past the stalls selling scarfs, badges, rosettes and rattles – and the guys selling the Golden Goal tickets. I always bought one.

Up to the stadium, and with 5/- in old money (25p) for my entrance fee into the Paddock, and another 4d for the matchday programme, I was set for another very special afternoon in the company of 40-odd thousand Liverpool supporters. And although the Kop looked enticing, I found my early spiritual home in the Paddock, standing halfway up the terrace, adjacent to the 18-yard box at the Anfield Road End of the ground. I watched the Reds from that 'spec' for the next 15 years or so before having a spell on the Kop itself – and ultimately a timely migration to the seats of the Main Stand.

Over the years, I've watched the Reds from every part of the ground, including the home dugout, of more later. Well, everywhere except the Boys' Pen – and I don't regret that particular omission. I wasn't brave enough! I also enjoyed 'watching' the Kop from the Paddock. They were an essential part of my afternoon's entertainment. The swaying of the crowd and the singing of the songs was a thing of wonder for this 11-year-old boy. And I knew I would ultimately become part of that world-famous institution when the time was right.

Liverpool beat Fulham 2-1 that September day, their first home win of the season, and my support for the club had gone up a notch. I wasn't able to attend every home match that season, but I racked up a decent number of games. And I was briefly on the Anfield injured list too when I fainted whilst watching the Reds play Newcastle United. I was lifted out of the crowd, led down the touchline by the St John's Ambulance team, and after a quick once-over, a slurp of water and a gigantic blast of smelling salts, I was dropped back into the Paddock to the sound of a few ironic local cheers.

I had the odour of those smelling salts in my nose for the next week – but I didn't miss a goal.

Back home, my day would be rounded off by walking up to the 'top shops' to buy a copy of the *Football Echo*. Pink in colour and read from cover to cover. It became a very special part of my Saturday football ritual. Especially spotting the paragraphs in bold type in the Reds' away match reports which highlighted the description of a goal having been scored. Hopefully for the Reds!

Whilst I was getting used to life in the big league, the Reds were making new strides in European competition. Having won the FA Cup the previous season, they had qualified for the European Cup Winners' Cup. Liverpool reached the semi-final of the competition via two-legged successes over Juventus, Standard Liège and Honvéd of Hungary.

A new goal machine was unleashed on European football – well, not quite, but Liverpool full-back Chris Lawler scored twice against the Belgian champions and another against Honvéd. Lawler would spend his career popping up with vital goals for Liverpool, 61 in all, including 11 goals in 66 European ties. He even scored on his England debut.

The semi-final was the Battle of Britain – Celtic v Liverpool. A match-up of huge proportions.

The first leg was a narrow 1-0 win for Celtic but the Reds triumphed in the second leg, Tommy Smith scoring from a free kick on the hour to level the aggregate score and then Geoff Strong, bravely limping from a leg injury, rising to head home the vital winner five minutes later. The game was played in monsoon conditions turning the pitch into a mudbath.

The atmosphere at Anfield that night was highly charged, and got out of hand when a late 'goal' from Celtic's Bobby Lennox was ruled offside. The Celtic fans rioted at the end of the game, throwing bottles and cans on to the pitch in their hundreds. My dad, on police duty in the stadium that night, said that the following day the joke in the station was whether the officers present at Anfield should charge overtime for handling the crisis, or just get the money back on the empties!

Ironically, the final itself was held at Hampden Park, and a relatively small crowd of 41,657 watched a low-key game in which the Reds went down 2-1 to Borussia Dortmund.

The match had gone into extra time after Roger Hunt had pulled the Reds level midway through the second half. The Germans' extra-time winner came from a lob by Libuda which struck Liverpool's bar and then went into the net off captain Ron Yeats.

The next time Roger Hunt would line up against Dortmund stars Hans Tilkowski, Lothar Emmerich and Siggi Held would be in another final held at Wembley later that summer … the *World Cup Final*!

Kop That – *Liverpool recorded their biggest post-war derby victory at Anfield, 5-0, where seven Scousers were in the line-ups. When they next put five past their neighbours at Anfield in 2019, only Trent Alexander-Arnold and Tom Davies were Scousers in the 28 who played.*

1966/67 – A HUNT FOR
THE BIGGEST PRIZE

THE SUMMER of 1966 will remain memorable for those of us fortunate to be around back then – this was the year when England won the World Cup. It is difficult to explain just how big a deal it was. England were finally top of the football tree. World champions – the best of the best. They hadn't managed it before – and they haven't managed it since. The country went crazy and Alf Ramsey – later Sir Alf, of course – and his victorious team were national heroes.

The 16-team tournament had been held in England that year. It was played across eight venues nationwide. England, themselves, never had to set foot out of Wembley Stadium. One of the other venues was Goodison Park. And it hosted the reigning world champions Brazil, Pelé et al.

I have been privileged to attend many World Cups since in various personal and professional capacities, travelling thousands of miles in the bargain. But in July 1966, my mum, my brother, David, and I took the 81 corporation bus along Queens Drive, and walked the last half mile or so to Everton's home ground. It was Brazil v Portugal – billed as Pelé v Eusébio. The champions needed to win to stay in a tournament that was being graced by the Portuguese. It was a fantastic feeling to be at the World Cup, albeit in my own backyard.

On the night, Pelé was kicked off the pitch and Eusébio delivered a double coup de grâce. Brazil out, Portugal would fall on their sword against England in the semi-final. Liverpool fans had a heightened interest in proceedings with three Anfield men in Ramsey's squad. Gerry Byrne was allocated the number 15 shirt but never actually played, Ian Callaghan the number 20 jersey – he would play once – and perhaps most interesting of all, Roger Hunt would wear number 21 and play in all six matches. He would also score three goals, including both against France in their vital group game.

Everybody at Anfield knew the true value of Roger Hunt: hard-working, full of honest endeavour and a goalscorer. Ramsey recognised all those qualities in the modest man from Golborne. The southern-based press tended to fall behind that goalscoring genius Jimmy Greaves, but an injury sustained against France kept him on the sidelines on English football's historic afternoon.

Hunt and Geoff Hurst were chosen ahead of Greaves – and the rest, as they say, is the stuff of legend. Roger Hunt was actually told he would be playing in the final in a whispered conversation with Ramsey on the eve of the match as the squad made their way into a cinema to watch *Those Magnificent Men in their Flying Machines*. Anything to calm the nerves.

Eight different English clubs were represented in the final against West Germany that famous afternoon, including Blackpool and Fulham. It wouldn't happen now, would it?

Celebrations went on for days up and down the country, but within a fortnight the new season was swiftly upon us with the traditional curtain-raiser, the FA Charity Shield. Liverpool had won the league, and Everton the FA Cup, so the Charity

Shield was staged on Merseyside at Goodison Park in front of over 63,000 fans.

It was a filthy afternoon, but remains so memorable, as before the match, Roger Hunt and Everton's fellow World Cup winner Ray Wilson ran around the pitch holding the World Cup aloft. As BBC's Kenneth Wolstenholme said of the trophy on the day they won it, 'It's 12 inches high, solid gold and it means England are the world champions.'

And there it was, the World Cup itself, right in front of our eyes on a rainy afternoon at Goodison Park. It remains one of my favourite moments of watching football. It was a genuine 'I was there' moment. Indeed, as I type these words, I have a framed colour photo of that special time right in front of me.

Liverpool and Everton captains, Ron Yeats and Brian Labone, followed behind our World Cup heroes with the Football League Championship trophy and the FA Cup respectively. Liverpool went on to win the match – and the only goal was scored by ... Roger Hunt. Naturally.

In the New Year Honours list, Alf Ramsey would be knighted and England captain Bobby Moore received the OBE. The Kopites went one further and knighted Liverpool's star striker themselves. 'Sir Roger Hunt, Sir Roger Hunt, Eye-Aye-Addio Sir Roger Hunt!'

Spin forward 40 years or so and I was now sitting in my office as chief executive of the Football Association. One of the first things I did on moving in was to have a huge photograph mounted on the wall of Bobby Moore, on the shoulders of his victorious England team-mates, holding the famous Jules Rimet trophy aloft.

I also worked, with the national press and government officials, to try and get medals for the England squad players who didn't play in the 1966 final – the 'other 11', including Liverpool's Ian Callaghan and Gerry Byrne. Back then only the

11 players who played in the final received medals – winners or runners-up. We put pressure on FIFA to do justice to the players who had been part of previous World Cup final squads, but not played in their respective finals. And I was delighted when, in 2009, Callaghan and Byrne, and their fellow squad members, were invited to 10 Downing Street to receive their belated 1966 World Cup winners' medals from the then Prime Minister Gordon Brown.

Later that evening, the players attended England's World Cup qualifier against Andorra at Wembley. At the function beforehand I spotted the two Liverpool men and as I walked towards their table they both waved, and laughing called out,

'We've got them – at last!', holding their precious medals aloft.

After three glorious seasons, Liverpool's 1966/67 one itself had turned out to be something of a damp squib. In the league their defence of the title fell away with just one win in their last five games. Their European Cup ambitions had come to a dramatic halt on a foggy night in Amsterdam when a young Dutch forward called Johan Cruyff made the headlines by leading his Ajax team-mates to a staggering 5-1 first-leg lead in their European Cup second-round tie.

Ajax, or A-jax as we all wrongly pronounced it, because their name was the same as a popular household detergent, fittingly took the Reds to the cleaners. Of course, Bill Shankly rallied the troops and nearly 54,000 fans crammed into Anfield a week later to witness 'the great comeback'. But it was not to be, as the precocious 19-year-old Cruyff scored twice in a game that ended 2-2.

In the FA Cup, Liverpool were back at Goodison Park in March for a fifth-round tie with Everton which unusually was played on a Saturday evening in front of nearly 65,000 fans. Such was the interest in this game that it was beamed live into Anfield where another 41,000 spectators watched – the combined attendance over 105,000.

On a very windy night, causing one of the huge screens at Anfield to go walkabout during the match, the Reds were blown out of the FA Cup by a goal from Roger Hunt's World Cup-winning colleague Alan Ball.

So, all in all, an indifferent season for the Reds, but the signing of future Liverpool great Emlyn Hughes from Blackpool in February would prove to be a brilliantly shrewd move by the Reds' master strategist, Bill Shankly. Emlyn would end up playing over 650 games for Liverpool – and captain both his club and country.

Kop That – *Roger Hunt scored 18 goals in 34 internationals and was on the losing side on just two occasions. Only Luis Suárez and Milan Baroš have a better goals per game ratio for players who won more than 20 caps in their time at Anfield.*

1967/68 – GOING FOR A SONG

THE NEW season marked another first for me, as I made my way to Anfield for Liverpool's Inter-Cities Fairs Cup second-round tie with West German side TSV 1860 Munich. No mugs either the Germans. Runners-up in the previous season's Bundesliga and narrowly beaten two seasons before by West Ham United in a memorable European Cup Winners' Cup Final at Wembley Stadium.

This was, of course, a time when only a country's champions entered the senior competition, the European Cup, and other big sides spread themselves out between the Cup Winners' Cup and the Fairs Cup. So, there were always plenty of big hitters in both competitions.

Liverpool had comfortably beaten Malmö of Sweden in the competition's first round but expected a tougher assignment against TSV, former Bundesliga champions. In goal for Munich that night was Yugoslavian Petar Radenković. He was a vastly experienced and talented keeper. And in more ways than one it would seem. Music lover Radenković even had a top 20 record in the German pop charts. His popular song 'Bin I Radi Bin I Konig' might not have worried The Beatles too much, but it certainly added some colour to his reputation.

Mind you, it didn't help him much that night at Anfield as red-hot Liverpool scored hit after hit, sending the Germans packing in a remarkable 8-0 win. My own European debut had turned out a real treat as early goals from Ian St John and a diving header from Tony Hateley set the tone for the evening. Tommy Smith added a 43rd-minute penalty.

Radenković got a tremendous welcome from the Kop as he took to the field for the second half. They also demanded he gave them a song – but he was too busy picking the ball out of the net.

Five goals in 25 second-half minutes – including three in five minutes from Hunt (two) and Thompson – sent the German team home in a spin.

Radenković left the field to a sympathetic ovation from the Kop – and perhaps he had briefly enjoyed his trip to Liverpool, then the epicentre of the pop-music world, despite balls flashing past him at a rate of knots at Anfield. 8-0 was a stunning first-leg scoreline. Game and tie emphatically over. TSV restored some pride with a 2-1 second-leg victory, with Ian Callaghan on the scoresheet – his third goal in the tie.

However, Liverpool's progress in the competition came to a swift end when they were beaten in the next round by Hungarian side Ferencváros 1-0 away before Christmas, and then by the same score on a snowy surface at Anfield in early January.

My only other memory of that day is spending the afternoon on 'snow-clearing' duty, helping make safe the paths of houses up and down our street and earning some pocket money in the bargain – and then being frozen to death in my normal spec in the Paddock watching the Reds struggling to come to terms with both their sprightly opponents and the Alpine Anfield surface.

It was one of those evenings when they were destined not to score.

One month earlier I had been at Anfield to witness a unique moment in the famous stadium's history – and a goal that remains one of the most bizarre I have ever seen … no, *the* most bizarre.

And once again, wintry weather played its own crucial part in proceedings. Liverpool were playing Leeds United on a snowy pitch in December. With those two teams there was always a special intensity about their matches, and this latest league encounter was no different.

Roger Hunt got the Reds in front after 16 minutes before Leeds United's goalkeeper, Gary Sprake, contrived to concede a goal that will go down in Anfield folklore. With half-time fast approaching, Sprake, whose career seemed a never-ending mixture of classy and clumsy, picked up a back pass on the edge of his penalty area in front of the Kop and went to throw it out to full-back Terry Cooper. Whether his attention was distracted by Hunt lurking nearby, Sprake seemed to turn as he was releasing the ball and in so doing threw it into the far corner of the net. His own net.

There was a momentary hush in the stadium while everybody took in what they had just seen – I clearly remember Leeds United's big Jack Charlton staring at referee Jim Finney to see what decision was forthcoming.

'Goal' – and the Anfield crowd went potty. Sprake had allowed a slippery ball to get out of his control – and the rest is history. As he sped down the players' tunnel to face the music in the Leeds United dressing room, the stadium's PA system blasted out two inspired choices as its half-time entertainment. And, of course, the Kop reacted swiftly to both, serenading the forlorn Welsh goalkeeper with two hits of the moment, The Scaffold's 'Thank U Very Much', and the bittersweet, appropriately titled Des O'Connor ballad 'Careless Hands'.

Sadly, Gary Sprake never really lived that goal down – a moment when a snowy pitch and a slippery ball combined to send his throw-out back across his body and into his own net. Luckily for him, though, there were no TV cameras at Anfield that day and so his misfortune was spared a national armchair audience.

But for the 39,676 frozen folk there that afternoon, myself included, it was an unforgettable moment, that's for sure.

Kop That – *On a musical note, the referee in the TSV rout was one Albert Sing, whilst on a footballing one, Gary Sprake would finish the season as a European winner as his club defeated Liverpool's conquerors Ferencváros in the final.*

1968/69 – THE
BLONDE BOMBSHELL

ALUN EVANS made his first impression on the Anfield faithful wearing the colours of Wolverhampton Wanderers. His youthful pace and precision left Ron Yeats in his wake and Tommy Lawrence in his goal, both beaten and wondering 'who is this guy?'

Those of us there all wondered the same, because at the time, the Midlands side's stars were the likes of striker Peter Knowles and his flamboyant sidekick Derek Dougan. Evans was a fresh face and a new name. That precocious show of teenage talent in a league game between the Reds and Wolves in the autumn of 1967 also took the eye of the shrewdest man in the stadium that afternoon – Bill Shankly.

And within ten months Alun Evans, at the tender age of 18, was to become Shankly's latest recruit, and at £100,000 the most expensive teenager in British football. He signed for Liverpool on 16 September 1968, celebrated with a plate of chicken and chips, and five days later made his debut for the Reds against Leicester City at Anfield.

It took him just ten minutes to get off the mark with a goal in front of a delirious Kop. Bizarrely, it was Liverpool's *third* goal of the game as the home side blasted their opponents aside

– and Ian Callaghan even added a fourth two minutes later. Alun Evans's take on his dramatic debut? 'What a team, what a day, what a crowd.' And all of us there agreed.

Evans had got off to a flyer – and he scored two goals in his next league match, ironically against his old club Wolves at Molineux. 6-0 to Liverpool on that memorable day. Evans celebrated his 19th birthday a couple of days later, and then helped Liverpool to a 4-0 win at Burnley the following weekend. What a start for this blonde-haired bombshell, who soon became very popular with the Liverpool fans, and a pin-up for his female followers.

He also instantly became one of my favourite players. I was just 14, had blonde hair and in my back-garden kickabouts I allowed myself to believe it could be me playing up front for the Reds. Thankfully, Shankly picked the right teenager!

Evans scored five in his first nine games for Liverpool, but the goals all but dried up in the remainder of the 1968/69 season – and towards the end of the campaign he got himself sent off after an altercation with Coventry's veteran defender, Maurice Setters.

What followed off the field was more painful and disruptive to Evans's subsequent progress at Anfield. Enjoying an evening out at a Midlands nightclub in December 1969, he was the innocent victim of a violent, unprovoked attack which left him with serious facial injuries. It left him with both physical and mental scars and Evans's Liverpool career became an unsteady series of highs and lows. 'Flaxen-haired flop' was one of the crueller headlines.

For those like me who were big fans, key moments stand out. His two goals in an FA Cup fifth-round replay at Leicester City, his stunning Anfield hat-trick against Bayern Munich in the European Fairs Cup – Beckenbauer, Breitner, Maier, Muller et al. – and a brilliant goal against Bayern Munich a year later which won him German TV station ARD's 'Goal of the Month' competition. And, of course, his key role in Liverpool's famous win over arch-rivals Everton, in their 1971 FA Cup semi-final at Old Trafford.

Evans had been a key architect of Liverpool's semi-final win but his trip to Wembley was less successful, his FA Cup Final appearance being cut short when he was substituted midway through the second half. Alun Evans's career at Liverpool finally came to a close on 22 January 1972. Ironically, his last game was against his old club Wolves at Molineux. He was off to Aston Villa and later settled in Australia. A 'nearly, not quite' career at Anfield but his September 1968 arrival at the club excited the fans who always seemed to have a soft spot for their blonde bombshell.

One of the great fun things to do around this time was to go and watch the Liverpool first-team squad going through their paces at the club's training ground at Melwood. Every half-term holiday my mate Andy and I would get a couple of buses to West Derby and make our way over there. And, more often than not, we were allowed into Melwood and got the opportunity to see the players up close. Remarkably, very few other people took advantage of these opportunities and we were able to see our heroes practising their skills and lapping the training ground. And, of course, there were always the famous five-a-side matches between the players and the staff. Those matches never ended until the staff had their noses in front.

The best part of these half-term treats was when Bill Shankly would come out of his office and wander over to us and exchange some pleasantries – typical of the man, and super-memorable for us. At the end of the session we would collect the autographs of the players, take some photos with the old Kodak Box Brownie before the squad boarded the coach to take them back to Anfield for lunch.

All seems very innocent now, and not a corporate gig in sight. Happy days.

The Reds met their Yorkshire rivals in a late-season midweek game at Anfield that would decide that season's title race. It was Liverpool's last throw of the dice – they needed to beat Leeds to have any chance of knocking Don Revie's side off top spot. The atmosphere that night was simply electric, but the home side just couldn't find their way through a tough Leeds defence.

At the end of the match there were remarkable scenes when, having celebrated their title-clinching draw with their own visiting fans, the Leeds players were making their way off the pitch. Revie briefly spoke to captain Billy Bremner and pointed towards the Kop which was still packed to the rafters. Bremner, rather gingerly, slowly took his players towards the Kop, not knowing what reception to expect, only to be greeted by a huge ovation and a resounding and repetitive chant of 'Champions, Champions, Champions ...'

It went on for several minutes – and Don Revie later described it as one of the most emotional moments of his long career in football. 'They must be the best supporters in the world,' he said, and sent a telegraph to Anfield the following day with the same message.

Bill Shankly also went into the Leeds United dressing room after the players had enjoyed their celebrations on the field and sportingly complimented them on their deserved title win. Mind you, he did say that on the night 'the best team had drew'!

It was another gesture appreciated by Leeds United – their first league title win – and not the last away team to clinch the title at Anfield, as history would bear witness.

Kop That – *Evans became only the third Liverpool player to score on his league debut in the 60s, and joined Geoff Strong and Tony Hateley in scoring both against the Reds and then for them in the decade.*

1969/70 – CHANGE IS IN THE AIR

LIVERPOOL GOT off to a cracking start to the new season, winning seven of their first nine league games and drawing the other two. Hopes were high. Would this be another serious title tilt for Shankly's men? It certainly seemed so.

And, yes, as it happened the league championship trophy would end up on Merseyside that season – but across Stanley Park at Everton. Liverpool's campaign would offer much, but ultimately fail to deliver. Change was in the air for the Reds. As a supporter, the season still offered some special moments, but some carry a sting in their tail. Try these on for size.

12 August: Liverpool 3 Manchester City 2 – second game of the season, late goals from Hunt and St John clinching a thrilling victory for the Reds.

Also memorable for City's cheeky chappy Mike Summerbee dropping his shorts in front of the Kop, when City were leading 2-1 with just six minutes to go. No doubt, the bottom fell out of his world with Liverpool's late goal flourish!

16 September: Liverpool 10 Dundalk 0 – a European midweek massacre for the Irish club and standing in the Paddock my dad and I were beginning to lose count of the score!

25 October: Liverpool 4 Southampton 1 – the Reds were drifting to a 1-1 draw with the Saints when they introduced Roger Hunt as a substitute with 15 minutes to go. The Kop roared their approval and 'Sir Roger' scored two goals in two minutes, his eye for a chance and his coolness in execution steering Liverpool to victory. Everybody there knew we were watching somebody coming to the end of a great Liverpool career – and giving of his best to the last.

15 November: Liverpool 2 West Ham United 0 – special recognition for the club as the BBC chose this game to be the first *Match of the Day* programme broadcast in colour. Experienced producer Alec Weeks, who had directed the first *Match of the Day* – Liverpool v Arsenal in 1964 – was back at Anfield for this groundbreaking TV moment.

Weeks enjoyed covering football at Anfield 'because if the game is boring, I can always point the cameras at the Kop'. The late evening show came live from Anfield itself, David Coleman being joined by Bill Shankly and the Liverpool team. All in glorious colour. I went to the match and then stayed up to watch the show – on a black-and-white TV!

26 November: Liverpool 3 Vitória Setúbal 2 – trailing 1-0 from the first leg of their European Fairs Cup tie, the Reds' task got even harder when the Portuguese visitors scored goals either side of half-time.

Bring on the cavalry! Roger Hunt and Alun Evans came off the bench, Tommy Smith scored with a penalty, and in a hectic finish Evans and then Hunt scored, the latter with the last kick of the match. It was to be Roger Hunt's 285th and final goal for the Reds. A move to Bolton Wanderers beckoned. So, 3-2 on the night, 3-3 on aggregate. And when the referee blew the final whistle, nobody moved. Not the players nor the crowd.

The players were eventually led off the field by the referee, but we all stayed behind waiting for ... well, something. And that something came via the public address system telling us the tie was over and that Liverpool had been knocked out on away goals. We drifted away slowly.

6 December: Everton 0 Liverpool 3 – one of those great derby wins. No goals at half-time, then Emlyn Hughes scored with a header early in the second half. What then followed was another headed goal that has gone into derby match folklore. Peter Thompson crossed from the left and Everton full-back Sandy Brown sent a bullet header ... bang into his own net. It was an absolute belter.

Unfortunately, for Sandy, the match was being covered by the BBC for *Match of the Day* and therefore his goal, *that* goal, is preserved for history. Bobby Graham, perhaps surprisingly an ever-present in the league for the Reds that season, added a clever third. It was a great day to be a Red at Goodison.

13 December: Liverpool 1 Manchester United 4 – a week after Liverpool had thrashed the Toffees, Manchester United did a similar number on the Reds. Gentler times perhaps – and Bobby Charlton's superb finish for their fourth goal brought applause from all around the stadium.

I got to know Bobby well in future years – a great man – and, one time, he sent me a copy of a new book: *Bobby Charlton's Most Memorable Matches.*

He had signed it inside the front cover: 'To Brian, Do you notice none of the games had us beating Liverpool! Best Wishes Bobby.'

21 February: Watford 1 Liverpool 0 – an FA Cup quarter-final: Liverpool red-hot favourites to progress against Second

Division opposition in Watford. The two teams had met each other earlier in the season in a Football League Cup tie at Vicarage Road with Liverpool 2-1 winners. This time it would be different. On a ploughed field of a pitch, an ageing Liverpool side looked leggy and laboured and home side Watford took full advantage.

Barry Endean's decisive second-half headed goal sent Watford unexpectedly into the semi-finals and Liverpool's season into oblivion. Shankly was furious and he knew he had to act decisively.

21 March: Liverpool 0 Everton 2 – revenge for Everton in a run of wins that steered the Blues to the title. I watched this game from behind the goal at the Anfield Road End, packed with Evertonians, having missed out on a ticket for the Paddock. Not a great place to be when Everton's Alan Whittle scored a goal right in front of us. Joe Royle had scored the first Everton goal in front of the Kop. A long afternoon.

8 April: The Gerry Byrne testimonial – the final match of the season at Anfield marked the end of the career of a true Liverpool great, Gerry Byrne. Byrne signed for Liverpool in 1955, playing over 300 matches for the Reds. He was best remembered for bravely playing through the pain of a dislocated shoulder in the 1965 FA Cup Final. A superb full-back, who made two appearances for England. On a rainy night at Anfield nearly 40,000 of us turned out to say thank you.

The final score between Liverpool and the All Stars XI was 8-8, and two men particularly took my eye. One, the great Sir Stanley Matthews, lined up on one wing for the All Stars, and on the other, unknown to most of us, a speedy young man, with a distinctive high-stepping stride – Skelmersdale United's Steve Heighway. He would be a pivotal part of Liverpool's future. But on that 'opening' night he actually had to ask one of his team-mates which end the Kop was!

Gerry Byrne's career had drawn to a close, and for some of the other Liverpool greats of the 60s time was also running short – change was in the air.

Bill Shankly's magnificent Team of the Sixties had given Liverpool fans a decade of excitement and achievement – ten seasons of wonderful moments of titles won, of a famous cup finally lifted, of travelling the world over, of being a superb band of brothers, driven on by a mercurial manager. Individually, and collectively, the players had given of their best – time and time again. And so had the supporters. The Kop had become as famous as the team itself. Huge, loud, committed and quick-witted – a terrace like no other in football.

Bill Shankly was the architect for the sea change in fortune and fame for the club from Liverpool 4. The most charismatic of men, as honest and straight-talking as they come, a leader, a giant in the sport he loved. Dedicated, grounded and brilliant. And very much a man of the people. His next job would be to construct a new side, with new faces and new ambitions. And it was a challenge he would rise to.

Kop That – *Some 50 players made appearances in the 1960s, with Roger Hunt playing most games (386) and scoring most goals (235).*

1970/71 – SHANKLY'S NEW ARMY

EVERY FAN has a favourite match they have witnessed – a match that stands out from the rest. A match that stays long in the memory. A match that almost defines the club they follow – or the special nature of a certain fixture, rivalry or competition. And if you are a Liverpool fan like me, with 60 years of unforgettable occasions to pick from, then any choice of game is open to be fiercely contested by others who will not share the same view. That is the fun of being a supporter, and everybody's divine right. It is my choice, not your choice – and that's that.

Anyway, by my reckoning, I have roughly 3,500 matches to choose from since I became a novice Red back in the autumn of 1961 – so plenty of choice then! One of the standout matches for me at the start of the new decade was Liverpool's epic 3-2 win over Everton at Anfield in November 1970.

The scale of Shankly's rebuilding programme for the Reds was clearly illustrated in this match – and the enormous impact the new arrivals could make. Back in March of that year, Everton had convincingly beaten Liverpool on the way to securing the league championship.

The Liverpool team that took the field eight months later had a quite different look and feel about it. Seven changes of personnel – Alec Lindsay at left-back, Larry Lloyd at centre-half, John McLaughlin and Ian Ross in midfield, Brian Hall and Steve Heighway on the flanks and £110,000 signing from Cardiff John Toshack leading the line.

This was the 'new' Liverpool team – and lots of attention was focussed on the two new wingmen, Hall and Heighway. Both young men were university graduates, refreshingly honest and hard-working, affectionately nicknamed 'Little Bamber' (Hall) and 'Big Bamber' (Heighway) after the presenter of TV's popular *University Challenge*, Bamber Gascoigne. They would go on to make nearly 700 appearances for the Reds between them, and made early positive impacts, with Everton as their prey.

After a goalless first half, the first derby match of the season burst into life soon after the restart with Everton scoring two goals in quick succession, Alan Whittle and Joe Royle on target again at Anfield. The young Reds now had a mountain to climb, and captain Tommy Smith, only 25 himself, drove his raw recruits forward. High-stepping Heighway, who had recovered from a bad migraine on the morning of the game, showed a direct style and then spotted a shooting gap. One goal back.

Seven minutes later it was Big Bamber's cross that was met by new boy Toshack, rising by degrees to head home past Everton's Andy Rankin. 2-2. It was the Welshman's first goal for Liverpool.

At this point the Kop was going potty, an unbelievable sound, and all of us there were just urging the now rampant Reds to deliver the coup de grâce. And it came on 84 minutes, Lindsay's cross, Toshack's head and Chris Lawler, cool as a cucumber, finished decisively. The place went bonkers.

I've watched the TV highlights of that game many times since. It was filmed for ITV's Sunday afternoon show. And I'm so glad it was captured for posterity. For me, even half a century later, it remains an all-time Anfield memory – a real highlight – and will make my list of favourite games for certain. And it ended on a rather personal footnote.

As we all celebrated Lawler's winner wildly in the Paddock one of my brand-new 'school shoes' went flying, and was never seen again. I hobbled my way home and then had a bit of explaining to do to my mum. The 'money doesn't grow on trees you know' argument came heavily to the fore, but nothing could wipe the smile off my face that day.

If Big Bamber helped swing the league derby match in Liverpool's favour in November, it was Little Bamber that was the unlikely hero when the Merseyside rivals met in the FA Cup semi-final at Old Trafford in March. Both teams had been in European action in the midweek before the big Old Trafford clash. Liverpool had completed a two-legged victory over Bayern Munich, while Everton had suffered a surprise exit from the European Cup at the hands of unfancied Panathinaikos.

Saturday's FA Cup semi-final saw Everton go ahead through Alan Ball – and the Blues looked on course for a Wembley place. As often is the case in FA Cup football, fate then took a hand. Early in the second half, Everton's captain Brian Labone limped off with a thigh strain and the dynamics of the game changed dramatically.

Firstly, Alun Evans raced through to equalise, then provided a cross contested by Rankin and Toshack, the resultant ball dropping for Brian Hall to screw past Howard Kendall on the Everton goal line. His first goal for the Reds – the winning goal for Liverpool – and a new chant was born. 'He shot, he scored ... and all the Kopites roared, Brian Hall, Brian Hall.'

As we all eased out of the Stretford End, news spread like wildfire that Stoke City had beaten high-flying Arsenal in the other semi-final. Without disrespecting the side from the Potteries, it seemed the easier of the two potential opponents in the final. But as we all piled into my dad's old Morris Minor, we heard Arsenal had equalised with a last-gasp controversial penalty. The Gunners would win the replay – and by the time the FA Cup Final came around the famous north London side had been crowned league champions and had their sights on the double.

An FA Cup Final ticket. Back in those days it was the Holy Grail. It was one thing your team getting to the most prestigious game of the season – it was a whole different thing getting there yourself. I had been to Wembley the year before when we went on a school trip to watch England play Northern Ireland, but seeing your own team in the FA Cup Final – that would be something special.

As luck would have it, I got a ticket via a lucky number on the end of a coupon given out at a match against Newcastle United at Anfield a few weeks before the final. I say I got lucky; in fact it was my brother, David, who got the coupon as I was on another school trip, this time to the Netherlands to play football, and missed the game. High-level diplomacy, well, furious family rows, took place in the days building up to the final, on 'who deserved the precious ticket most' before I secured the prize – and on Saturday, 8 May set off on a Football Special from Lime Street Station to Wembley.

To be honest, travelling on my own to the match (discounting the other 15,000 fans!) was a little bit daunting – but with my precious ticket stuffed strategically down my trousers for safekeeping, off I went. It was a blistering hot day. In fact, Shankly later blamed the Reds' 2-1 defeat on the texture of the players' shirts. 'They couldn't breathe in them.'

Whatever, the young Reds didn't quite hack it on the day. Heighway scored the first goal of the game in extra time, fooling Arsenal goalkeeper Bob Wilson at the near post. I worked with Bob for many years at BBC and ITV and often reminded him of that goal, and he would remind me of the final result. Touché. After the match was finished, we all scrambled back to the station adjacent to the stadium and off we went back to Merseyside.

Twenty-four hours later, the faithful gathered in their hundreds of thousands in the city centre to welcome home the gallant losers and listen to Bill Shankly giving one of his famous orations in front of thousands and thousands of fans. 'Since I come here to Liverpool, to Anfield, I have drummed it into the players, time and again, that they are privileged to play for you, and if they didn't believe me, they believe me now.'

We lapped it all up – hung on his every word. He was a simply inspirational figure, the like of which you wouldn't see again until a certain German gentleman arrived like a whirlwind in Liverpool over 40 years later.

Kop That – *In 1974, Brian Hall would become the first Liverpool player to score in a second FA Cup semi-final, whilst Steve Heighway would become the first from the club to score in a second final.*

1971/72 – A STAR IS BORN

I HAVE never been a fan of pre-season friendlies – no matter whether you dress them up as something else or crown them with a huge trophy at the end of a set of meaningless games. In this scenario, size doesn't matter. These days they often involve the team and its entourage travelling across the globe to fulfil a lucrative sponsorship deal or to spread the gospel of the Premier League or the club itself.

Teams across Europe start their seasons at different times so you often see your team playing against a club either already someway in to their latest campaign or barely back from their sunbeds. Back in the 1950s and '60s Liverpool would go on extravagant post-season tours including USA in 1953 and 1964.

Into the sixties and Bill Shankly's pre-season fixtures for the Reds invariably involved away matches against German, Scandinavian, French or Scottish opposition. He wouldn't have many of them either – and travel times would be manageable. And there was no need to 'sell the brand' back then.

Whilst that would be the build-up for the first team, Liverpool's reserves would play matches against local teams or turn out in the odd pre-season testimonial. And that's how I found myself at Prenton Park on 31 July 1971 to see Liverpool's second string against Tranmere Rovers. And what was just supposed to be a way of killing time before the real stuff started a fortnight later became something of a revelation because one player stood out amongst the rest.

He was a player who Liverpool had bought in the week of the previous season's FA Cup Final. It was a transfer that barely raised an eyebrow, or made a headline amidst cup final fever but it was this latest recruit that Shankly said of later to be THE young man that lit the fuse under his new breed of Reds. 'He "ignited" the side.'

Kevin Keegan's rise from the relative mediocrity of playing for Scunthorpe United to becoming one of the game's most sought after stars is a remarkable one. Shankly and his backroom boys had spotted Keegan in a sequence of FA Cup games for Scunthorpe against Tranmere Rovers earlier in that season. His potential was recognised and his signature was on the end of a contract by the beginning of May.

At Prenton Park that July afternoon in 1971, the match programme had Keegan lining up in a Liverpool side with veterans like Tommy Lawrence and Ron Yeats, established strikers Bobby Graham, Alun Evans and Jack Whitham, and a fledging Phil Thompson was also in the team.

On that afternoon, Keegan gave us a matinee masterclass. He was perpetual motion, a midfield dynamo and will o' the wisp. I later learned Ronnie Moran, in charge of the reserves that day, criticised him for his indiscipline! Liverpool won the match, and the winning goal came from a penalty, earned when Keegan was upended in the box.

Whilst hard taskmaster Moran might have had reservations about Keegan's non-stop performance I can tell you the young Doncaster lad was the only topic of conversation amongst Liverpool fans on the ferry back across the Mersey that afternoon.

To this day I can remember being totally beguiled with this recruit to Liverpool's ranks. 'Who is that guy?'

Shankly was kept informed of Keegan's progress and in the traditional match between the first team and the reserves held at Melwood ahead of the starting weekend, the little man started in the first team, helping them to a seven-goal haul, and helping himself to four goals. On the Thursday before the Reds' opening game of the season against Nottingham Forest at Anfield, Shankly asked young Keegan, 'Where do you want to play on Saturday – for the first team or the reserves?'

'I haven't come to Liverpool to play in the reserves,' responded Keegan, never short on self-confidence, and two days later he made his league debut for the Merseyside giants. And in the 12th minute he had scored his first league goal for the Reds. It was a bit of a scruffy goal to be honest but that didn't matter – it was scored at the Kop end and in front of BBC's *Match of the Day* cameras.

A star was born. Keegan would enjoy a remarkable career at Anfield, his partnership with John Toshack being the stuff of legend. He would be a human dynamo on the field – and a decent human being off it.

Every autograph request was positively received – and every request for a photograph rewarded with a smile. He was also commercially astute, as football made its early footsteps into 'selling the star'. Whether it was an aftershave advert with famous fellow-sportsman, Henry Cooper, 'Splash it on Henry' … or a tilt a the hit parade with his single 'Head Over Heels', Keegan was in and around everything.

Including the penalty area. He scored 100 goals for Liverpool in 323 appearances in all competitions and laid on goals aplenty for his team-mates, especially Toshack. And yet Keegan's desire to play abroad after six successful seasons gracing the Anfield pitch was greeted frostily by many of the Liverpool faithful.

Typical of Keegan's sense of occasion, the little Yorkshireman's final game for Liverpool was their biggest and possibly his best. The 1977 European Cup Final against West German champions, Borussia Möenchengladbach played in Rome was the high-water mark for Liverpool FC at this stage of their vibrant history. More on that later, but suffice to say Keegan turned in a match-winning performance and his man-marker, German maestro Berti Vogts, was turned inside out.

The 1971/72 season in which Keegan made his baptism of fire was further indication that Bill Shankly was moving from his first great Liverpool side to developing a special new team. The league season itself started mundanely with just five wins in their first 12 games but their form in the second half of the campaign was outstanding.

Thirteen wins and two draws in 15 consecutive matches from late January thrust the Reds right into the heart of the title race with two games remaining. It was a remarkable sequence in which they had only conceded three goals but, in their final two games, both away, against Derby County, the eventual champions, and Arsenal, the Reds failed to score and came up agonisingly close to winning Shankly's third league championship. He only had a season to wait for that to happen.

Kop That – *Three Scunthorpe players in that era would later captain England – Kevin Keegan and Ray Clemence at football, of course, and Ian Botham at cricket.*

1972/73 – GET THE
SILVER POLISH OUT!

MANCHESTER UNITED, Manchester City, Leeds United, Everton, Arsenal and Derby County – six different English clubs had won the league championship since Bill Shankly's men had lifted that precious piece of silverware at the end of the 1965/66 season.

That sequence of different clubs underlines the fact that back in the 1970s winning the league title was never the relatively closed shop which it could be argued the Premier League is these days – the miracle of Leicester City excepted. Back then it seemed to be a tight race between three of four clubs as the season turned into the home straight. Nobody would be 20 points ahead, that's for sure.

In the six seasons following the Reds' last title triumph, Shankly's men had finished fifth, third, second, fifth, fifth and third respectively. Close but no cigar. In fact, Anfield had been a trophy-free zone for some little time – but that was about to change.

In the autumn of 1972, things were changing for me too. I had left my school, Quarry Bank, and found myself at the University of Liverpool studying for a degree in economics. I was genuinely concerned I might be totally out of my depth in such a learned institution but was determined to give it my best shot. If the lectures were going to be challenging – and they were – meeting fellow students from all over the country was a really refreshing experience.

And among them, of course, plenty of football fans, each with their own personal 'take' on their own club's result from the previous weekend. From having an hourly/daily/weekly/monthly discourse with mates who were either Liverpudlians or Evertonians, now the fortunes of Coventry City, Wolverhampton Wanderers, Norwich City and Fulham were part of my Monday morning coffee break ritual with my new mates. It was fascinating to hear their thoughts on their own teams' fortunes, but they also took advantage of being based in a football-mad city like Liverpool and matchday trips to both Anfield and Goodison Park were a regular part of their unofficial curriculum.

And those among them who decided to take in an early December fixture, ahead of the Christmas holidays, between the Reds and Birmingham City at Anfield were treated to 'the game of the season'.

I was there too, having cried off with a 'very heavy cold' after only being named as substitute for my Old Boys team's latest game (after another extended run of indifferent form!). In grassroots football a late Saturday morning cry-off is never appreciated by your team-mates.

And, when you are also clearly spotted on BBC's *Match of the Day* highlights later that evening, standing in the crowd and throwing the ball back into play at a game being played on that very same afternoon, my team-mates let me know what they thought in no uncertain fashion! A fair Kop you might say.

The *Match of the Day* cameras had made a lucky selection as the Liverpool–Birmingham City tussle turned into a mini-classic. Behind 3-1 in the match, the Reds finally got their noses in front late in the game with a goal by John Toshack. 4-3 the final score.

One of Liverpool's other goals that day was scored by Peter Cormack, a clever midfield player who seemed to play on his tiptoes. Bought from Nottingham Forest in the close season, the talented Scotsman became one of my favourite players in his four-season stay at Anfield – and more importantly in his first season he scored winning goals in critical matches on Liverpool's route to the title. Two single-goal wins over Everton and Crystal Palace were secured by Peter Cormack goals, as was a point in a tight 1-1 draw with Norwich City. Cormack again on target.

And he would score the vital opening goal in a 2-0 win over arch-rivals Leeds United in an Easter Monday clash that all but clinched the Reds' third First Division championship in the reign of Bill Shankly. It was a day to get to the match early and I was there two hours before the kick-off, securing my normal spec in the Paddock – part of a crowd that was just short of 56,000 fans. An even bigger crowd witnessed a goalless draw against Leicester City the following Saturday, which definitively clinched things for Liverpool, and the post-match scenes were memorable as the crowd rose as one to the architect of this latest achievement.

As Bill Shankly approached the Kop, the noise ratcheted up in volume. The fans' acclamation for their favourite Scotsman was as emotional as it was genuine. Remarkable scenes followed, with Shankly returning the homage shown to him. With his arms outstretched and a Liverpool scarf around his neck, it was a supreme moment for Shankly. But he also had his eyes on another prize – European domination.

Bill Shankly was desperate for Liverpool to make their mark in European football. The club would become world-famous for their exploits in European competition. Anfield

'European nights' became the stuff of legend – and Shankly's Reds got the ball rolling.

In eight seasons of European football, Liverpool had already experienced the highs and lows of meeting Continental rivals. Memorably hammering European champions Inter Milan at Anfield, then losing controversially at the San Siro; beating Celtic in an all-British European Cup Winners' Cup semi-final on a rainy night on Merseyside; then, ironically, losing their first European final against Borussia Dortmund on a rainy night in Glasgow.

Being taken to the cleaners by Ajax, and a young Johan Cruyff, in the thick fog of Amsterdam.

Winning and losing ties on the toss of a coin – against FC Cologne and Athletic Bilbao respectively – and reaching another European semi-final before losing to domestic rivals Leeds United with a single first-leg goal scored at Anfield.

By 1972/73 Liverpool were becoming seasoned campaigners in European football. They breezed through UEFA Cup ties against Eintracht Frankfurt, AEK Athens, Dynamo Berlin and Dynamo Dresden, before beating Tottenham Hotspur in a tight semi-final. Liverpool led 1-0 from the home leg, and the teams met again just two days after the Reds' big Easter Monday league win over Leeds United. Liverpool lost 2-1, but Steve Heighway's vital second-half goal got his team through on the away goals rule. The two-legged final pitched Liverpool against Borussia Mönchengladbach – the first leg at Anfield.

This tie will be remembered for its false start – rain had fallen on Merseyside in the days leading up to Anfield's big night. The pitch was sodden but Austrian referee Erich Linemayr adjudged it fit to play on. However, following further downpours after the kick-off the game was abandoned 27 minutes into the first half and quickly rescheduled for 24 hours later. We were all told to keep our ticket stubs and bring them with us the following day to gain free admission. The attendance of 41,169 for the rescheduled match suggested not everybody could make it to Anfield two nights running.

But those of us that did saw Liverpool deliver a Shankly masterclass. The canny Scotsman had spotted a weakness in the Germans' defence in the brief time they had been on the pitch the night before and replaced pint-sized Brian Hall with the lanky John Toshack.

The match turned into a triumph for Shankly – 3-0 – Keegan notching twice and Larry Lloyd adding a third. Keegan also missed a penalty on the night. Three minutes after Lloyd had scored, Ray Clemence made a tremendous save from a Jupp Heynckes penalty – a save that was as vital as any goal scored that night. Not least because the return leg in Germany proved to be a tough night for the Reds – Heynckes was on target twice in the first half for Borussia and throughout the second half Liverpool were on the rack.

But somehow the Reds saw it through and Shankly walked around the perimeter of the stadium to greet the fans a very happy man, the UEFA Cup in his hands – a European champion at last.

Kop That – *Larry Lloyd, in the Anfield final first leg, became the first of only two Liverpool players to score their only European goal in a final – Markus Babbel followed him in 2001.*

1973/74 – SHANKLY'S OWN WEMBLEY WIZARDS

AS LIVERPOOL began their new season campaign with a narrow home win over Stoke City, Kopites were blissfully unaware that they were witnessing the opening game of Bill Shankly's final season in charge of his beloved team. That seismic change was 11 months away, and what a shock it would be – we can all remember where we were when we heard that bombshell. But let's not get ahead of ourselves.

The autumn of 1973 found the country in turmoil. Unrest in the coal mines had led to an overtime ban. As stocks dwindled, the country at large felt the effects. The speed limit was reduced to 50mph, petrol coupons were issued and street lighting was reduced by 50 per cent. Theatres and cinemas had to switch off exterior signs and publicity showcases – and football took a kicking too. The use of floodlights was banned, and midweek games were moved to the afternoon with crowd figures plummeting as a result.

To make matters worse, in October England had failed to win their crucial World Cup qualifying game against Poland at Wembley and were out of the following summer's tournament in West Germany. And, closer to home, Liverpool had tumbled out of the European Cup, being given a two-legged football lesson by Yugoslavs Red Star Belgrade. That brace of defeats led to a Boot Room inquest that opined that the game had to be played 'from the back'. Defenders had to be creative as well as destructive. 'The Europeans showed that building from the back is the only way to play,' said Shankly.

Things briefly brightened for the Reds in the first week of December as they beat Hull City in the League Cup fourth-round replay played in front of just 17,120 spectators on a Tuesday afternoon.

Of course, those of us studying hard at university (!) managed to slip away in time to see the match get underway at 2pm – a kick-off time reflecting the need to manage any extra time that might be needed on a cold winter's afternoon with hours of daylight getting shorter.

Those of us there felt pleased with ourselves – of course, the rest of the population was at work, school or queueing up to fill their cars from an ever-diminishing supply of petrol. What we did witness at Anfield that day was a small piece of Liverpool FC history. Their 3-1 win over Hull City included a hat-trick from Ian Callaghan.

Liverpool's longest-serving star played over 850 games and scored just 68 goals in them. A brilliant winger turned midfield dynamo, 'Cally' was the bricks and mortar of Shankly's sides of both the 60s and 70s, and would also play an important role in Bob Paisley's early seasons in charge of the Reds, including their iconic 1977 European Cup Final triumph in Rome. On this afternoon in December 1973, Cally's hat-trick was completed in the 73rd minute, following two goals he had scored in the opening 20 minutes of the first half.

Four days later Liverpool went to Goodison Park to play in the first derby match of the season.

More than 56,000 crammed into Goodison Park that afternoon, kick-off 2pm, and the game was won by a single goal for Liverpool scored by a one-hit wonder Alan Waddle. Deputising for the injured John Toshack, Waddle, who had joined the club that summer from Halifax Town, got on the end of a Callaghan cross and beat David Lawson in the Everton goal.

Waddle, a limited but likeable player, covered for Liverpool's injured Welshman 16 times that season but only scored once, his only goal a winner in a derby match, his place in the history secured. Over the next three seasons he just made six more appearances for LFC, all as a non-scoring substitute, before moving on. Nothing subsequently matched his own special career moment – the winning goal in a Merseyside derby. Nothing more needed.

It was the second half of the season that really set things on fire for the Reds, culminating in a trip to Wembley, and another FA Cup Final. In truth, it was a cup run that started with a couple of troublesome ties in the third and fourth rounds – relatively comfortable home draws against Doncaster Rovers and Carlisle United went to unexpected replays.

The South Yorkshire side had come to Anfield bottom of the Fourth Division, 90 places below their famous Merseyside hosts. Surely it was a done deal that Liverpool would roll them over easily? 'Cricket score' – that type of thing. Well, Doncaster-born Kevin Keegan did his bit, scoring an early goal, but precocious Rovers equalised and then went ahead. They led the match for nearly 40 minutes before Keegan pulled the Reds, faces and shirts, level.

In the dying seconds Rovers' marksman Peter Kitchen hit the crossbar with a clever lob, and Liverpool escaped an FA Cup defeat that would have been up there with their infamous Worcester City debacle in the 1950s.

The replay was relatively straightforward, a 2-0 win, the same score as in their fourth-round replay at Second Division

Carlisle United, the first match at Anfield having ended goalless.

Ipswich Town were put to the sword in the fifth round, and then a single John Toshack goal beat Bristol City, who had beaten runaway First Division leaders Leeds United in the previous round.

Liverpool would finish runners-up in the league to Don Revie's men, who had enjoyed a long unbeaten run from a cracking start in August.

The FA Cup semi-final against Leicester City took us to first Old Trafford for a 0-0 draw that Liverpool dominated, and then in the midweek to Villa Park. Shankly's message to his team before the replay was as colourful as it was cunning. 'Imagine that you're getting battered by George Foreman (the world heavyweight champion at the time), then the lights go out and you have to go through it all again – that's how Leicester feel.'

I was at both matches and certainly the replay was an exciting affair, including a fantastic goal from Kevin Keegan in a 3-1 win. Memory fails me to how I got there and back on the night but somehow you always did. And so, I had to go on another hunt for that most elusive of commodities – an FA Cup Final ticket. Always a challenge. And in 1974, believe me, a spare ticket to watch Liverpool meet Newcastle United in the FA Cup Final at Wembley Stadium on the first Saturday in May was nigh impossible to get your hands on.

I suffered many false dawns, and too many false promises, in the weeks ahead of the big day – and was beginning to give up hope. I'd resigned myself to a long stretch watching *FA Cup Final Grandstand* from start to finish. Then 48 hours before the big game my dad came home from work with a sealed envelope and a wide smile.

'There's something in it for you,' said Dad. And, sure enough, there was. A terrace ticket, behind the goal at the tunnel end of Wembley Stadium where the mass ranks of Liverpool fans would be standing, swaying and singing. Perfect.

As was Liverpool's performance on the day. Newcastle United's star striker, Malcolm Macdonald, had mouthed off in the week of the game about how his team had nothing to fear from their Merseyside opponents. By the end of the game the Kopites rang out a chorus of 'Supermac is only good when it's raining!!'

Liverpool simply put the Geordies in their place with a three-goal second-half blast. It was a very one-sided final, that's for sure. 'Goals pay the rent and Keegan does his share,' BBC TV's David Coleman purred, as Liverpool deservedly took a 55th-minute lead. Steve Heighway then scored in his second successive FA Cup Final.

And in the 88th minute a masterful move, involving a marvellous sequence of passing, delivered the ball on a plate for Keegan to grab his second. 'And Newcastle were undressed.' Coleman again. Their crestfallen team included two Anfield legends to be: Terry McDermott and Alan Kennedy.

Bill Shankly was caught on cameras moving his arms around on the bench as if guiding a plane into its parking slot, the Anfield faithful repeatedly chanting his name. At the end of the game, two supporters even raced on to the pitch, knelt down and went to kiss his feet. 'Ay, polish my shoes while you're down there, lads,' Shankly quipped.

As a proud 14-year-old boy living in Glenbuck, Ayrshire, a young Bill Shankly would have rejoiced on the day in 1928 when a makeshift Scotland team went down to Wembley Stadium and hammered the much-fancied England team 5-1.

On 4 May 1974, Shankly's 70s side had put on their own outstanding display. Bill had his own team of 'Wembley

Wizards' and he must have been proud as Punch as his players conjured up their own dazzling magical show.

In the glorious aftermath of the final, both at Wembley itself and then back home in Liverpool the following day, in front of tens of thousands of adoring fans, Bill Shankly was acclaimed like never before. And, once again, just by raising his hands, he was able to bring a rapturous crowd to absolute silence and his subsequent victory oration held them spellbound.

It was a simply glorious time. Nobody would have guessed then that the next trick up the great man's sleeve was to be a showstopping vanishing act.

Kop That – *On 14 occasions a Liverpool player has been voted the Football Writers' Footballer of the Year, with Ian Callaghan being the first recipient in 1974.*

1974/75 – SHOCK WAVES
AND STILL WATERS

WHEN THE media were summoned to Anfield on Friday, 12 July 1974 for an unscheduled press conference, there was no sense of what news was about to be delivered. But perhaps the timing of the gathering gave it an added sense of theatre – noon. High noon.

Liverpool chairman John Smith made the staggering announcement that Bill Shankly was leaving his beloved Anfield. One of the most charismatic figures in the history of British football was retiring. 'Guided by my conscience. My conscience is honest so if I do something, I'm doing the right thing. Coming to my decision was like walking to the electric chair.'

Shankly talked of feeling tired and of the pressures being intense. Of his desire to spend more time with Nessie, his wife. His decision was national news and stopped the Red half of Liverpool in its tracks. Myself included. That day I was doing the latest shift at my summer holiday job in the famous Schofields lemonade factory, in Dalrymple Street just off Scotland Road.

I was helping load lorries with crates of cream soda, dandelion and burdock, and orangeade. I say helping, more like hindering, as the regular staff worked at a pace I couldn't keep up with – and they knew it. Still, they fired the crates at me like bullets from a gun. Character-building stuff for this second-year student of economics – and some.

Anyway, come a few minutes past 12 noon that day, with crates of fizzy pop whizzing past my ears, a guy ran into the depot and shouted 'SHANKLY'S RETIRED!!!!' The conveyor belt came to a complete halt. The staff were stunned – even the Evertonians.

I was devastated. Shankly was a bigger hero for me than any of the great players who served under him so brilliantly. Still is. I took the rest of the day off and like many others couldn't quite get my head around it. Liverpool *without* Shankly? How does that work?

Liverpool had actually signed a player on the day he retired – Ray Kennedy, from Arsenal, who would become an important piece in the post-Shankly jigsaw.

Bill Shankly would lead the Liverpool team out at the FA Charity Shield match against Leeds United at Wembley Stadium, a game memorable for Kevin Keegan and Billy Bremner being sent off for fighting, and would be feted by his adoring Anfield fans the following April in a testimonial match between Liverpool and a team picked by his old managerial foe Don Revie.

If truth be told, Bill Shankly initially found retirement a difficult pill to swallow. It became known that he would regularly threaten to resign in football's close seasons, and then be persuaded not to. Only this time he had seen it through. In the early days following his big decision, he would still turn up at Melwood, making it confusing for the players who now had a new boss.

Over time, Shankly would go to watch matches at Anfield, even standing on the Kop on one occasion, Goodison Park and Prenton Park, and was a welcome guest at games up and down the country. As time passed, gradually his influence and profile naturally diminished. Poignantly, in 1977, when Liverpool brought their first European Cup back to a wildly excited city, Shankly was on the extreme edge of the victor's balcony, left of centre stage.

Bill Shankly died on 29 September 1981, aged just 68. I was privileged to attend his memorial service held at Liverpool Cathedral, an event laced with warmth and respect for the great man.

At Anfield itself, the Shankly Gates and the lifelike statue erected outside the Kop are two fitting lasting epitaphs. A thousand words have been written and spoken about him. I love these delivered by that late, great broadcaster Bryon Butler: 'Lord of the fanatics, all Scot and Scouse, a legend in a tracksuit, the embodiment of Liverpool, the master of Anfield ... a man who turned a game of sweat and blood into a faith.'

Shankly himself put it this way: 'I wanted results for the club, for the love of the game, to make people happy.' And he did.

Back in August 1974, Liverpool had replaced Shankly within a fortnight, not with the latest big managerial name but with somebody very reluctant to actually take the job. Bob Paisley turned the job down twice before finally, at a third time of asking, succumbing to the dual offensive of Liverpool chairman John Smith and secretary Peter Robinson.

Paisley, a quiet, unassuming individual, had been heavily immersed in life at Anfield for over 35 years. Born in Hetton-le-Hole in County Durham, coal-mining territory in England's industrial north-east, Paisley excelled at sport at school. His early football adventures saw him play as a 20-year-old wing-half for Bishop Auckland in the FA Amateur Cup Final against Willington.

Sunderland seemed an obvious destination, and it would seem they told him they were interested. Only for the Roker Park club not to follow it up because they felt he was too small.

George Kay, the then Liverpool manager, didn't share that view and snapped him up for the Reds.

The apprentice bricklayer had found his football home, but all that was put on hold as king and country called – and Paisley was off to war. In World War II, Paisley would serve in the Royal Artillery and then the Eighth Army at El Alamein in Egypt. It would help shape his take on life.

When hostilities came to an end Bob Paisley settled back at Anfield and he kick-started a professional career of 277 games for the Reds, scoring just 13 goals.

Mind you, one of those rare goals was in an FA Cup semi-final against Everton. Famously, Paisley was left out of the Reds' line-up for the 1950 final itself against Arsenal at Wembley.

His name had actually been printed in the cup final programme, but he wasn't selected on the big day, having missed four games through injury following the semi-final win. He was devastated. He told manager George Kay he was fit to play. And he did, but four days after the final, in the Reds' final league game of the season.

Retiring in 1954, Paisley started life behind the scenes at Anfield, firstly using his building skills before taking an interest in physiotherapy and medical matters. He worked his way through the ranks including trainer, reserve team coach and through to assistant manager by 1974. But when it came along, he didn't fancy taking on the big job. It was partly out of respect for the outgoing Bill Shankly, who he hoped would change his mind about retiring and return, and because he didn't feel he had all the attributes needed to follow such a legend.

Smith and Robinson kept trying to persuade him, thinking whatever deficiencies he may think he had, there was a strong set of individuals in and around him to help him – Joe Fagan, Ronnie Moran and Reuben Bennett. And Paisley was ultimately persuaded but, as he said, 'It's like being given the *Queen Elizabeth* to steer in a force ten gale.'

The players themselves were unsure. Many were disciples of Bill Shankly, loved how he motivated them, his all-embracing style and his winning mentality.

Paisley's early team talks were short, sketchy and uninspiring. He stumbled around opponents' names and left his team unsure what was expected of them – individually and collectively. There was a story that after a couple of months he actually asked to be relieved of the role, but the Liverpool board stood firm, and stood behind him. And they were proved right.

When he retired nine years later Bob Paisley OBE had become the most successful manager in British football history.

Kop That – *In Shankly's 783 games in charge in all competitions, the Scot used just 71 players, with Ian Callaghan making 660 appearances throughout the period.*

1975/76 – A MODEST SUCCESS

BOB PAISLEY'S first season in charge of 'the big heads' had been a bit of a curate's egg – some good, some not so good.

They did finish second in the league. They did land the club's biggest-ever win, an 11-0 drubbing of Norwegians Strømsgodset Drammen in the Cup Winners' Cup. But they were knocked out early in both domestic cup competitions, and were out of Europe before Christmas.

Paisley was still viewed with some scepticism by both his players and the fans alike – myself included. Off the field, bringing former headmaster Tom Saunders into the inner sanctum had proved a good move, and, on the field, Paisley had decided to develop a more football-playing back line.

It was in his second season when a combination of his innate knowledge of the game and his propensity to try new things and new players started to deliver the goods. But the 1975/76 season didn't start well. A 2-0 defeat to QPR at Loftus Road, coupled with a dismal performance in the capital and ructions in the away dressing room after it, didn't augur well for the forthcoming campaign.

Two of the big influencers in the Liverpool dressing room, Tommy Smith and Liverpool captain Emlyn Hughes, simply didn't get on, and made no bones about it. Smith thought Hughes had too much access to the new Liverpool manager, and he probably did, and Hughes didn't care what Tommy Smith thought.

While that internal feud went on and on, Paisley, aided by his Boot Room team, started to change things around on the pitch in his second term. Goalkeeper Ray Clemence and full-back Phil Neal played all 42 league games, Phil Thompson, Kevin Keegan and Emlyn Hughes 41 each, the evergreen Ian Callaghan 40 matches and Steve Heighway made 39 league appearances.

But elsewhere things were changing. In an inspired move Paisley moved misfiring striker Ray Kennedy back into midfield, a masterstroke which bore fruit for the next six seasons. And he introduced local boys Jimmy Case and David Fairclough into first-team action with spectacular results.

Case fancied himself as a forward, but the Boot Room saw him more as a hard-tackling midfielder who could get a fair share of goals as well. A qualified electrician by trade, Case was spotted playing for South Liverpool and was snapped up by the Reds. David Fairclough was a speedy forward with a mop of red hair. Tall and talented he made a big impact, especially when coming off the bench as a substitute.

Paisley, whose affection for horse racing almost matched his love of football, would have described his new unlikely talisman as an 'improving leggy colt' with a big finish. He would ultimately be tagged as 'Super Sub', something he resented, but the evidence of his debut season, 1975/76, gave merit to the argument.

Fairclough started five league matches and came on as substitute in another nine, and in a title-winning sequence of scoring notched seven goals in an eight-game run, with four of them having come off the bench. It was a remarkable achievement, including a wonderful twisting and turning run and shot that secured a late win over Everton, and yet Fairclough's most famous Liverpool goal was still a year away.

I witnessed Paisley's first title-winning season from a new perspective. I had finally made the move from the Paddock to the Kop. This was a big moment in my support for the Reds and I had already notched up 15 years' commitment to the cause. Scrapbooks, programmes, autographs, photographs, newspaper cuttings, annuals, ticket stubs, badges, bubblegum cards, rosettes, scarfs and rattles – I had collected the lot, and still have lots of them to this day. More of that later. Now it was time to take leave of my special place in the Paddock and be part of something totally unique.

Whatever your team, wherever you sit or stand in a stadium, you tend to 'own' your space, be defined by it, get used to watching a match through that specific prism, from that angle, and around the same folk, so moving your spec is not a decision a real football fan takes lightly.

For me to become a Kopite was almost a rite of passage, time to be part of the choir, not the audience. Time to be part of the prematch rituals of the most famous terrace in world football. Time to 'try and suck the ball into the net for the Reds'. Time to watch in awe as young lads scrambled over the fence between the Boys' Pen and the Kop then jumped between the girders, high above our heads. The ones that held the roof up!

Big matches seemed bigger matches when standing on the Kop. You got there earlier, tried to find the perfect spec, then realised during the motions of the game, you had moved 20 yards up and 30 yards across from where you originally marked your spot, and without really noticing it.

The noise was deafening, the banners magnificent, the songs seemed to emerge from the epicentre, and then spread left and right, and new songs were learned over several weeks

– no Wikipedia in those days – until we were all word-perfect. And, of course, then there were the bragging rights. If you met a football fan from another club, you just puffed your chest out and said you were a Kopite. Enough said.

The Kop also had its own mix of slightly less than fragrant odours wafting up and down the famous terrace. Perspiration, okay, sweat ... and lots of it, fried onions straight out of the burger buns, meat pies, beer drank, and beer spilt ... and finally, and how can I put this delicately ... pee ... and lots of it! Ah yes, the age-old problem of having had a skinful before the game and then landing yourself among 15,000 people tightly packed together like sardines for the next two hours. The rolled-up *Liverpool Echo* is no myth.

Bob Paisley had got his Reds, quietly and modestly, to a remarkable season finale. The closing weeks of the campaign would see his side compete in a two-legged European final, and a remarkable one-match shoot-out for the First Division championship.

Liverpool's final match of the season was away to Wolves. The Reds needed to win, or draw 0-0 or 1-1, to be confirmed champions; anything else and the team that inflicted a 2-0 defeat on the Reds on the opening day of the season, QPR, would be crowned unlikely champions. Oh, and Wolves needed to win the match to retain their First Division status. They created a special match programme for the game, and splashed across the front cover was 'Wolverhampton Wanderers FC Proudly Present THE GREAT FIRST DIVISION DRAMA'. Curtain rises at 7.30pm.

Nothing much on the game then! And, of course, in those days there was no live TV coverage of the match, even though it was a title decider, not that it would have stopped the thousands of Liverpool fans heading down the M6 to be part of what promised to be a special night. When we arrived at Molineux, turnstiles were gradually getting slammed shut, but we just managed to get through one which was still open, and joined the massed ranks of Liverpool fans behind the goal.

In the match itself, Warrington-born Steve Kindon put Wolves ahead with a blistering shot in the 13th minute – unlucky for some. And for the next hour it seemed it would be that way for Liverpool. Back in a London TV studio a group of QPR players were preparing to uncork the champagne.

It was a fretful night for us Reds watching our heroes struggle, until the 76th minute when Kevin Keegan wriggled beyond Wolves' despairing defenders and slotted the ball home. 1-1.

His strike partner John Toshack nudged Liverpool ahead in the 85th minute and Ray Kennedy put the game and the title to bed a minute from time. At the end of the game, thousands of Liverpool fans spilled on to the Molineux pitch to celebrate – I had not done that before and haven't done it since – and then we all joined the longest traffic jam in Western Europe. And did a mass conga down the M6. Who cared? We were champions again.

For Bob Paisley it was a great triumph which he handled in his usual modest way. A fortnight later, he was a European champion as well, as Liverpool lifted the UEFA Cup with a second-leg 1-1 draw against Bruges.

The first leg in late April at Anfield had been dramatic – the Reds had trailed 2-0 to the Belgians early in the first half before delivering one of those special European comebacks the club have now become famous for. Playing towards the fervent Kop, with its occupants at full voice, Ray Kennedy pulled one back in the 59th minute before substitute Jimmy Case levelled matters two minutes later. Astonishingly, three minutes after that, Steve Heighway was pulled down in the box and Kevin Keegan stepped up to score a penalty and put Liverpool ahead 3-2.

It was one of those memorable occasions when us Kopites felt we had tried to suck the ball into the opponents' net. And succeeded.

Kop That – *By a remarkable coincidence, Bob Paisley's first championship as a player and then as a manager came after the Reds won their final league game of the season at Molineux.*

1976/77 – EUROPEAN GLORY

'RUB YOUR eyes again. Liverpool last night became the champions of Europe. It was a memorable, unbelievable and unforgettable occasion.'

One of Fleet Street's finest description of the events in the Stadio Olimpico in Rome on the evening Liverpool Football Club lifted the European Cup and were crowned as the kings of European football. And it was all those things and more – back then, we couldn't have dared dream the Reds would go on to win club football's most prestigious trophy another five times. Every one of them special.

But this was the first time, and that made it extra special. Wednesday, 25 May 1977 – an historic day for everybody with an affection for the Anfield club the world over.

Liverpool were now sitting proudly centre stage on football's top table – the elite of the elite.

It was estimated 25,000 of us were there to witness football history being made on that sultry Italian evening – and another half a million people would give our triumphant gladiators the thumbs up when they paraded their hard-won booty around Liverpool the following evening.

Nine months earlier. 30 August 1976, to be exact. Bank Holiday Monday. It is 5pm. I have just arrived in Barrow-in-Furness and the streets are empty. Obviously my 'big-money transfer' from working part-time on a garage forecourt in Liverpool to starting life as a junior reporter on a small daily newspaper in Cumbria was not headline-grabbing stuff.

But it was for me. It was the starting point of the next 40-odd years of my life – a career in which I would work for some of the most prestigious media and sporting organisations in the country, hold down some important public positions, become the subject of media attention myself, witness iconic sporting moments right up close, and meet many of my heroes – and rarely be disappointed.

All while having a wonderful time turning my childhood passion for sport into a lengthy and rewarding career. I'd always harboured ambitions to be a sports reporter. While watching the 1966 World Cup tournament on TV, as a 12-year-old, I would type out short match reports on my much-loved Petite typewriter. On leaving university, I had tried very hard to break into my chosen profession, with no luck, whilst my mum and dad quietly humoured me and wished I'd settle down and get 'a proper job'.

Anyway, my big break came when I was recruited as the youngest and least experienced reporter on the news desk on the *North-West Evening Mail*, and what I lacked in experience I made up for with enthusiasm. Armed with a sharp pencil, a reporter's notebook and a newly minted press pass, I was ready to take on the world, or a small part of Cumbria at least.

My new job did come with its downsides. The opportunities to see the Reds regularly were clearly diminished – although, on my second night in my new town, a trip to watch Barrow FC at Holker Street ended with me having a post-match beer with Liverpool heroes Ron Yeats and Tony Hateley, both seeing out their playing careers in the quieter waters of the Northern Premier League. And I would routinely race back to Liverpool every Saturday evening to take my place in the Sunday league pub team Storrsdale FC the following day.

Its players were drawn from those lads who enjoyed a pint or two in The Storrsdale, a pub managed by a former Liverpool player, and subsequent scout for the Reds, Norman Low. And we played in an old Liverpool FC away kit, white shirts, black shorts, red socks, which my dad had got from an old police pal who worked at the Liverpool County FA. It did take a little persuasion for some of the Evertonians in the team to actually wear it, but we got there somehow.

If for some reason I couldn't make it back to Liverpool I would turn out for a side in the Barrow Sunday League. And, on one such occasion, I spotted a well-known face watching the action from the touchline. Emlyn Hughes.

Emlyn was born in Barrow and still had family up there. The town was proud of its famous 'son' and every time we wrote about him in the *Evening Mail*, which was just about every night, we had to preface his name with 'Barrow-born'. I once omitted it from a story I was writing and got a dressing down from the editor. 'Emlyn Hughes is one of ours and never let our readers forget it,' said the boss. 'Don't you mean Barrow-born Emlyn Hughes?' said a cheeky young Scouser pushing his luck!

Living in a remote town like Barrow did throw up the odd curveball, perhaps most frustratingly on the night Liverpool played those great French champions, Saint-Étienne, in that epic European Cup quarter-final. I was determined to get to the game and got permission to leave work in good time to make it. The problem was the guy I was travelling from Barrow with, a local Liverpool-mad solicitor, got delayed at some court proceedings, and by the time we got in his car we were pushing it to make it to Liverpool in time.

Travelling from Barrow to anywhere takes a while before you hook up with the M6, and a tractor can pop up at any stage en route and slow you down to a snail's pace. And, sure enough, one did that night. We got to Liverpool very late, deserted the car about half a mile from the ground and sprinted up Priory Road, arriving just minutes before the kick-off only to be greeted with all the turnstiles slamming shut.

Locked out and lucked out, we tried every which way to get inside Anfield that night but failed, and then listened, with mixed emotions, along with a couple of thousand other frustrated souls, as the capacity crowd inside the ground went crazy as Kevin Keegan scored in the second minute to level the tie on aggregate. We stuck around for another 15 minutes outside the ground, hoping by some miracle the turnstiles would open again, before, crestfallen, we slowly headed back to the car.

There were no tractors to get in our way as we travelled *back* to Barrow, and we listened on the car radio as David Fairclough scored his famous tie-clinching goal on 'one of the greatest nights in Liverpool's history!' Or words to that effect from the exuberant commentator. The first cut is the deepest. There were long periods of silence in the car on that return journey.

Liverpool's season went from strength to strength. Another league championship was clinched the week before Paisley's men met Manchester United in the FA Cup Final. The treble was on because the Reds had also won through to the European Cup Final, to be played in Rome four days after the big domestic showdown between Liverpool and Manchester United. I went to both matches, and although we lost to United, with my old school and Liverpool University mate Steve Coppell in their ranks, and despite an often-forgotten superb goal from Jimmy Case, any disappointment was tempered by the fact I'd be setting off by train to Rome on Monday teatime.

It was a real adventure. If Saturday's journey had been to 'Anfield South', as Wembley Stadium became dubbed given Liverpool's regular visits there, this one was to Anfield

Further South – the Stadio Olimpico in Rome. And we were going to Italy by rail. Our train tickets had 'Rome and back' printed on the front, which was comforting to know. And, as a procession of engines pulled out of Lime Street Station, the sense of excitement, both in the packed carriages themselves and from those waving us off on the platform, was palpable. Train after train left Liverpool. Spirits were sky-high; there was no thought of us losing this one.

We arrived in Rome at 6am Wednesday morning tired but excited, and spent the hours before the match visiting the sites of this famous city, counting down the hours to the kick-off. When we got into the stadium itself, it became clear that we probably outnumbered the supporters of fellow finalists Borussia Mönchengladbach by about four to one.

When the Liverpool players came out to warm up they were blown away by the colour and noise coming from the legions of Liverpool fans in the stadium. The match itself was tremendous. Liverpool went ahead in the first half through Terry McDermott, and the Germans equalised early in the second half.

Liverpool's second goal was legendary stuff as veteran Tommy Smith, of all people, headed in a Steve Heighway corner. A penalty won by the outstanding Kevin Keegan, playing his final game for the Reds, and netted by Phil Neal completed the scoring and the celebrations had already got underway as Barrow-born(!) Emlyn Hughes lifted the European Cup – a stylish trophy that truly befits the accomplishment of winning it.

What a night to be a Liverpudlian! Mind you, in what seemed to be a late change of plans by the Italian police we were all back on the trains and setting off out of Rome by midnight. And the train went through West Germany without stopping – probably wise that.

Over 40 hours later we arrived back in Lime Street Station, exhausted, starving, thirsty, in need of a hot shower, and still chuffed to bits. We were just a little bit too late to get across to Anfield to catch Tommy Smith's testimonial, but not too late to get to The Storrsdale before closing time, have a couple of pints and reflect on a fantastic few days. Memorable.

Kop That *– After adding the European Cup to other trophy wins, Ian Callaghan in 1977 won a third England cap a record 11 years and 49 days after his second, which was gained during the 1966 World Cup campaign.*

Bill Shankly enjoys a cuppa with some potential future stars.

Liverpool players all ears for the traditional Monday lunchtime FA Cup draw.

Liverpool legend Ken Dodd entertains the Reds on cup final eve.

Half-term treat – school children watch their heroes train.

'Please pick me, boss.'

Bill Shankly and his main men.

Bob Paisley takes his first steps as the Reds' new boss.

Kenny Dalglish signs for Liverpool – an Anfield legend has arrived.

Bill Shankly in a thoughtful mood.

Kevin Keegan and Ray Clemence enjoy European Cup glory.

King Kenny clinches the league title – and the FA Cup is to follow.

Ian Rush celebrates an FA Cup Final goal – the double is won!

'A cup final with your name on it.'

Gérard Houllier lifts the UEFA Cup.

John Barnes – a special player.

Michael Owen – a striker supreme.

*Robbie Fowler –
'one of our own'.*

1977/78 – THE SCOTTISH SPINE

AS THE July summer sunshine in 1977 drove millions to the beaches both here and abroad, the pop charts were topped by a song that had a familiar ring about it. 'So You Win Again', Hot Chocolate's number one hit, could have been the mantra for the reigning European champions as they returned to Melwood for preseason training in preparation for another campaign. Their previous glorious achievements were already destined for the history books.

The Boot Room always looked forwards not backwards – no room for complacency, no time for backslapping, no 'show us your medals' – last season was past; the attention now was on the here and now.

Life had changed in the weeks after Liverpool had won the European Cup. Their man of the match in Rome, Kevin Keegan, had made good his ambition to play abroad by moving to Hamburg. He had signposted his attention to be an English football export at the start of the previous season and probably had loftier sights than the rather unfashionable German team, but he became as great a favourite there as he had been at Anfield – and twice won the Ballon D'Or, European Footballer of the Year, while there.

Bob Paisley had lots of time to think about how to replace Keegan and chose to call time on the big man/little man strike force. So, John Toshack's days leading the line at Anfield were numbered too. The player they targeted to kick-start another campaign of 'winning again' was Celtic's Kenny Dalglish. At 26, Dalglish was ready to leave Parkhead and test himself in English football's top division. And Liverpool's transfer strike force of chairman John Smith and secretary Peter Robinson set out to get him.

Celtic were not keen to sell but a British transfer record fee of £440,000 loosened their grip on their mercurial talent and off he headed to Anfield.

Eleven years earlier a 15-year-old Dalglish had spent a few days at Liverpool and he had taken in the 1966 FA Charity Shield match between Everton and Liverpool as part of his trip. Dalglish's formal debut for Liverpool was also in the FA Charity Shield, this time against Manchester United at Wembley Stadium.

When the real action got underway, he was a smash hit. He scored within seven minutes of his league debut at Middlesbrough and netted again in the following two home matches against Newcastle United and West Brom.

I remember a particularly clever goal he scored against Chelsea at Anfield inside 90 seconds of the game starting. He played all 42 league games in his first season, 62 games in all, scoring 31 goals.

Dalglish also made goals for his team-mates – 'assists' as they are called now. His ability to hold up a ball and find a red shirt with a killer pass was also in his armoury. This book will capture many of the great times we were spellbound by King Kenny, also marvel at his move from pitch to the management hot seat, and also register the immeasurable compassion and leadership he showed when the Hillsborough disaster devastated a club and a city. The knighthood he was awarded in 2018 was fully deserved.

Over the years I've got to know Sir Kenny Dalglish and his family well – good people, who rarely put themselves first. Back in 1977, as Kenny Dalglish settled into his new environment, so too did another Scot, a former Partick Thistle player who would become one of Liverpool's all-time great players.

Alan Hansen was a natural athlete – a Scottish international, at various levels, at four different sports. Football was just one of them. But Liverpool made their move for this ball-playing, intelligent centre-back towards the end of the 1976/77 season, an annual unofficial transfer 'window' for LFC who used some of their purchase power to offset corporation taxes that came their way at that time of the year.

Hansen didn't start the new season in the first team but ended it playing in a European Cup Final. He would later captain Liverpool's double-winning side and have a remarkably successful 'second' career as one of the leading football pundits on British television. Paisley might have been fortunate to pick out Hansen the footballer; I was lucky enough to be in the driving seat at the start of the erudite Scotsman's broadcasting career at BBC TV Sport that spanned over two decades. Always a team player – and fun to be around.

Bob Paisley always had his eye on Graeme Souness to become his midfield general, leader and enforcer. Having started his career at Tottenham Hotspur, Souness was now at Middlesbrough and LFC kept their tabs on his progress. They made their move for him in January 1978 – he scored a stunning goal for the Reds against Manchester United at Anfield in February, BBC *Match of the Day*'s Goal of the Month, and made central midfield for Liverpool his home until he moved to Italy in 1984.

A suave, stylish dresser, a driver of smart cars, a man with an eye for the good things in life – that was Graeme Souness. Called 'Charlie', short for Champagne Charlie, his then girlfriend, Mary Stävin, was the reigning Miss World. But Souness, the footballer, was all-consuming when he crossed that white line on a Saturday afternoon or Wednesday evening. Paisley knew he had a player who could handle himself, control his team-mates and dominate his opponents, sometimes with subtle skills, sometimes with brute force.

In Dalglish, Hansen and Souness, Bob Paisley had out-and-out winners – they made nearly 1,500 appearances for the Reds between them, and like Shankly before him, in Yeats and St John, Paisley had built a Scottish spine at the heart of his team. The 1977/78 season itself was a curious mix – runners-up in the league but without ever being real contenders, and an embarrassing defeat in the FA Cup third round against Chelsea.

On the upside Liverpool had convincingly won the European Super Cup, beating Kevin Keegan's Hamburg 7-1 on aggregate, including a stonking 6-0 home win in the second leg, with a hat-trick from Terry McDermott. Liverpool's approach to the Football League Cup had always been a bit patchy. They first played in the inaugural competition in 1960/61 but then opted out of it until 1967/68.

As its status grew – not least with the final moving to Wembley, replacing the previous two-legged affair – it became a trophy worth winning. And indeed, Liverpool did just that, winning it four successive times in the early 80s.

Their first final came in March 1978, against Nottingham Forest, and their outspoken gifted manager Brian Clough. Clough, and his sidekick Peter Taylor, had taken Nottingham Forest out of the Second Division and would win the First Division championship in their first season back. A remarkable achievement by any measure, and having shared a goalless draw at Wembley with Paisley's men, Forest went on to win the replay at Old Trafford with a disputed penalty. Nottingham

Forest would become a thorn in Liverpool's side for the next few seasons.

Clough, like Paisley, was from the north-east. Both real football men – but vastly different characters. If Paisley was quiet, uncommunicative and essentially shy, Clough was the opposite. He was a headline maker, a man of opinions, charismatic and TV gold. Every self-respecting stage and screen impressionist at that time had to have 'Brian Clough' in their act. They'd have struggled with Bob. Mind you, Terry McDermott would seem to have got his voice and unusual gait off to a tee.

Liverpool would return to Wembley in May to play in the European Cup Final against Belgian champions, Bruges – a European final on home soil.

En route the Reds had beaten Dynamo Dresden, Benfica and their opponents in the previous year's final, Borussia Mönchengladbach, and two years on from beating them to win the UEFA Cup, Bruges stood between Liverpool and a second European Cup Final win.

As a Liverpool fan it was a slightly weird experience – having spent the best part of a week getting to and from Rome by train the previous year, now it was less than three hours before the train from Liverpool pulled into London. I know I felt it was less of an adventure than the previous year, but a European Cup Final was a European Cup Final. And who knows when we would be in another one!

What I do remember of the occasion was that Wembley Stadium seemed to be owned by Liverpool fans on that evening. If 25,000 Liverpool fans had made it to Rome, more than double that number were there at Wembley to see Liverpool crowned European Cup winners again.

To underline that nothing stands still in football, the team fielded for the big night showed no less than five changes from the Reds' Roman conquest.

Into the starting line-up had come Phil Thompson, Alan Hansen, David Fairclough, Graeme Souness and Kenny Dalglish – out of the team Joey Jones, an injured Tommy Smith, Ian Callaghan, Steve Heighway and Kevin Keegan.

The decisive moment in the game came midway through the second half when Souness played a neat ball into Dalglish, who with poise and precision neatly chipped it over the outrushing Bruges goalkeeper into the net.

Job done. And our 'Football Special' had us back in Lime Street in the early hours of the morning. Still tired, hungry, thirsty and needing a hot shower, but home sweet home.

So, Liverpool *had* won again.

Kop That – *In October 1977, Kenny Dalglish scored for the away side (Scotland) in a World Cup qualifier defeat of Wales at Anfield. The game was switched to Merseyside after crowd trouble at Cardiff.*

1978/79 – ANOTHER TROPHY IN ANOTHER HAUL

ON 21 June 1978, the world premiere of *Evita* took place in London's West End. The smash-hit musical concentrates on the extraordinary life of political leader Eva Perón, the wife of post-war Argentinian president Juan Perón. Unusual concept perhaps, but Eva's rags to riches story and the wonderful songs and score from the gifted Tim Rice and Andrew Lloyd Webber made it the hottest ticket in town.

And that was still the case a year later, when having recently settled in London I thought I would treat myself to a matinee performance of *Evita*. I rather foolishly bought a ticket from a tout outside the theatre. 'Best seat in the house, mate!' he told me. When I actually went in, I climbed up one set of stairs after another before eventually finding my seat right on the very back row of the theatre. I reckon I was nearer Argentina itself than the front of the stage!

Lesson learned.

Four days after *Evita* had made its triumphant debut in London, over in Buenos Aires, the country's football-mad population were wildly celebrating host nation Argentina winning the 1978 World Cup with a 3-1 win over the Netherlands in the final. It was a World Cup shrouded in controversy, with the country itself having been the subject of a military coup in 1976 and the troubling 'disappearance' of over 5,000 people as the dictatorship took hold. Argentinian World Cup stars included Osvaldo Ardiles and Ricardo Villa, and in a huge headline-grabbing coup, newly promoted Tottenham Hotspur bought both of them ahead of the new English season.

Two World Cup winners, heroes in Argentina, were now centre stage in a new country, but the talented duo got a very clear idea of how tough things might get in the overture and opening acts of the season. Anfield legend Tommy Smith, often seen as a pantomime villain himself, gave the two new imports a 'special' welcome when playing against them for his new club Swansea in a League Cup tie at the Vetch Field in the early days of the new campaign.

Within two minutes of the start of the match, Tommy's chest-high tackle on Ardiles, playing his fourth match on British soil, nearly cut the diminutive South American in half. The canny Argentine midfielder, who had studied law at university, must have wondered whether he had just been a victim of a common assault.

A few days later, Ardiles had recovered enough to be in the Spurs line-up, with Ricky Villa, at Anfield to meet Liverpool, who were looking for their fourth straight league win of the new season.

And, boy, did they get it. 7-0. Liverpool were brilliant that sunny late summer afternoon. The rampant Reds simply swamped Spurs and wrapped up their victory with a swift passing move climaxing in a pinpoint Heighway cross, and a brilliant header from Terry McDermott, the player who had started the move way back in his own half. Paisley described it as 'possibly the best goal ever scored at Anfield'.

Liverpool's left-back that day was close-season signing Alan Kennedy, who played for Newcastle United against the Reds in the 1974 FA Cup Final. Kennedy would take a while to settle in at Anfield but by the end of his time there had made legendary contributions to Liverpool's rich history, especially in their famous European story.

Liverpool's defence of their European crown started with an all-English clash with league champions Nottingham Forest. This always looked the trickiest of ties – Brian Clough's team had already bloodied Liverpool's nose in the previous season's Football League Cup Final.

And, for sure, they were at it again, with a decisive 2-0 win over the Reds in their European Cup first round first leg at the City Ground. A late goal from Forest full-back Colin Barrett put some clear water between them and Paisley's men. The Liverpool manager was furious. He thought his team had fallen into the trap of chasing down an English league result rather than settling for a 1-0 European away result.

And it proved fatal. Liverpool went for it in the second leg at a fully cranked-up Anfield but could not get past a solid Forest defence. 0-0. The Reds brief, but glorious, reign as European champions was temporarily halted. And on that week's Friday night football show *Kick Off*, presenter Gerald Sinstadt signed off with, 'On a very sad week for Liverpool Football Club,' and up came the closing refrain, 'The party's over. It's time to call it a day. They've burst your pretty balloon …'

To the dulcet tones of Johnny Mathis, the Granada TV programme went off the air with a series of moody black-and-white photographs of disappointed Liverpool players at the end of Wednesday's defeat to Nottingham Forest. There was a furious backlash from Liverpool supporters, and for many years that followed whenever the Reds took a handsome lead the Kop would often belt out 'Gerald Sinstadt, Gerald Sinstadt. How's the party going NOW?!' And quite often Gerald was there to hear it. Awkward.

If European glory was beyond the Reds this time, their performance in the league was peerless.

They won the First Division title by eight points from runners-up Nottingham Forest. Their 3-0 win at Leeds in their final game of the season gave them 68 points – then the biggest total ever reached in the First Division in its 90-year history. Their goal difference of 69 was another all-time best, and their 85-goal haul in their 42-game programme won them a £50,000 prize from a national newspaper.

The statistics roll on. Paisley only used 15 players across the league season – and two, David Fairclough and Sammy Lee, only started four games between them. And the Reds only let in 16 goals in the 42 games, and just four in their 21-home-game schedule. They remained unbeaten at Anfield. Their final record for the season of 30 wins, eight draws and just four defeats gave the new champions 68 points.

Of course, two points for a win was in operation then, but converted to three points (and accepting they played four games more than is the current convention) they would have ended up with a points tally of 98. They are the facts and figures, but the style of their football won huge acclaim too from fans and the media alike. 'The statistics are incredible, the quality of their football breathtaking. They maintained it to the last kick of the season.' Four players: Ray Clemence, Phil Neal, Ray Kennedy and Kenny Dalglish, played in every game, and Graeme Souness only missed one match.

Fittingly, Liverpool clinched the title at Anfield with a 3-0 win over Aston Villa on the 40th anniversary of manager Bob Paisley signing as a young player for the Reds back in 1939. The match programme highlighted the anniversary with Liverpool chairman John Smith writing, 'Bob has worked his way from the bottom to the top, and his behaviour and attitude to the game have set a wonderful example ...'

We all travelled midweek to Elland Road for the Reds' final game of the season. The Leeds United players gave the champions a guard of honour before the game and the West Yorkshire crowd gave the Reds a huge ovation. Undoubtedly, that was both recognising the achievement of that evening's opponents and also returning the compliment for how the Kop had so graciously cheered the Leeds United side when they clinched the league title at Anfield ten years before.

Liverpool won the game at a canter and our travelling support, in its thousands, gave its heroes a rapturous reception on the final whistle. Time for another party!

Kop That – *Between March 1972 and April 1978, Everton scored just one goal in 13 league derbies. In 1978/79 they ended the drought by winning 1-0 at Goodison and drawing 1-1 at Anfield.*

1979/80 – DEPARTURES
AND A DREAM JOB

ON 1 August 1979, Barrow-born Emlyn Hughes signed for Wolverhampton Wanderers, ending 12 years of spectacular service for Liverpool Football Club.

I saw Hughes's first game for Liverpool in February 1967, against Stoke City at Anfield, and also watched his last game for the Reds in an FA Cup semi-final replay against Manchester United at Goodison Park in April 1979. During that period Hughes played over 650 games for Liverpool and I must have watched literally hundreds of them. His unrelenting enthusiasm, his never-say-die attitude and superb athleticism made him a personal favourite of mine.

I loved that we all called him 'Crazy Horse'. Legend has it that a wild rugby-style tackle, grabbing Newcastle United's winger Arthur Bennett around the neck, in Hughes's early days at Anfield earned him that colourful nickname, and it stuck. Hughes's dad had been a rugby league international so perhaps his gifted footballing son had something about that sport in his DNA as well as for the round ball.

Shankly had been at Bloomfield Road to watch a young Emlyn Hughes make his debut for Blackpool and had wanted to sign him for Liverpool there and then. He got his man a year later, and ultimately made him captain of the Reds. Emlyn was not universally popular in the Liverpool dressing room, but the club's supporters loved him, and he went on to captain his country and be voted the Football Writers' Footballer of the Year in 1977.

With two European Cup winners' medals, two UEFA Cup winners' medals, four league championship medals and an FA Cup winners' medal all won at Anfield, he typically added a League Cup Final winners' medal to complete the haul in his first season at Wolves. On his first return to Anfield as a Wolves player Hughes received a fantastic reception from the crowd, and then it was business as usual – a home win.

When he finally retired from football, I got to know him well through our mutual work at the BBC – he approached those jobs with the same enthusiasm he had for his football, especially as a long-time team captain on *A Question of Sport*. And we bumped into each other all the time when he, his wife Barbara and his family took a month-long trip to Australia to watch the 2003 Rugby World Cup – and he loved the fact England won it.

Emlyn Hughes sadly died from a brain tumour, a young 57-year-old, the following year, and, four years later, whilst still in my position as chief executive of the Football Association, I was invited by Barbara and the Hughes family to help unveil a statue of him that had been erected in a prominent position in the town centre of Barrow-in-Furness. They reasoned my Barrow, Liverpool, BBC and FA connections charted both my life and his. It was an absolute honour to be asked to be part of that special day.

August 1979 had also proved to be the month I left Barrow-in-Furness. Almost three years to the day that I'd arrived as a wet-behind-the-ears reporter on a small local newspaper, I was off to London, and the next stage of my professional adventure – a job at the BBC.

The opportunity to have a six-month contract working for BBC TV Sport was a chance not to be missed, and a risk worth taking. I turned down a couple of other good job offers from top provincial newspapers to try my luck at the sharp end of top-class broadcasting and never regretted it – my six-month contract turned into a happy 18-year, long-term stay.

In those days, when viewers only had BBC or ITV to choose from, the licence-funded corporation had built up a fantastic reputation for their sports coverage – and they had most of broadcasting's best presenters and commentators, and the lion's share of the best sporting events, both here and around the world.

For older readers of this book, can you imagine walking down a corridor with David Coleman's unmistakeable voice booming out of one office, Peter O'Sullevan's out of another, Murray Walker trying to make the coffee machine work, Bill McLaren looking for his commentary notes he had put down somewhere, Harry Carpenter picking up flight tickets to get to the next big fight in Las Vegas, Eddie Waring taking off his trilby hat having come straight off a train from Leeds, Peter Alliss and Jimmy Hill practising their golf swings in the reception area, while John Motson and Barry Davies pored over that month's *Match of the Day* commentary rota to see who had got which game?

Indeed, in my first few days, Coleman came out of his office and barked, 'Hey, I believe you're the new lad – a Scouser, eh? Well, welcome to the first team. Work hard and you'll be fine.'

Fanciful? Not really – that was your average day at the BBC Sport offices in Shepherd's Bush in the early 1980s. And I was absolutely in my element.

One Saturday evening I'd had a beer in my hand watching *Match of the Day* in my digs in Barrow; within weeks I was actually working on the iconic programme as an assistant producer in the exciting buzz of BBC Television Centre in London. I would have paid *them* for the experience, but they were paying me.

What working at the BBC gave me over the next two decades was a different insight into how sport and football worked, and the opportunity to meet and get to know many of the key movers and shakers in it. And, given Liverpool were top of the pile for a lot of the time I was there, my dealings with the key people and players at Anfield became normal business, and very satisfying it was too.

Over the course of my first season on *Match of the Day* 1979/80, Liverpool would appear 14 times, in the league, FA Cup and Charity Shield, and score no less than 38 times. Mind you, it was a fantastic volley from Norwich City's Justin Fashanu against Liverpool that would win the BBC's famous Goal of the Season competition.

I quickly got the hang of most things, although some of the technical stuff was a bit more difficult. Thankfully, there were plenty of more experienced people around to help me. And they did. What I was blessed with was a strong editorial instinct and a lifetime's passion for sport and sports broadcasting which gave me a decent base to work from.

On the last Saturday of the 1979/80 season, Liverpool's match with Aston Villa was the main attraction on that evening's *Match of the Day*. The Reds romped home 4-1 with their Israeli international Avi Cohen experiencing the unusual feat of scoring for both teams on the same afternoon. It clinched another league title for Liverpool, four in the last five years for Bob Paisley's men.

My task on that evening's programme was to put together a closing musical montage encapsulating all of Liverpool's best moments of the season, and to the glorious strains of Gerry

Marsden's 'You'll Never Walk Alone'. Nice work if you can get it. I was chuffed as the resulting sequence went on air, but there was a surprise awaiting me. As all the presenter, pundit, commentary and production credits rolled across my lovingly crafted montage, a new name popped up on the screen for the first time ... *Brian Barwick*. It was a really special moment, and one that the programme team had held back from telling me was just about to happen.

You earned your 'credit' in those days, and it was the programme's way of saying, 'You're one of us!'

Kop That – *Liverpool lost in the FA Cup semi-final that season to Arsenal, doing so in a third replay at Highfield Road, Coventry, the only time a semi-final has been staged at this now-defunct ground.*

1980/81 – WINNERS AND WINE GUMS

LET'S START this chapter with an important date – 30 May 1980. There's no doubt plenty was going on the world over on this particular day, which was a Friday actually. But, probably of most interest to Liverpool fans is on that day a certain Steven George Gerrard popped into the world at Whiston Hospital on Merseyside. The rest, as they say, is sporting history.

The following month the 1980/81 First Division fixtures came out, and for the first time in my life, I spent more time looking out for Liverpool's away matches rather than the forthcoming season's matches at Anfield. Quickly scanning down the list I noted the dates of the matches at Tottenham Hotspur, Arsenal and Crystal Palace. Only three teams from the capital in a league of 22 clubs. An unusually low number. Add Brighton as an 'outlier' and that was your lot. Not very promising.

Now living in London, and working on BBC's *Match of the Day*, which in a new rotational arrangement with ITV had moved to Sunday, my chances of seeing the Reds play live were limited.

Although the programme was to be transmitted at teatime on Sundays, the production work on the show straddled both days of the weekend. The odd weekend off, a midweek game or a cup tie were my limited opportunities – the Reds would play 11 cup ties across the FA Cup and the Football League Cup that season, but only one of them in London – at Wembley Stadium against West Ham United in the Football League Cup Final, the clubs having already met in August in the FA Charity Shield.

Down the years I've got used to it, and follow the promotions to, and the relegations from, the top division with great interest. As I write this midway through the 2020/21 season there are seven London, or nearby, teams in the 20-team competition. The other day I scribbled down all the London teams I've watched Liverpool play, some many times over, plus the clubs or grounds located close by. It works out something like this: Arsenal, Brentford, Brighton, Charlton, Chelsea, Crystal Palace, Fulham, Luton, Millwall, Oxford, QPR, Reading, Tottenham Hotspur, Watford, West Ham United, Wimbledon ... and Wembley.

A welcome addition to my new London-based life was a parcel that would arrive religiously every Tuesday morning during the football season from my dear old mum. It contained the matchday programme from Liverpool's latest game, the famous *Football Echo* from the previous Saturday, Monday's *Liverpool Daily Post*, which always had the most comprehensive reports/reviews and stunning matchday photographs, a brief note on family life back home, and, unfailingly, a quarter-pound bag of Maynards wine gums. Had to be Maynards. For future reference I like the green, black and, of course, the red ones best.

The only downside to receiving this thoughtful weekly gift was the herculean task of unravelling the brown paper and its wonderful contents from the half a roll of Sellotape my mother used to secure its safe passage. Occasionally, even a master safe cracker couldn't have found their way into the thoughtful treasure trove of stuff that lay beneath Mrs B's unyielding super-wrap.

Liverpool's league form in the 1980/81 season by their own high standards was poor. They finished fifth in the table, their lowest position for ten seasons. In a campaign riddled with injury problems, the Reds drew a remarkable 17 games, lost eight and won only 17. Their final points tally was 51 points in the last season when two points for a win was in operation. In 1978/79 they had famously conceded only 16 goals – two seasons later they were letting in 42 goals. Perhaps the fact they used no less than 23 players in league matches throughout the season underlined the problems facing Paisley due to injuries and inconsistency of form.

One new area of achievement was winning the Football League Cup for the first time. The Reds' history in this competition had been patchy at best – one final in their 14 previous attempts. However, Liverpool reached the 1980/81 Football League Cup Final, playing West Ham United at Wembley. A 1-1 draw came with two late goals in extra time, the first for Liverpool from Alan Kennedy in the 118th minute and an equaliser from the Hammers' penalty hotshot Ray Stewart in the final throes of the game. And with no penalty shoot-out in those days, it was off to Villa Park for a midweek replay a few weeks later.

This time, Liverpool nailed it. One down, goals by Kenny Dalglish and Alan Hansen turned the game around, and secured the first of what would be four successive triumphs in domestic football's 'second' cup competition. That would qualify as taking the competition seriously!

However, it was in the European Cup that Liverpool came into their own once again.

An easy-looking first round tie against Finnish side Oulun Palloseura started with a surprising 1-1 draw in the away leg on a pitch heavily criticised by Bob Paisley. The return leg at Anfield, on a perfect early-season pitch, was a wholly different matter, both Terry McDermott and Graeme Souness hitting hat-tricks in a 10-1 win.

Next up an intriguing tie against Scottish champions Aberdeen. Under the tutelage of one Alex Ferguson, the team from the granite city had knocked the two Glasgow giants, Rangers and Celtic, off their perch. He had done a remarkable job with his Aberdeen team, but he recognised this would be a much sterner test.

And it was. The latest 'Battle of Britain', as the press tagged the tie, was virtually over in the first five minutes of the Reds' away leg, Terry McDermott scoring with a beautiful chip from a through ball from David Johnson. Aberdeen huffed and puffed but couldn't blow the Reds' defence down.

The second leg got worse for Ferguson's men, losing 4-0 for a 5-0 aggregate score. It was a lesson learned for the Scottish champions, and a bad memory stored away for Fergie which he would, no doubt, draw on many times when planning Manchester United's attempts on knocking the Reds off 'their bloody perch' in years to come. As you will read later, I got myself caught up in that sporting rivalry and Fergie proved to be a formidable opponent, both for the Anfield men and yours truly.

I was at Anfield for Liverpool's next challenge in the European Cup against Bulgarian champions CSKA Sofia, memorable for another Graeme Souness hat-trick, including two absolute belters – unstoppable shots. 5-1 in the home leg and a 1-0 win on the road. The drama in this European Cup run came in the semi-final. Drawn against German giants Bayern Munich, the first game at Anfield ended goalless, and marked the European debut for a young Ian Rush, who was making his early strides as a Liverpool player having been signed from Chester.

I don't think any of us watching this callow chap would have thought he would develop into a free-scoring machine, and a genuine Liverpool legend. In fact, it took him time to settle in at Anfield and fight off his natural shyness. If Ian Rush lacked a little self-belief, it was not something his Central League team-mate Howard Gayle lacked when he was unexpectedly thrust into the limelight in the Reds' legendary semi-final second leg against Bayern.

Paisley's injury woes meant he had to put out something of a makeshift side against the Germans, whose confidence of winning the tie was evident with their match programme giving travel and hotel details for the final in Paris.

In came reserves Richard Money and Colin Irwin for Alan Kennedy and Phil Thompson, and when Kenny Dalglish was injured early in the first half, Paisley turned to another reserve, Howard Gayle, as his surprise replacement. The 22-year-old talented if mercurial striker ran the Bayern defence ragged, his direct approach, tackling back and sheer power-pack energy unsettling the German side. So much so that he became a target for their defenders and to protect him, and keep 11 Liverpool players on the pitch, Paisley substituted the substitute. But Gayle had made his mark. And Liverpool went on to win the tie with a coolly taken goal by Ray Kennedy, and even Rummenigge's late finish couldn't turn the game in the Germans' favour.

Paisley, a man for whom understatement was a byword, went one better that night. 'That,' he said, 'was the greatest performance we have given in Europe. Everything was going wrong for us, and the players did everything right and showed real character.' None more so than Howard Gayle.

And so, we were off to Paris. Support Liverpool and see the world. Or, at least, Europe and its major, magnificent capitals. The tour T-shirt had Rome, London and Paris printed on the back and a liver bird on the front. Thousands of us descended on the French capital, once again a level of support which totally outstripped the tickets allocated to the club. The match itself got a tremendous build-up. Liverpool v Real Madrid had a real ring of authenticity about it. The Reds were looking for their third win in club football's top competition against the Spanish club who had won the first five finals.

The game itself? A bit of a damp squib. The two teams cancelled themselves out and the game looked to be heading for extra time when Liverpool's Kennedy Boys did the business. With nine minutes left, Ray Kennedy took a throw-in deep in Real Madrid's half. His namesake, Alan, received it and went straight for goal, past an ineffectual challenge, and he thumped a cross shot over the Madrid keeper, and the game was won.

Quite what Alan Kennedy was doing that far up the pitch given the state of the game is still something of a mystery, but it was a spectacular goal. And there was no way back for the Spanish masters – a flash of individual brilliance had done for them. Olé!

Kop That – *Graeme Souness is the only Liverpool player to score a hat-trick in two games in European Cup/Champions League competition in the same season.*

1981/82 – THE CHANGING OF THE GUARD

THE SUMMER of 1981 was a time of significant change at Anfield. One of the team's key positions, that had been the property of one careful owner for the previous 11 years, was about to be vacated.

Ray Clemence, goalkeeper supreme, had played his final game for the club. Fittingly, it was in the Reds' winning European Cup side in Paris. It was his 665th appearance for the Reds, and yet another clean sheet. From establishing himself as Tommy Lawrence's replacement at the end of 1969/70, Clemence only missed six league games in the following 11 campaigns. He guarded his goal, and Liverpool's fortunes, with a calm, commanding presence. And many times it was his outstanding saves in a match that were just as important as any goals scored by his team-mates at the other end of the pitch.

Clemence was a brilliant sweeper keeper and also knew how to protect himself in the hurly-burly of the six-yard box when burly opponents, up for corners and free kicks, flew across his path. Ray Clemence decided after the final in Paris it was the moment to move on from Anfield. 'It just felt the right time,' he said.

And so, on the August day when he signed for Tottenham Hotspur, I was sent by BBC's *Grandstand* to track him down in north London and get him back to BBC Television Centre for a live interview. Not for the first time, or the last, my growing professional connections with Liverpool Football Club got me to the right hotel where Ray was staying, and he was happy to travel back across London to speak to David Coleman about his big transfer move to Spurs. In later life, in my time as CEO of the Football Association, I had the privilege of working with Ray, who by then was England's goalkeeping coach under Sven-Göran Eriksson.

One of the most endearing images of Ray Clemence was a photograph of him when, as a young player at Scunthorpe United, he was snapped while stacking deckchairs on the beach at the nearby resort of Skegness during the close season.

A hugely contrasting image of his replacement at the same age would have captured Bruce Grobbelaar as a young, conscripted soldier in the Rhodesian Army fighting in the bush against rebel forces in the country's civil war. Grobbelaar was just 17 when he joined the army, and he grew up very quickly in circumstances that were no place for a teenager. Life and death were part of the daily stuff of being in the challenging theatre of the Bush Wars. He and his fellow conscripts fought the enemy in the heart of the jungle, and many died in that challenging terrain. The young soldiers slept rough, caked themselves in animal dung as camouflage and survived on a diet that included wild animals they killed themselves, poisonous snakes and flying ants. Grobbelaar watched comrades killed in action, and stayed alive himself by returning mortal fire on his enemies.

In his fascinating autobiography, *Life in a Jungle*, Grobbelaar reflected on his young army experiences. 'Surviving a war makes me think I'm lucky, I'm fortunate. A lot of people haven't been. When I came out of the military, I thanked God I came out unscathed …'

Having served an extended two years in the army, Grobbelaar resumed playing football in his own country before joining Durban City in South Africa. Next stop on his global football journey was Canada, where he enlisted as a goalkeeper for the Vancouver Whitecaps. They were being coached by the former Blackpool and England keeper Tony Waiters. Waiters had also spent some time at Liverpool as a coach and subsequently made LFC aware of the qualities of his new protégé.

Bob Paisley and Tom Saunders checked out the Whitecaps' Grobbelaar, when he was on a loan spell from his Canadian club at Crewe Alexandra, and later paid Waiters's club £250,000 to sign him in March 1981. Grobbelaar played three away matches in the Central League for Liverpool Reserves before the end of the 1980/81 season, then, as a result of Clemence's surprise departure, the Zimbabwean was thrust into the limelight, and straight into the Liverpool first team, at the start of the 1981/82 season. He would play all 42 league games in that first season, although his contrasting style to his distinguished predecessor entertained and alarmed in equal measure.

In the week building up to the start of the season I went up to Anfield to interview Liverpool's new goalkeeper for BBC's *Football Focus*, and after completing the chat and having been tipped off he was a bit of a showman, I asked him to perform some tricks with a football which we would film for inclusion in the piece.

He proceeded to spin a ball on one finger, another ball on another finger, and juggle them left, right and centre around his body. It was stuff worthy of a Harlem Globetrotter. 'It was (in the USA) I developed my repertoire of pre- and in-game gymnastics and clowning: climbing the goalposts, handstands, spinning the ball on the tips of my fingers. I understood my duty to entertain as well as keep goal. It was ingrained in the American sporting culture.'

Over time the Anfield Boot Room gently persuaded him to tone down most of his jovial excesses (!) whilst accepting it was all part of the make-up of the man. The Everton fans were a little crueller, nicknaming him 'The Clown' – a tag that stuck.

Grobbelaar was joined by Mark Lawrenson, 24, and Craig Johnston, Ian Rush and Ronnie Whelan, players all under the age of 24 challenging for slots in the first team. Lawrenson was Liverpool's record signing, from Brighton, and I watched him play in a 'Reds v Whites' match behind closed doors at Anfield a few days before the start of the season.

Having arrived early for my interview with Bruce Grobbelaar, I was just biding my time, when Bob Paisley spotted me and invited me into the ground to watch the back end of the game. We both sat on the Paddock wall inside Anfield before retiring to the dugout to shelter from the strong August sunshine. What became clear in those few minutes was how much Paisley thought of his new signing, Mark Lawrenson. And so it proved – at the end of the forthcoming campaign, Paisley highlighted Lawrenson as his player of the season for 'his attitude and adaptability' to whatever role he was given.

It was really a season of two halves for the Reds, and they faltered badly up to and into the Christmas period – on Boxing Day they were 12th, with only 24 points, after 17 games. And a 3-1 home defeat against Manchester City, with sloppy goals conceded, seemed to sum up everything that wasn't right with the Reds, including the erratic form of their shiny new goalkeeper.

Under new captain Graeme Souness, a 4-0 third-round FA Cup win at Swansea a week later seemed to kick-start the under-fire champions' season. They completed their league programme with 87 points, taking 63 out of a possible remaining 75 points, including 11 successive wins. It was a remarkable turnaround, and the Reds also retained the Football League Cup, which was enjoying the first of what has proved to be one of many new names, the Milk Cup.

Liverpool came from behind to win an exciting extra-time 3-1 win over Tottenham Hotspur, with Anfield legend Ray Clemence in the Londoners' goal at Wembley. Liverpool's goals came from Ronnie Whelan (two) and Ian Rush – clear signs a new broom was sweeping through the Anfield first team.

At the end of the game, Liverpool collected not one, but two cups, deposed skipper Phil Thompson lifting the newly fashioned Milk Cup and new captain Graeme Souness raising the long-established Football League Cup itself. And, on the lap of honour, the Kop's emerging new favourite, Bruce Grobbelaar, responded to his fans' calls by walking on his hands to celebrate the Reds' Wembley triumph, whilst clutching his medal in his teeth.

Ironically, in May, Tottenham Hotspur also provided the opposition at Anfield on the day Liverpool clinched their 13th league title. Liverpool trailed to a magnificent goal from Glenn Hoddle at half-time, and ahead of the match restarting, Ray Clemence received a spine-tingling reception from the Kop as he made his way to the goal he was defending in the second half. Indeed, the whole ground rose to salute him. It was a truly memorable moment brilliantly captured for posterity by the BBC *Match of the Day* cameras.

Then it was down to business – Lawrenson headed home an equaliser in the 51st minute, Kenny Dalglish added a second four minutes later and Ronnie Whelan rounded things off three minutes from time. 3-1. It was another magnificent second-half comeback, which mirrored their season as a whole – a poor first half, which also included being beaten

SIXTY YEARS A RED ... AND COUNTING!

by Flamengo in the World Club Championship, and a spellbinding second half.

So, Liverpool picked up the league championship trophy and the League Cup, and former Anfield iconic keeper Ray Clemence was there in person on both occasions to witness the presentations first-hand. Meanwhile, the man who replaced him was walking on air – and on his hands! Of course.

Kop That – *Ian Rush became the second Liverpool player to score 30 goals in a full debut season. Kenny Dalglish was the first.*

1982/83 – CUPS AND CAPS

AS THE 1981/82 domestic season wound down, attention eagerly turned to the forthcoming FIFA World Cup which was to be held that summer in Spain. On the last Saturday of May England beat Scotland 1-0 in their annual Home International Championship clash, this one at Hampden Park. I attended the game for the BBC and having finished my duties there managed to jump a lift back to Liverpool with Phil Thompson, Phil Neal and Graeme Souness.

Having sorted out the 'what ifs' of the afternoon's game, their conversation soon turned swiftly to the World Cup. Souness had been chosen in the Scotland squad along with Alan Hansen and Kenny Dalglish, whilst Terry McDermott would be joining Liverpool's two Phils in Ron Greenwood's England squad. I wasn't left out of the conversation on the forthcoming tournament as I, too, was heading to the World Cup, and I reminded them that my team, BBC TV Sport, would be at the final whoever was in it!

On the Sunday, crowds were out in Liverpool in huge numbers, not for the now traditional triumphant homecoming of one of our two Merseyside football clubs, but because of the Papal Visit to the city of His Holiness Pope John Paul II as part of a tour of the UK. It is estimated more than a million people turned out to greet him on that Sunday.

The Pope arrived by helicopter at Speke Airport, met by an enthusiastic crowd, estimated at 150,000. His hugely successful visit took in both the Anglican and Metropolitan cathedrals, and he was warmly welcomed by the adoring throngs who lined the street, five or six deep, as he was driven through the city in the famous 'Popemobile'.

And later that evening in a genuinely surreal moment, as my mate Greg and I were walking down a deserted lane to our local pub in Allerton, a stream of police motorcyclists went roaring by us followed by the Popemobile itself, with the Pope still on board.

The vehicle was heading for the Archbishop's Residence for an overnight stay, and as it slowed right down to turn into the grounds, from just ten yards away, Greg and I paid our respects, which the Pope kindly acknowledged. Our very own unscheduled private audience.

I enjoyed working at the World Cup, based initially with the Northern Ireland team in Valencia, who provided one of the shocks of the tournament by beating hosts Spain, before moving across to be with the England party in Madrid, and once they, too, had exited the competition, staying on to watch the final itself.

Back home, the country was just getting over the ordeal of the Falklands War, which had ended the day after the World Cup had started. And times were really tough in the great city of Liverpool – government policy seemed set on a course to 'manage it into decline', the economy was in a wretched state and jobs were at a premium.

In a thought-provoking TV drama series, *Boys from the Blackstuff*, Liverpool playwright Alan Bleasdale told a bleak, hard-hitting five-part tale of a group of Scousers struggling to make sense of the predicament they found themselves in. Actor Bernard Hill played Yozzer Hughes, unemployed and losing his mind. 'Gizza a job, I can do that' was his trademark line, and he, heartbreakingly, delivered it to anybody he spoke to, including his 'lookalike' Graeme Souness, who along with Sammy Lee had a cameo role in this much-acclaimed series.

Not for the first time, or the last, football would provide some well-needed respite to a hurting community, and the two Merseyside clubs gave their supporters a sense of pride and achievement.

At Liverpool Football Club, they were handling the news that Bob Paisley had decided that the 1982/83 season would be his last as Liverpool manager. It gave the club some time to select his replacement, which in due course was named as Boot Room stalwart Joe Fagan – a popular choice. Paisley's last season would see another three trophies head Liverpool's way – the FA Charity Shield following a 1-0 win over Tottenham Hotspur, the Milk Cup with a win over Manchester United and the championship again, his sixth title success in nine years. The Milk Cup Final win in extra time came courtesy of a wonderful goal from Ronnie Whelan, his third goal in consecutive League Cup finals.

And, after the match, as the Liverpool team lined up to collect the trophy, captain Graeme Souness invited Bob Paisley to lead the players up the stairs and be presented with the cup. Off came his cap and he made his way up the 39 steps to the Royal Box, something denied him back in 1950, and he proudly lifted the cup aloft. A marvellous gesture from his players.

The league campaign included a famous 5-0 derby match win at Goodison Park, with Ian Rush scoring four of the goals past his Welsh team-mate Neville Southall. I missed that game because I was in the company of Mickey Mouse, Donald Duck and the Pirates of the Caribbean – Disney World in Florida, on my honeymoon with Gerry, whose work as a film editor on my weekly *Football Focus* items led to a happy marriage – 38 years and counting. She is a bit of a football agnostic really but can feign keen interest if required, which has been needed many times down the years given the jobs I have found myself in.

In the week leading up to Bob Paisley's last home match as manager of Liverpool, against Aston Villa, he unexpectedly agreed to BBC TV Sport's Alan Parry and myself shadowing him on his daily business as part of a *Sportsnight* main feature for the following Wednesday night's programme. Paisley gave us great access to his professional and family life. What became clear was that this shy, private individual had never forgotten where he had come from.

That was beautifully personified on the matchday itself when as hundreds of guests were enjoying the rich fare and corporate hospitality in the various suites in the stadium, we filmed an elderly Anfield retainer carrying an old wooden tray on which there was a bowl of soup and two pasties. Bob's lunch. Nothing fancy, just warm and filling. In the room marked 'Manager' Bob, in his cardigan, was deep in thought as his lunch arrived.

A couple of spoonfuls of soup later, and he settled down to write out, in longhand, his team line-up for this his last match in charge at Anfield. Grobbelaar, Neal, Kennedy, Thompson, Lawrenson, Hansen, Dalglish, Lee, Hodgson, Souness and Johnston, with Nicol as substitute. They were a set of wonderful images that captured the man – an ordinary man in an extraordinary job, and with an extraordinary record of achievement.

Earlier in the week we had gone to the Woolton home he shared with his wife, Jessie. They had been married since 1946 having met on a train journey. The Paisleys had two sons, Robert and Graham, and a daughter, Christine, and we filmed Bob enjoying playing with his grandchildren. At home he was very much husband, dad and granddad. Bob also gave us permission to film in the Liverpool dressing room on the build-up to the kick-off. It was very rare to get that type of access back in those days so my instructions to the cameraman were plain and simple – 'shoot everything that moves!'

And, whether it was Graeme Souness talking to coach Reuben Bennett, Phil Thompson bending and stretching, Alan Hansen reading the matchday programme or Kenny Dalglish being quietly congratulated by Paisley having been announced the FWA Footballer of the Year, it was fascinating footage which still pops up in sports documentaries to this day.

Before the start of the game Liverpool were presented with the Football League Championship trophy, and captain Souness handed it straight to Bob Paisley, who took the plaudits from the packed crowd, and both sets of supporters. The match itself ended 1-1 and we made our way to the Boot Room to film our closing sequence.

Joe Fagan, the man who would replace Paisley, spoke first. 'When Bob took the job, he didn't know how he was going to handle it – because Bill had such a strong personality and character, and Bob was different. But he did brilliantly, getting the right players, setting them and the staff up right – and six titles, well, it is unbelievable really.'

On cue, in walked Paisley himself carrying a beautiful silver service – teapot, sugar bowl and cups and saucers. With a little chuckle he said, 'A present from the Villa for me – I think I'll leave it here with you guys, a bit of class for the Boot Room.'

Cups, now that was what Bob Paisley was all about – three European Cups, one UEFA Cup, one Super Cup, three League Cups, six Charity Shields and *six* league titles. That's real silver service.

Kop That – *Jerzy Dudek, the hero of Istanbul, dedicated his Champions League medal to fellow Pole John-Paul II. Jerzy claimed the Pope was a follower of the club and he calls his save in the Final as the 'hand of the Pope'.*

1983/84 – SMOKIN' JOE
AND A ROMAN HOLIDAY

JOE FAGAN was born in Liverpool in 1921, and like his nickname-sake world heavyweight champion 'Smokin' Joe' Frazier, he could pack a punch. At a travelling fair, the young Joe Fagan knocked out the 'house' boxer and everybody else who came his way that night.

However, just like his more illustrious boxing exponent 'Smokin' Joe', our Scouse version finally met his match, and a flat nose was the resultant lifelong memento of that pugilistic encounter.

Football seemed safer. And, subsequently, Fagan's nickname had more to do with him always seeming to have a cigarette on the go more than anything else. And, after a steady if unspectacular playing career, interrupted by service in World War II, Joe joined the backroom staff at Anfield in 1958 and worked his way up through the ranks.

By the summer of 1983, 25 years on, he had arrived at the pinnacle of his career, named as the new manager of Liverpool Football Club. Joe was a little bit reluctant at first, like Bob Paisley had been, but he had the confidence of those 'upstairs', and the players were also very fond of him. He had the dressing room very much on his side, but they also knew he was no soft touch.

Fagan's first season turned out to be a thumping big triumph, an unprecedented treble – league champions, Milk Cup winners and European Cup winners. A remarkable achievement for a modest man, a product of the Boot Room, who still lived close to Anfield itself.

And those on-field successes gave the city of Liverpool itself a much-needed boost as it continued to struggle through tough economic times, heavy unemployment, a seemingly hostile government and a sense of being singled out for the rough end of any deal. But Liverpool, or rather Merseyside, would have its day in the capital and show its resilience, and a united front, when the Reds and Blues came together at Wembley in the spring of 1984. And it would leave a lasting impression.

And so, to those three big prizes. First, the league title, 'our bread and butter' as Shankly always called it. Fagan's men claimed their seventh title in nine years – their third in a row. They collected 80 points from their 42 games, three more than runners-up Southampton, and had a goal machine up front in Welsh sharpshooter Ian Rush. Over the season, he scored 47 goals in all competitions for Liverpool, two goals for Wales and unofficially 50 goals in all if you count his successful penalty in the European Cup Final shoot-out.

Rush notched a phenomenal 32 goals in 41 league games – he scored five goals against Luton Town at Anfield, four against Coventry City and three in a televised Friday night match on an ice rink of a pitch at Aston Villa. He scored the Reds' first league goal of the season, and fittingly, their final league goal of the season too. Liverpool clinched the title with a 0-0 draw at Notts County – it was the second part of their unique treble done and dusted.

The first part of this special three-prong achievement had been duly delivered in March, and memorable it was too. Holders Liverpool had a marathon trek to that season's Milk

Cup Final. A two-legged round-two tie with Brentford, three tight matches before seeing off Fulham in the next round – I saw all of them and the Reds were lucky to proceed. They needed replays to knock out Birmingham City and Sheffield Wednesday respectively and then squeezed through a tight semi-final double-header with an inspired Walsall.

On the night of the second leg at Fellows Park a wall collapsed behind one of the goals and fans, young and old, spilled over on to the ground. Thankfully, there were no serious injuries but perhaps it was a portent of later, more significant incidents of that nature to come.

It had taken Liverpool 11 matches in all to reach the Milk Cup Final, but the prize was an all-Merseyside Wembley occasion against Everton, a prospect that absolutely electrified the city. The build-up to the game lasted over a month and, when the big day came, 'The Friendly Final' as it was dubbed, may not have delivered a winner on the pitch but the whole occasion showed a watching nation, and, no doubt, a few uneasy politicians, just how proud Scousers were of their city.

Fans of both persuasions travelled down together from Liverpool to London by train, plane and automobile, we drank together, laughed together, sat alongside each other at Wembley, and when the match finished as a 0-0 draw, Alan Hansen surviving a legitimate penalty claim, we all joined together in a spine-tingling impromptu chant of 'Merseyside, Merseyside, Merseyside'. Club loyalties were put to one side.

Those unique post-match Wembley moments still resonate to this day. It was an afternoon of Mersey pride, Mersey pride, Mersey pride. The players themselves, having shaken hands with the royal guest, the Queen Mother, did a joint lap of honour and left the business of the Milk Cup alone until the replay the following Wednesday evening.

The 100,000 fans that witnessed the action at Wembley were slimmed down to 52,000 for the replay at Maine Road. The game was won by a single goal scored by Graeme Souness, and he lifted the Milk Cup, before it went back to the Anfield trophy room, theirs for keeps. Liverpool now four-time, back-to-back, winners of the competition.

Everton would go back to Wembley in May to win the FA Cup, and the Merseyside giants would meet again under the Twin Towers in August 1984 in the following season's FA Charity Shield, the Toffees winning this time 1-0.

The final leg of the treble took us all back to Rome, the scene of Liverpool's iconic first-ever European Cup Final success. This time it wasn't to play a German side, but an Italian side – AS Roma. UEFA had picked the venue for the final months ahead of the game itself and so when the Reds came through a tough semi-final with Dinamo Bucharest, and Roma beat Dundee United over two legs, the die was already cast. Liverpool would be playing Roma in the Italian side's own stadium. Not ideal.

Ahead of the final, Liverpool took the players to Israel for a few days' 'R and R'. Rest and relaxation, or as it turned out 'reckless rumbling', as the squad ended up in a punch-up among themselves on one particularly lively night out in Tel Aviv. All sorted the following morning.

BBC TV Sport sent Alan Parry and myself out to Rome to grab some post-match interviews for *Sportsnight* as the game itself was going to be broadcast live earlier on ITV. And we needed to get that message to the team when they arrived at the Stadio Olimpico. Alan and I managed to gain access to the tunnel area, and the Liverpool players, as they went out on to the pitch an hour before the kick-off. We just joined at the rear of the group and kept walking and found ourselves earnestly digging our heels into the playing surface as the Italian security guards looked quizzically at us thinking their team were going to have an easy night if those two guys at the back were in the Liverpool squad.

The match itself, like many finals, was no classic but the penalty shoot-out provided a memorable sequence of Bruce Grobbelaar's 'wobbly legs' act and a winning penalty from Alan Kennedy, the second time he had scored the clinching goal in a European Cup Final.

Alan and I secured our post-match interviews amid the usual media scrum, and we both got a sense that Liverpool's captain Graeme Souness may just have played his last match for the Reds. Job done, Alan and I set off for the hotel where the club was staying but not before we had been chased down a now deserted road by some angry Roma 'ultras' – it was our turn to have 'wobbly legs' and wobbly everything else. In truth, it was very scary.

We actually took shelter in a local fire station, and they kindly organised a taxi for us. Thankfully, we weren't asked to go out on a call with them. Having already feigned being a pair of world-class footballers, dressing up as a couple of Italian firefighters might have just been one step too far. Back at the hotel where Liverpool were staying, we joined our own family and friends and enjoyed a long and memorable evening.

Sadly, on arriving back in the UK the following day I was to learn that my father had passed away earlier that morning. The man who set me off on my lifelong passion for football and for Liverpool Football Club had died suddenly from a short illness. It was devastating.

Kop That – *Graeme Souness is one of five players to have ended their Anfield careers with a European Cup/Champions League winners' medal – Kevin Keegan, Ray Clemence, Jimmy Case and Vladimír Šmicer being the others.*

1984/85 – HEYSEL

A FORTNIGHT before Liverpool's fifth European Cup Final against Italian giants Juventus at the Heysel Stadium in Brussels in May 1985, I caught a train from Waterloo Station to take me to the Reds' away match in the league against Southampton. The league title was already destined to go across Stanley Park to an inspired Everton side that had also qualified for the European Cup Winners' Cup Final against Rapid Vienna in Rotterdam. The Blues' epic semi-final second-leg win over Bayern Munich at an ecstatic Goodison Park, a landmark victory for the Toffees, had really whetted the appetite of the Everton fans, and they looked forward to both lifting their first European trophy, which they duly did, and then competing in the senior competition, the European Cup, the following season.

Everton had won the league title with an impressive 90-point haul, some 13 points clear of the Reds in the runners-up slot. The Blues, under manager Howard Kendall, were building up a real head of steam. This in a season when at one stage in October, champions Liverpool were languishing in 17th place – this, remember, the team that had won three titles on the trot.

With the likes of former Ipswich midfielder John Wark, who scored hat-tricks in three competitions that season, and

Luton Town's diminutive striker Paul Walsh settling into life at Anfield, the Reds had risen to 14th by mid-November, tenth by December and with a steady late run in the second half of the season to second place, but way short of the runaway Blues.

Attendances had really suffered at Anfield, through a damaging combination of their own unconvincing form, perhaps supporters' over-familiarity with success and the harsh economic reality of life on Merseyside at that time. This still a period when most of the attending Anfield faithful still came from the local area, and numbers were down.

A decent run to the FA Cup semi-finals, beaten in a replay by ultimate winners Manchester United, an early exit from the Milk Cup, a trophy they had dominated, and another World Club Championship defeat in Tokyo, this time to Argentinian side Independiente, left the European Cup as Liverpool's last chance of silverware. And perhaps an opportunity to take that wonderful trophy home for keeps.

A relatively smooth trek through the competition would pitch them in the final against Juventus, who had already beaten Liverpool in that year's Super Cup. Two former Liverpool captains who had lifted the European Cup had now left Anfield, Sampdoria for Graeme Souness, and Sheffield United for Phil Thompson. The ever-present Phil Neal would captain Liverpool in their fifth European Cup Final. He already had four winners' medals, and even though a full-back had scored in two finals.

And the final would be the last game in Joe Fagan's two-year reign as the club's manager. He was retiring and, perhaps in a surprise move, Kenny Dalglish would be taking up the reins as player-manager.

Back on that train journey to Southampton a fortnight before the Reds' fateful game in Brussels, I bumped into

Liverpool chairman John Smith and chief executive Peter Robinson, who'd been in London on business.

'Looking forward to Brussels?' I asked. Neither man reacted enthusiastically. 'The stadium's not up to the match, Brian – it's too old and not safe,' said Robinson. Robinson, a vastly experienced football man, who never used two words when one would suffice, was somebody always worth listening to. 'We've told UEFA all this, but nothing has happened.'

Recalling his words a fortnight later as the tragic events at the Heysel Stadium transpired, his thoughts, and those of his chairman John Smith were grimly accurate. Having travelled over to Brussels with friends, it was clear to us that the Heysel Stadium was not a modern facility and given the wide choice of venues available to UEFA it was one they would deeply regret.

My pals and I got into the stadium early, and we were on the side of the pitch, at the same end, but opposite where the tragedy unfolded. Fans taking a run at another set of the opposition's supporters was sadly not unusual in those times – 'hooliganism' had become a curse on the game. And, certainly still fresh in many Liverpool supporters' minds was the vicious treatment they had received at the hands of some Roma fans after the previous year's final.

Anyway, at Heysel, it became clear that a prematch charge by some Liverpool fans in Blocks X and Y had caused a serious problem, brushing through a flimsy fence of chicken wire and into a set of Italian fans standing in Block Z. Tickets for this block deemed 'a neutral zone' had been largely bought by Belgian-based Italians and local people. And as people tried to escape the trouble a wall collapsed, the terrible outcome being the death of 39 people, the majority of them Italian, and a further 600 people injured.

Although probably only 150 yards away, it was not possible for us to sense the scale of the tragedy, and without the aid of modern social media and suchlike, accurate news was at a premium. Incoming supporters brought the latest update – it went from 'some injured', to 'some injured and some fatalities', to 'many dead and hundreds injured'. It seemed unreal that such a tragedy had occurred so close to where we were standing.

The atmosphere inside the stadium had become febrile, the Juventus fans, sited at the other end of the stadium, inflamed and angry. Joe Fagan and Phil Neal made public address announcements appealing for calm from the Liverpool supporters in the ground.

For me, the match was now totally immaterial, but UEFA, in conjunction with the Belgian police, decided the game should go ahead, heavily delayed though it was. The right decision? Well, it bought UEFA and the Belgian authorities some time to think how they were going to manage the post-match dispersal of fans, many outraged, some looking for revenge.

Some forethought by the authorities might have prevented the trouble happening in the first place, but now they had to get around 50,000 people out of the stadium, out of the city and out of Belgium safely.

The match itself didn't matter – Juventus won 1-0, a Michel Platini penalty. The right team won.

For Liverpool and English football, it was a desperate night. And Prime Minister Margaret Thatcher was not slow in condemning Liverpool Football Club and other English clubs and calling for them to be banned from European competition.

After 21 seasons of unbroken European competition, Liverpool Football Club voluntarily withdrew from the following season's UEFA Cup. And then more severe sanctions were imposed by UEFA on all English clubs: a five-year ban from European competition, and a further year added for the Anfield club.

There were many innocent victims from that night of shame, not least a brilliant Everton team who, no doubt, would have done themselves proud in the European Cup the following season. That resentment still lingers. Some 14 Liverpool fans were ultimately brought to justice after a long-running legal process. Belgian police and football administrators from both the Belgian FA and UEFA were also brought to book.

For those of us there, it was a distressing situation and many of us felt slightly ashamed as we made our way through the airport terminal in Brussels to catch our planes home. It was on the tarmac at Speke Airport that one of the most poignant sights was the retiring Liverpool manager Joe Fagan in floods of tears, being helped to disembark by Boot Room colleague, Roy Evans. Joe, like many of us, was coming to terms with what had happened. And how his two-year tenure in the hot seat at Anfield had ended so brutally and tragically.

Kop That – *Between 1981/82 and 1986/87, Ian Rush was the club's leading scorer in all competitions, except in 1984/85, when John Wark led the way with 27 goals.*

1985/86 – AT THE DOUBLE

THE FIRST 11 days of May 1986 were among the most special of the 20,000-plus days I have followed Liverpool Football Club, not least because of the privileged position I was able to witness it all from as the Reds clinched the league title at Chelsea one Saturday, and the FA Cup at Wembley Stadium the following Saturday. The double. And they landed it by beating off the stern challenge of their close neighbours Everton to both prizes in the bargain.

Liverpool, under the new leadership of player-manager Kenny Dalglish, had landed the much-feted double. Only Tottenham Hotspur in 1961 and Arsenal in 1971 had achieved this landmark sporting feat in the 20th century to that point. Dalglish had started in his new role the previous August as the club tried to get back on its feet after the despair of Heysel.

Also back at the club was Bob Paisley, in a consultant capacity, and Dalglish very much valued the input of another Anfield elder statesman, Tom Saunders, as well. 'It's my opinion but it is your decision,' Saunders always told the canny Scotsman when they discussed football matters.

Dalglish, always his own man, accepted the challenge of his new role, whilst accepting he could no longer be at the centre of all the banter and fun in the dressing room. And he made significant changes. Firstly, he made Alan Hansen

140

his new captain, a move that upset the previous skipper, the long-serving Phil Neal, who ultimately left to manage Bolton Wanderers.

That other European Cup hero, fellow full-back Alan Kennedy, was also on his way out of Anfield – Sunderland his destination.

Steve Nicol took up the right-back berth and Jim Beglin slotted in at left-back. The big change came in midfield where Jan Mølby played centrally and directed the traffic around him. Dalglish got the best of the hugely skilful Great Dane.

One big dilemma was whether to select himself for the team. Now 34, Dalglish was still a hugely important part of this Liverpool side, but having briefly started the season on the pitch, he had only played intermittently for the lion's share of the season. He preferred to start games rather than come on as a substitute, but he still rarely chose himself in either capacity. With Dalglish's Boot Room colleagues urging him to play, it was when he picked himself in the famous number seven shirt in nine of the last 11 league games of the season that the Reds' title challenge really came alive.

And it was a formidable challenge as they had to chase down reigning champions Everton, who had comfortably beaten Liverpool at Anfield 2-0 on the last Saturday of February. At that stage of the season the Blues looked home and hosed to repeat their championship success of the previous season. They had eight points more than their Anfield rivals. But what followed next for the Reds was a miraculous 12-game run of 11 wins and one draw, and Kenny Dalglish was at the heart of it all. Liverpool leapfrogged over Everton into first place and then, a midweek 'Night of Destiny', as the *Liverpool Echo* called it, put clear water between themselves and Howard Kendall's Blues.

We were at Filbert Street and witnessed the Reds land a vital 2-0 win over Leicester City. On the same night, and at the same time, Everton were playing at relegation-threatened Oxford United. All the transistor radios among the Liverpool fans were tuned into the game at the Manor Ground, and huge cheers went up when we heard that Oxford had scored a late goal to unexpectedly win the game. It was the defining moment of the title race. It meant that if Liverpool won their final league game of the season on the following Saturday, away at Chelsea, they would be crowned champions.

And, having completed my duties as the new producer of BBC's Saturday lunchtime *Football Focus*, I made my way over to Stamford Bridge in the hope of watching a little bit of sporting history being made. As only happens to gifted people like Kenny Dalglish, it was his telling contribution that Saturday afternoon that became the stuff of legend.

There was only one goal in the game – it was scored by Liverpool, it came in the 23rd minute, it was a brilliant volley from the boot of Kenny Dalglish, and it clinched Liverpool's 16th league title. A special goal from a very special player. And manager.

On the final whistle the Liverpool players celebrated in front of their travelling fans. And I was on the pitch too trying to grab some instant reaction for BBC *Grandstand*'s *Final Score* segment. Gradually, the triumphant Liverpool players left the field and headed for the dressing room, and I followed them down the tunnel to help get more interviews. Knocking on the dressing-room door, I heard an unmistakeable Scottish voice. 'Brian, come in, what do you need?'

Once inside, Kenny gestured to me to sit next to him, and I quietly observed the suitably wild celebrations of the new English champions. Amid all the shouting and singing, Kenny ripped off his famous number seven shirt and threw it playfully in my direction. I caught Kenny's shirt, and, shortly after, beginning to feel I shouldn't overstay my welcome at somebody else's party, I thanked him for inviting me in and made my way to the door. Ronnie Moran, as always treating every win as just normal business, was picking up the sweat-soaked jerseys strewn around the floor. And he spotted the errant shirt in my hand, and asked me to throw it in the skip with the rest of that day's dirty kit. Without a second thought, I duly obliged.

I still think about how lucky I was that afternoon being allowed to share those private dressing room moments, and how unlucky I was not to still be the owner of that famous number seven shirt from that famous afternoon!

The following week was spent up on Merseyside putting together a 25-minute film which would be broadcast as part of the build-up on BBC TV's *Cup Final Grandstand*. It was another pinch yourself moment. In 1965, as a ten-year-old schoolboy, I had got up early to bag my chair in the living room, and never budged for over five hours as Liverpool won their first-ever FA Cup Final on our black-and-white TV.

Now, some two decades later, I had been trusted to deliver a compelling opening sequence, capturing on film a special week in the life of Liverpool, Reds and Blues alike. I wanted it to be memorable, affectionate, witty, unique and Scouse – as much heart went into it as head. Laced with orchestral versions of Beatles music, it literally romped along but had the occasional poignant moment too, as on one evening, we caught a stunning sunset over the River Mersey. I was proud of that short film, and I hoped I had done justice to my city, and both sets of fans.

Like everything else these days, in researching this chapter, I found the film on YouTube. And enjoyed it all over again.

On the morning of the match, I sent up-to-date pictures of the players relaxing at the team hotel ahead of the afternoon's stresses and strains and followed behind the team coach on its journey to Wembley. Once the players had reached the dressing room area, my job was all but done and my *Grandstand* bosses let me off for the rest of the day, and I was able to join some mates and watch the final in the best way possible – as a fan.

The match itself was dominated by Everton in the first half and then, inspired by a masterful midfield display from Jan Mølby, and a terrier-like performance by unsung hero Kevin MacDonald, Liverpool took a firm grip on the game in the second half. Two goals from Ian Rush – Everton's nemesis – and another from Craig Johnston delivered the goods, and the double was landed. What a remarkable first season for Liverpool's player-manager, Kenny Dalglish.

I joined both teams on a plane they shared back from Heathrow Airport to Merseyside the following day. When the clubs had booked the British Airways Boeing 757 several weeks before, it probably seemed a good idea to share the cost, but for the Everton players it must have been tough – Peter Reid actually ducked out and made his own way home – although there was no excessive behaviour from the victors – too hungover I would have thought.

The two teams were welcomed home by hundreds of thousands of people – red and blue – and I was on board the Liverpool bus, once again, grabbing interviews, but paused in that work when we got to Childwall Fiveways, a major roundabout system near my family home, because I knew that was where my mum would be standing at the roadside – that's where she always watched the homecomings – red and blue. Sure enough, I spotted her, and mischievously Kenny pushed me to the front of the bus where, among others, I briefly had the FA Cup itself for a travelling companion.

That nine days – from Chelsea to Childwall – I think they call it 'living the dream'.

Kop That *– Kenny Dalglish's league record in his first season as manager was played 42, won 26, drew ten, lost six – with 88 points, of all Liverpool's managers in their first full season in charge, Kenny's average of 70 per cent points gained exceeds all others, with Jürgen Klopp next with 67 per cent.*

1986/87 – NOT IN A RUSH

THE SUMMER of 1986 produced one of the most controversial moments in sporting history, and one of the finest. And all in the same 90 minutes.

England's 1986 World Cup campaign in Mexico had started badly – beaten by Portugal in their first group game, then held to a goalless draw in the next game against Morocco, everything came down to their last group game, against Poland. Ah, Poland and World Cups – it had never been a good mix for England. The Poles' famous 1-1 draw at Wembley back in 1973 had effectively knocked us out of the 1974 World Cup finals before we'd even qualified for them.

But, 13 years later, on a boiling hot day in Monterrey, Everton's Gary Lineker scored a sensational first-half hattrick in a 3-0 win over the Poles that put England through to the last 16, and gave Lineker a huge step towards winning the competition's Golden Boot and a late-summer move to Barcelona. Paraguay were beaten next, Lineker scoring twice and Peter Beardsley, a future Liverpool star, notching the other in England's 3-0 win in the Azteca Stadium in Mexico City.

The World Cup quarter-final between England and Argentina took place in the high altitude of the Azteca Stadium, and it remains a match remembered for Maradona's subtle cheating and sheer class. With the game at 0-0, the brilliant Argentine jumped and deflected a cross into the England net with his hand. England goalkeeper Peter Shilton immediately cried foul, but the referee and linesman were satisfied, wrongly, that there was nothing untoward about the vital goal. The goal stood, and still to this day the controversy rages on.

Maradona later confirmed he had handled the ball, calling it 'The Hand of God', and back home in Argentina, still smarting from the outcome of the Falklands War, it only heightened his status as a national icon. Four minutes after that 'goal', Maradona showed his absolute genius in beating five England players in a mazy run from his own half before guiding the ball into the net. It is up there as one of the greatest goals of all time. England clawed one goal back but were on the plane home, whilst Maradona went on to guide Argentina to win the World Cup.

Back in Liverpool, that summer it was another world-class player that was making headlines.

Ian Rush had signed for Juventus in a £3.2m deal – a British record fee. The Welsh striker who had set the Kop alight with his scoring prowess was on his way to play in Italy – in Serie A, where goals were at a premium and defences ruled.

Rush was on his way out of Anfield, but not immediately. Despite having been bought by one of the biggest clubs in European football he was loaned back to the Reds for one more season.

He would join Juventus in late July 1987 having delivered a farewell season like no other for the Anfield faithful, many of whom were sad he was leaving to play abroad.

Previous, and future, such transfers of iconic Liverpool players were not as well accepted by the fans as Ian Rush's move to Italy was. In 1976, when Kevin Keegan made it clear he saw his future playing outside of the country, and indeed in later years when Steve McManaman did the same, the reaction to the duo was less warm from the Anfield faithful.

Many Liverpool fans had sympathy with the 'Rushie Must Stay Campaign' – a group of them formed a committee and handed out leaflets asking supporters to sign a petition with three questions:

1) Why are Liverpool selling *Ian Rush*?
2) Which person is responsible for the sale?
3) What efforts have Liverpool made to keep him?

I think it is clear player-manager Kenny Dalglish wanted to keep him, that Rush had been offered an eye-watering deal from Juventus and Peter Robinson (PBR) got a record fee and an extra season of the top striker's services through good negotiating. Ian Rush put his heart and soul into what, at the time, he thought would be his final season at Anfield. Of course, as we know, after one season at Juventus he made his way back to Liverpool Football Club and scored and starred for the team for another *eight* seasons.

Typically, Rush scored the equalising goal in the 1986 FA Charity Shield in a 1-1 draw with Everton. And the Liverpool fans' reaction to him at Wembley on that day underlined that their respect and affection for him was very much intact. And, for the striker himself, it was business as usual in the first league game of the season at Newcastle, as he scored both goals in a 2-0 win. He played all 42 league games in his farewell season scoring 30 goals, including the late winner in his final home game against Watford, a game in which he captained the team, and all four sides of the ground rose to say their goodbyes. Rush was very emotional and threw his shirt into the Kop.

During the season he had inflicted his normal pain on Everton and Wales team-mates Neville Southall and Kevin Ratcliffe. Liverpool played the Toffees six times during the season, and Rush, having scored in the Charity Shield, followed it up with two league goals against them, the winner in a Littlewoods Cup quarter-final and five goals in the two-legged ScreenSport Super Cup Final held over from the previous season, and used as a temporary replacement for what would have been England's European qualifiers.

Rush scored twice in a 3-1 first leg at Anfield, and a hat-trick in a comprehensive 4-1 win at Goodison Park. Six matches and no less than nine goals against Everton. They couldn't wait to see the back of him!

The Reds finished runners-up behind eventual champions Everton in the league and went out in the FA Cup third round against Luton Town in a tie that went to three matches, two of them on the dreadful plastic pitch at Kenilworth Road. Those surfaces were in their early stages of development and the home side had a significant advantage. The Littlewoods Cup, formerly the Milk Cup, once again gave Liverpool a strong chance of success, and some startling personal achievements.

In their second-round first-leg tie at Anfield the Reds beat Fulham 10-0, with midfield man Steve McMahon scoring four goals, as well as missing a penalty. In the next round, McMahon scored a hat-trick in the Reds' 4-1 win over Leicester City. Jan Mølby landed the unusual feat of scoring a hat-trick in their fourth-round tie against Coventry City.

But it was a hat-trick with a difference – all penalties, and all placed to the left of the Coventry keeper, ex-Red Steve Ogrizovic. 'Oggy' would have his own big day at Wembley later that season when Coventry City upset the odds to beat Tottenham Hotspur in the 1987 FA Cup Final.

The Littlewoods Cup Final matched Liverpool and Arsenal and things got off to a good start for the Reds with Ian Rush putting them ahead. That in itself should have guaranteed Liverpool success, because in the previous 144 games in which

Rush scored the Reds had never lost. However, a double strike by the London side's ex-Celtic star Charlie Nicholas gave the Gunners the edge and the new trophy.

For Ian Rush it was a rare disappointment, but he would still have some important days left in him at 'Anfield South'. But first, he went to Italy for a new sporting adventure, in what turned out to be a one-season sojourn at Juventus – and he went with everybody's best wishes – and it was greeted with delight when he came back home so quickly.

Kop That – *Ian Rush scored a record 25 goals in 36 derby games – he scored in 15 of those games in which the Reds won 12 and drew the other three.*

1987/88 – LIVERPOOL'S
FIVE-STAR B & B

I FIRST met a young John Barnes in the week of the 1984 FA Cup Final as Watford prepared for their big day out at Wembley against Everton. After a training session, we filmed an interview with Barnes in his tiny flat, and the Jamaican-born 20-year-old spoke excitedly about the upcoming cup final, and especially of his passion for Brazilian football, and their great stars past and present. Four weeks later he was playing for England against Brazil at the Maracanã Stadium in Rio de Janeiro, and scoring his first goal for the national side.

And what a goal! Drifting in from the wing Barnes left Brazilian defender after defender in his wake before slotting the ball home. It was a goal worthy of Brazil's most famous-ever player, Pelé, himself.

Barnes scored another eye-catching goal in Watford's FA Cup tie with Liverpool in March 1986 – and 15 months later he joined the Anfield ranks from Watford for a £900,000 fee.

It proved to be an inspirational signing – John Barnes was a player of true class, blessed with a sure touch, pace and poise, mixed with a flair for dribbling, hitting accurate crosses and with an eye for goal. His televised brace of brilliant goals

151

against QPR at Anfield in October set the seal on his special new relationship with the Kop.

John Barnes, the son of a Jamaican military attaché who was later based in London, also had the character and personality to handle some of the unacceptable racist abuse that he and fellow black footballers had started to become the subject of on the British football scene. At the end of his first season at Anfield Barnes won both the PFA and FWA Player of the Year awards and contributed hugely to another memorable campaign for Dalglish's men. In fact, Liverpool players won 96 per cent of the total vote in that season's FWA award.

Peter Beardsley's background was a little less exotic. Born in Newcastle, he joined Carlisle United, Vancouver Whitecaps, Manchester United and then the Whitecaps once again, before his home-town club Newcastle United saw something in him the others hadn't, and that playing alongside ex-Liverpool great Kevin Keegan had brought out in him. Beardsley made a big impact for England in the 1986 World Cup in Mexico and his form continued for Newcastle the following season. So much so that in the summer of 1987, Liverpool paid a British record transfer fee of £1.9m to secure his services. Unlike Barnes, Beardsley wasn't an automatic hit with the Liverpool fans. He won them over eventually, making goals, taking goals and showing a level of energetic commitment to the cause that was admirable.

Barnes and Beardsley – Liverpool's own new B and B.

Liverpool-born striker John Aldridge had joined the Reds from Oxford United in January 1987 and made a few appearances, mostly as a substitute, at the back end of that season. A bit of a Rushie lookalike, and certainly seen as a potential Rushie replacement, the former South Liverpool player Aldridge started the 1987/88 campaign like an express train, scoring 11 goals in the first nine league games of the season. He would go on to score a total of 26 league goals in 36 games and cement his place in the side. His double strike in the FA Cup semi-final against Nottingham Forest booked Liverpool yet another Wembley engagement, where he would have the misfortune of creating a new piece of FA Cup Final history.

Midfield stars like Steve McMahon and October recruit Ray Houghton added guts, guile and goals from midfield, as did Steve Nicol, his hat-trick at Newcastle United being one of the standout individual performances of the season. Nicol was an ever-present in the Reds' 40 league games, seven FA Cup games and three Littlewoods Cup games, and the versatile Scotsman played in six different positions. This was very much Kenny Dalglish's Liverpool side and they won the title in impressive form, including being the first team to win it *before* the traditional Football League Cup Final had been played.

Their style of football won plaudits from football folk the length and breadth of the country. They went through the season breaking club records – on Boxing Day their win at Oxford United took their unbeaten league sequence to 20 matches – a club record. And when Liverpool met Arsenal at Anfield in January 1988 it was before the biggest audience ever to witness a Football League match to that date.

The gate was 44,294 and 250 million other people watched the game via television. Ten countries took the match live, 45 more showing recorded highlights. The level of global interest in the Reds was growing all the time as the TV markets expanded. It was a fortuitous moment for BBC Enterprises to release *The Official History of Liverpool FC*, the full-length video documentary that I had produced, with John Motson as the film's narrator.

The BBC launched the new film with an exclusive screening at Anfield itself, with many of the club's famous names of past and present in attendance, and on the screen. It was a proud personal moment, and the video, a labour of love, became a big hit. In fact, it was heading for the Christmas number one in the fledgling video sales charts, only to be pipped by *Andy Pandy, Bill and Ben, and the Woodentops*, a compilation of the great days of *Watch with Mother*!

Anyway, the following June, John and I were both awarded a 'platinum disc' comprising of the video's cover shot of Kenny Dalglish for sales worth £300,000. We went on to make several more Liverpool videos, including *The Story of the Kop* and a three-part history of *Match of the Day*.

The Reds' unbeaten sequence in the 1987/88 season had continued, including equalling Leeds United's record of 29 league games without defeat set in 1973/74, with a 1-1 draw at Derby County. The Reds' unbeaten stint ended in a single-goal defeat, ex-Leeds hero Allan Clarke's brother Wayne scoring the winner for Everton at Goodison Park. The standout league performance for the Reds that season was against Brian Clough's Nottingham Forest at Anfield.

Having beaten them four days earlier in the FA Cup semi-final, Liverpool put on a stellar performance against the East Midlands side in the league four days later. They didn't just win the game – 5-0 – but their peerless display drew unstinting praise from some of football's greats.

'They must be the best of all time. That was the finest exhibition by any team in all my time of playing and watching the game.' Those were the words of Tom Finney, the man Bill Shankly named as the best player he had ever seen.

A visitor to Anfield that night, Michel Platini, said that in replacing Ian Rush with Peter Beardsley, John Barnes and John Aldridge 'they have traded one great player for three great players'.

Liverpool clinched the title with a Peter Beardsley goal in a 1-0 home win against Tottenham Hotspur in their 36th league game. The Reds were on course for their second double in three years and were red-hot favourites to beat unfancied Wimbledon in that year's FA Cup Final.

Although they had finished a very respectable seventh in the league and held Liverpool to a 1-1 league draw at their rickety old ground at Plough Lane, the Dons were seen as cup final makeweights.

Now, I had seen Wimbledon play a lot that season, and knew they would not be pushovers – their style of football was not pretty, but it was pretty effective. And so it proved. On the day Princess Diana was introduced to both sets of players as the FA Cup Final's guest of honour, the London side set about their business in typical fashion – hard and direct.

Two of Liverpool's players, Gary Gillespie and Nigel Spackman, wore protective headbands, having been injured in a clash of heads in their final league game of the season at Luton the previous Monday. Liverpool conceded a poor first-half goal, Dennis Wise's free kick being headed in by Lawrie Sanchez, and had already had a goal netted by Peter Beardsley disallowed by Brian Hill, the referee, not allowing an advantage having already blown for a foul.

Liverpool huffed and puffed but just couldn't find a way to capitalise on their superior share of possession. All that would seem to have changed just after the hour, when John Aldridge was brought down in the penalty area by Wimbledon full-back Clive Goodyear. It looked a soft penalty but was a potentially vital lifeline for the faltering Reds.

Up stepped the normally reliable spot-kick taker Aldridge himself. He had successfully converted 11 penalties for the Reds that season, including one in the FA Cup semi-final itself. At Wembley that afternoon, under a hot sun and under immense pressure, Aldridge's penalty, driven to the left of Wimbledon keeper Dave Beasant, was saved. Beasant went into Wimbledon folklore and Aldridge became the first player to miss a penalty in an FA Cup Final at Wembley.

On the final whistle, Wimbledon wildly celebrated their surprise victory, and the Liverpool players were left to reflect on 'what might have been'. As John Motson so cleverly coined it, 'The Crazy Gang have beaten the Culture Club.'

Kop That – *After injury forced Mark Lawrenson to retire in March 1988, the defender became Oxford manager, and so followed the bizarre 'achievement' of winning the league as a player before seeing Oxford relegated from the top flight as a manager.*

1988/89 – HILLSBOROUGH

SATURDAY, 15 April 1989 is a date that will be etched into the history of Liverpool Football Club as long as this well-respected and much-loved sporting institution continues to play football the world over and for many, many decades to come. It is a date that marked the saddest day in the club's history, and brought a city to a shuddering halt.

It also marked the start of a fight for truth and justice which took three decades, during which many grieving families showed with a real strength of purpose moral courage and dogged determination that those they had lost or were injured at Hillsborough would never be forgotten.

Saturday, 15 April 1989 should have been a routine working day for me. It ended up being something very different.

By now, I was the editor of *Match of the Day*, a job I could barely have thought I would aspire to when I started watching the much-loved programme back in the mid-60s – my Saturday evening treat. This particular April Saturday was a little bit different as it was an FA Cup semi-finals afternoon. Back in 1989, both games kicked off at 3pm and neither were shown live on TV – that, in itself, seems almost unbelievable now.

Liverpool were playing Nottingham Forest at Hillsborough, a repeat of the previous year's semi-final, whilst Everton and Norwich City were at Villa Park in the other match. Highlights of both games were going to be on *Match of the Day* that night. Desmond Lynam and Jimmy Hill, our highly experienced on-screen presentation team, asked whether they could attend one of the games in person and head back to the London studios in good time to prepare for that evening's programme. I agreed but asked them to leave the match ten minutes before the final whistle so they would avoid any predictable traffic snarl-ups. They plumped for Liverpool v Nottingham Forest at Hillsborough.

Back in London, I joined my BBC colleagues ready to simultaneously watch both games 'live' on two adjacent TV monitors, before working out the running order for that night's *Match of the Day*. We were joined by two guests, one a rabid Liverpudlian. We often hosted people on a Saturday afternoon who wanted to see their favourite team in action but, for whatever reason, couldn't get to the game itself – they would be made welcome and they tended to love the banter that flew between us all as the match action was relayed into BBC TV Centre.

Saturday afternoon was always fun. Not on this Saturday. As we watched the stadiums filling up it became clear how unevenly the Liverpool fans were distributed at the Leppings Lane End at Hillsborough, and we sensed something was amiss. As did our guests, both experienced people in the stadium business. Indeed, something was very wrong. And although the match at Hillsborough got underway, six minutes later it was brought to a halt.

What we then saw was the stuff of nightmares as people spilled on to the pitch gasping for breath, having freed themselves from the horrendous crushing on the terraces. Recognising the urgency of it all, supporters were assisting each other, some attempting emergency first aid. Advertising hoardings were used as makeshift stretchers. Anything that was at hand to help stricken fellow fans.

The police were far too slow to understand the real nature of the problem in front of them. Unacceptably so, as has been subsequently proved. The fans knew this was no crowd invasion; this was people fighting for their lives. And, very sadly, some didn't make it.

Watching the outside broadcast pictures coming out of the BBC unit at Hillsborough, I contacted my colleagues at BBC's *Grandstand* programme and told them that there was a major incident developing at Hillsborough and that they needed to be across it. They were already aware of it and communications between their studio gallery and the outside broadcast at Hillsborough started taking place, where a vastly experienced producer, John Shrewsbury, selected sensitive camera shots that commentator John Motson could talk over.

Motson, the football commentator, became Motson, the news reporter, and I contacted Desmond Lynam and Jimmy Hill and told them to stay at Hillsborough as long as was necessary to get as true a picture of events as possible before heading back to London. Back at base, I was speaking to my BBC bosses. They had a decision to make. Did they leave *Match of the Day* in the schedules or, as was more likely, run an extended late-evening news programme.

I fought hard to retain *Match of the Day*'s place in that evening's schedule, and won.

Obviously, there would be no football in a shortened show, but I felt the combination of Desmond Lynam's unrivalled broadcast authority, Jimmy Hill's seniority in football circles, John Shrewsbury's instinctive use of on-site pictures and up-to-the-minute interviews, and in my role as programme editor, with such a strong Liverpool background and knowledge of the football club, we would interpret the tragic events of the afternoon professionally and objectively. And with integrity and empathy.

I did hundreds of programmes during my career at the BBC, and treated every one of them seriously and wholeheartedly, but this was one programme I was determined to get as right as was possible. When we came off the air, I think we all believed we had done our best to deliver a contemporaneous, honest and authoritative piece of television. However, we all knew that what we had witnessed that day would change the world of football forever, and, much more importantly, the lives of those nearest and dearest to the innocent souls who had perished, while just going to see a football match.

A few days after the horror of the Hillsborough Stadium disaster, I made my way up to Anfield to pay my respects and lay a bouquet among the remarkable floral carpet of largely red and white flowers that already spread from the Kop down across the pitch. Many had messages of sympathy or hope attached to them. Other tokens of love – scarfs, shirts, rosettes and even teddy bears were placed lovingly on the ground. Marks of respect from clubs and supporters from up and down the country, and from across the sporting world. It was a truly amazing sight to behold. It is thought that up to two million people filed through Anfield during the club's eight days of mourning.

Whilst at Anfield I took the opportunity to spend a little time with Peter Robinson and Kenny Dalglish. I also witnessed first-hand how the Liverpool players, and their wives and girlfriends, spent time speaking gently to the shocked and grieving relatives and friends of those who had died or were injured in Sheffield the previous Saturday.

I returned to Liverpool to attend the Hillsborough Memorial Service held at Liverpool Cathedral and televised live to the nation. The moving service ended with a prayer, then a period of profound silence, followed by a young chorister singing solo the opening words of 'You'll Never

Walk Alone', before the rest of the choir and many of the congregation joined in. Tears flowed. Kenny, his wife Marina and his players would attend funerals and be there for those who had suffered such devastating losses for many weeks, months and years to come.

The fight for truth and justice would take decades. And the 97 who perished because of events on that day in April 1989, whilst going to a football match, will never be forgotten.

Eventually it was decided Liverpool FC should resume playing football. A Hillsborough Memorial Match was held at Celtic with the home crowd delivering another powerful rendition of 'You'll Never Walk Alone'. Fittingly, the first competitive match for the Reds was at Everton, who as neighbours had handled themselves with great empathy and dignity during this traumatic period, offering support and comfort. The whole city had pulled together as one.

The FA Cup semi-final with Nottingham Forest was ultimately replayed in front of a reduced capacity crowd at Old Trafford, and broadcast live on television.

Liverpool won the game and in so doing set up another all-Merseyside FA Cup Final. It fittingly proved to be a fantastic football match, the Reds winning 3-2 after extra time – Ian Rush once again proving to be Everton's nemesis.

Six days later I was at Anfield to witness a remarkable end to the league season. Title hopefuls Arsenal came knowing that nothing less than a 2-0 win would wrest the title from Liverpool, who once again were on the verge of landing the double. Playing their eighth match in 24 days, the Liverpool team contained the Gunners in the first half. However, in the second half the London side started to get on top. Alan Smith got an important first goal, and then with literally seconds of the season left, Michael Thomas scored the vital title-clinching second goal.

Arsenal, like Leeds United in the 1960s, had clinched the league title at Anfield, and once again the home crowd handled it with great dignity, applauding the new champions.

After all, we had all been reminded in the weeks that preceded the title decider that there were far more important things in life than the winning or losing of a single football match.

Kop That – *Prior to the 1989 FA Cup Final, no substitute had scored more than once in a final. Stuart McCall then became the first to score twice – shortly afterwards Ian Rush became the second.*

1989/90 – KOP THAT!
AND COP THAT!

STEVE COPPELL was a very little chap but a very big fan of Liverpool Football Club. So big, that even at 11 years of age and still under five feet tall, young Coppell used to watch his beloved Reds in Anfield's Boys' Pen.

Now grown men would have passed on that particular fortnightly adventure into the unknown, but Steve was determined to go to the match, and so the Boys' Pen it was. He later joined his older brother Kevin on the Kop but he wasn't much taller by then either. And his height, or lack of it, was why both Liverpool and Everton passed on him when he was put forward for trials at the two Merseyside clubs.

Steve was a very good footballer, a winger of craft and class, and he finally got his chance at Tranmere Rovers – the rest, you could say, is history. A move to Manchester United followed, with 322 appearances and 54 goals for them and 42 England caps and seven international goals, including playing in four of their matches at the 1982 World Cup in Spain.

Seriously injured on international duty, Coppell's career was cruelly cut short at just 28, but he was already recognised for both his natural football ability on the pitch and his studious interest in the sport when off it. He was perfect 'manager material' and in 1984 Crystal Palace chairman Ron Noades both spotted it and nurtured it.

And the unlikely pair proved to be a big success, which is how we get to September 1989 and Crystal Palace, just fresh from winning promotion from the Second Division, turning up at Anfield for an early-season midweek league game. For Steve Coppell it promised to be a special evening – bringing 'his team' to play against the team he had faithfully followed as a boy.

My relationship with Steve Coppell began when we played football together at Quarry Bank High School in Liverpool. Him an outstanding winger, me an average full-back. Subsequently we both went to Liverpool University to study economic history. I was in the year ahead of Steve, but we all took a close interest in his fledgling football career. I went to see his debut for Tranmere Rovers against Aldershot at Prenton Park, and it was big news when he suddenly joined Manchester United.

Old Trafford boss Tommy Docherty allowed Steve to finish his studies and play for United at the same time, which became an interesting angle for football reporters, and it is how I and a few Liverpool University mates ended up being interviewed for filmed features on both BBC's *Football Focus* and Granada's *Kick Off* show on the weekend Steve came to play for Manchester United at Anfield for the first time.

It proved to be a bittersweet experience for Steve – United lost 3-1, but he scored their consolation goal at the Kop end. Of course, he would have his own moment of triumph when he was part of the Manchester United team that beat Liverpool in the 1977 FA Cup Final. Now in September 1989, Coppell was bringing his bright Palace side to the place he had loved going to as a young football fan – Anfield.

And I was there that night, cheering on the Reds, of course, whilst hoping Steve's team would also have a decent night of it. It did prove memorable for Steve and Palace but for all the wrong reasons. The Reds turned on a masterful performance and beat the Londoners 9-0 ... 9-0!

Steve Nicol got the first for the Reds after seven minutes, Steve McMahon the next eight minutes later, and Ian Rush added a third on the stroke of half-time. Goals four and five came from Gary Gillespie and Peter Beardsley, respectively, and then came the highlight of the evening. John Aldridge had agreed to move to Spanish side Real Sociedad on 1 September and he was set to join his new club the day after the Palace game.

Dalglish named Aldridge as a substitute and when Palace conceded a penalty in the 67th minute, the Kop roared for him to be brought on to take it. On he came, and with his first touch he took the penalty, and scored.

And at the end of the game an emotional Aldridge, a Liverpool fan from his head to his toes, threw his shirt and boots into the Kop. Barnes, Hysén and Nicol had added three more for Liverpool on a tough old night for Steve Coppell and his Palace side. Not the return to Anfield he would have wished for.

Seven months later the teams met again, this time at Villa Park in the FA Cup semi-final. Following the tragedy at Hillsborough the previous season, the FA approved both semi-finals to be broadcast live on BBC TV. I was in charge of the BBC's FA Cup output that Sunday, and just as a piece of professional neutrality, I decided to be on site at the second semi-final between Manchester United and Oldham Athletic. I watched the first semi-final, between the Reds and Crystal Palace, which kicked off at midday, on a TV in a production caravan in the car park at Maine Road.

Liverpool and Crystal Palace was expected to be a 'nailed-on' win for the Reds, and all seemed to be going to plan when Ian Rush opened the scoring after 14 minutes. Palace responded well in the second half, scoring within a minute of the restart through Mark Bright, before going ahead with a goal from defender Gary O'Reilly.

In an absolutely absorbing cup tie, Steve McMahon levelled things up for Liverpool on 81 minutes before a penalty by John Barnes two minutes later had the Reds on course for a hat-trick of FA Cup Final appearances. But it was not to be. Andy Gray equalised for Palace two minutes from time, and Alan Pardew scored the vital winning goal in the 109th minute of the game. 4-3. Steve Coppell, always a serious observer of the game, had only jumped for joy when Andy Gray scored the late Palace equaliser, and sprinted down the touchline and out of sight on the final whistle. He left his celebrations for the privacy of the dressing room.

Back in Manchester, I was personally and professionally deflated. Personally because my team had lost in a semi-final they really should have won, and professionally because I didn't think the second semi-final I was now in charge of broadcasting would get anywhere close to the epic that had just finished at Villa Park. Well, not quite as good, but it turned out a belter at Maine Road too – a 3-3 draw.

On the day the FA Cup semi-finals were shown live on TV for the first time there had been a record 13 goals in two extraordinary matches. The day left me professionally exhilarated, personally disappointed and quietly chuffed for an old university pal, Steve Coppell. He had suffered the ignominy of a 9-0 defeat at Anfield but had taken Crystal Palace to their first-ever FA Cup Final. 'After losing to them 9-0 and 2-0 in the league I would have been happy with just 1-0. To get four goals against the best team in the country renews your faith in our players and everything they do,' said Coppell.

Crystal Palace would serve up another epic match in the final against Manchester United – 3-3 this time – before losing 1-0 in the replay at Wembley five days later. Liverpool typically brushed themselves down and went on to win the league title for the third time in five years – a remarkable feat for Kenny Dalglish, who also brought the curtain down on his own fantastic playing career with a cameo performance when coming on as a substitute in the 71st minute against Derby County in the final home game of the season.

Dalglish, a mere 38 years and 58 days, was cheered to the rafters by the adoring Anfield crowd. A class act as a player, a manager and a person. Manager of the year Dalglish had delivered Liverpool's 11th title in 18 seasons, and quite incredibly it was to be the club's last title success for the next 30 years.

Kop That – *In 18 seasons since 1972/73 Liverpool finished outside the top two only once – in the 1980/81 season – but they did win the League Cup and European Cup!*

1990/91 – KING KENNY STEPS OUT

THE FRONT page of the *Liverpool Echo* shouted out in big, bold type the story that would shock football.

KENNY QUITS!

'Kenny Dalglish drove away in tears from Anfield after announcing he was resigning as manager of Liverpool FC. He made the bombshell announcement at a specially convened press conference pointing to the pressures of the job being behind his sudden decision to quit. The news was greeted not only with total disbelief on Merseyside – but with complete amazement throughout the country coming hard on the heels of one of the greatest derby matches ever seen.'

Yes, Kenny Dalglish was leaving the club that he had become a legend at, both as a world-class player but also as a hugely successful manager. In 14 years at Anfield, Dalglish had exceeded all expectations in either role, however high those expectations had been set. Certainly Liverpool's greatest-ever player and, into his sixth season as manager, a serial trophy winner. Also, his magnificent selfless support for the casualties, the club and the city following the horror of Hillsborough made him a much-loved and respected figure at Anfield.

And yet two days after watching his team draw 4-4 in a spellbinding FA Cup fifth-round replay with neighbours Everton at Goodison Park (a tie they eventually lost), the iconic Scotsman was laying down his tools, and picking up his golf clubs. He realised he needed a rest from the stresses of the job, and he knew what was best for himself, his wife Marina and their four young children. Putting himself and his family first for once.

Shankly had left the club on a Friday, and now so had another iconic Anfield figure, Kenny Dalglish. I phoned the Dalglish home when I heard the shock news and his wife Marina took the call. Kenny had taken refuge on the golf course with LFC's chief scout Ron Yeats. She accepted my good wishes, and I left her with the thought that, after a short break (the Dalglish family went off to Disney World), if Kenny wanted a further platform to explain the reasons behind his decision, I could provide it.

And, sure enough, some three weeks later I took a call in the BBC *Sportsnight* office from Kenny saying he was ready to go on television and further explain his reasons for leaving Anfield. His interview with presenter Desmond Lynam led the show that night and I suppose it was an old-fashioned 'scoop'. For me, it was the sign of a mutual respect I had built up with the man who Bob Paisley described as 'the best player Liverpool had signed in the past 50 years'.

When Dalglish left Liverpool Football Club it was as reigning champions and current leaders of the First Division. And perhaps a short break would have been enough to recharge his batteries, and I think he probably thought that himself, but things had moved on at Anfield.

After a short spell in charge as a caretaker manager, long-serving Ronnie Moran handed over the reins to another iconic Scot whose playing career at Anfield had been one of outstanding achievement.

Graeme Souness had been manager at Rangers for five years and done extremely well at Ibrox. And when approached to replace his old friend Kenny Dalglish at Anfield he simply couldn't resist the challenge. For us Liverpool fans we just felt some comfort that the managerial baton was being passed to 'one of our own'. A former Liverpool great who knew the club values and expectations, who knew the power and meaning of 'This is Anfield'.

Personally, I have always found Souness to be a decent man to deal with: straightforward, experienced and intelligent, qualities he now shows as a senior pundit of Sky Sports football coverage. And back in 1991 it should have worked out well for him at LFC, but 33 months later when he left the club, Souness probably reflected on a missed opportunity and mistakes, albeit well-meaning ones, that stalled the Reds' relentless pursuit of being among the best of the best. He later admitted himself he was the right man for the job but at the wrong time.

A bit like Shankly in 1970, Souness felt he had to change the personnel – move players out, and move new ones in. He was concerned some of the players had lost their edge, were ageing or were simply not good enough. But not all those he replaced them with were of the quality of those that had left. He admitted later he tried to change too many things too quickly. And his training regime was considered too tough at times, bringing a spate of injuries.

And he also made some off-field mistakes, like when giving the exclusive story of his triple heart bypass operation, and subsequent complications, to *The Sun* newspaper, which they then published around the time of that year's Hillsborough anniversary. This was very damaging to his reputation on Merseyside, something he recognised and regretted.

There were good times too – winning the FA Cup with a Wembley win over Sunderland in 1992, even if, still in the early days of convalescence from his heart op, he had handed over control on the big day to Ronnie Moran. And he would take the Reds back into European competition after six seasons' omission post-Heysel.

All of that was ahead of Souness when he arrived at Anfield in April 1991. It was a season that saw Liverpool finish runners-up behind Arsenal, two defeats against the Gunners, and those other old adversaries, Nottingham Forest, being critical in the title race. It was still a remarkable sequence – in the last ten seasons duly completed Liverpool had finished first, first, first, second, first, second, first, second, first and finally second. Add four FA Cup finals, three of them as winners, and you get a sense of their domination in this period.

One of the key figures during that successful period, and indeed before it, was Alan Hansen. He had enjoyed being one of 'the three Jocks' – Dalglish, Souness and Hansen – and was one of Anfield's greatest players. He played 620 times for the Reds, captained the side, developed a great defensive partnership with Mark Lawrenson, and was one of the classiest and most cultured defenders in world football. A serious knee injury had kept him out of the team in the 1990/91 season and in March, just weeks after his regular golfing partner Dalglish had suddenly left the club, he decided to retire from football.

That interested me, as the BBC's Head of Football. I was always looking at ways to keep our coverage of the national sport current, contemporary and challenging. Desmond Lynam, the finest sports presenter of his generation, was now ensconced as the on-screen face of football on the BBC. Jimmy Hill and Terry Venables produced lively and, at times, controversial punditry but I was keen to add somebody fresh out of the dressing room. Alan Hansen fitted the bill perfectly. A much-decorated player, an intelligent man, telegenic and possibly looking for the next career step after 14 seasons at Anfield.

I contacted Alan, who had been doing bits and pieces of media work at BSkyB, and explained what I wanted from him – and he subsequently signed an exclusive contract with the BBC at the end of the 1991/92 season and stayed with the corporation for the next 22 years! Indeed, he became more famous as a football pundit than he was as a highly successful player – well liked by BBC colleagues, a good team player, well respected by the sport he had left and well loved by the TV viewers.

The Premier League was due to start in August 1992, and, having secured the highlights broadcast rights, *Match of the Day* was back in its familiar late-evening slot and Alan Hansen would become a Saturday night fixture. He would admit to being a nervous performer, certainly in the early days, but settled into the role and his analysis became an integral part of that much-loved show.

I think his mindset was one of stability – he stayed at Liverpool for a lengthy period and did the same at the BBC. He played with some of the very best at Anfield and, at the BBC, working with presenters of the quality of Desmond Lynam and Gary Lineker played a big part in that long-term TV commitment. And while other pundits had more time to make their points on other channels, nobody could hit the viewing figures that the BBC's football output delivered on a regular basis. And Alan was always keen to know the latest audience figures.

Dalglish, Souness and Hansen: three Anfield icons, whose lives had all changed direction in the early months of 1991.

Kop That – *Dalglish, by giving himself a substitute appearance in winding up his playing career against Derby, joined Alan Hansen as the only two Liverpool players to play in the 70s, 80s and 90s.*

1991/92 – A SILVER LINING

THE MAIN entrance at Anfield was something of a revolving door during the summer months of 1991. Graeme Souness was making his early moves in the transfer market and players were coming and going at a fair rate of knots.

Two big-money new men were a pair from Derby County – Dean Saunders, a Welsh striker, bought for a record transfer fee between English clubs of £2.9m, and England international centre-back Mark Wright, costing the Reds £2.2m. Saunders's father Roy, a half-back, had played 146 times for Liverpool in the 1950s, and Wright's father was a Scouser and thrilled his son was now playing for the Reds. One of Souness's former Rangers players, winger Mark Walters, joined his former boss at Anfield as the Scotsman tried to reshape his first-team squad.

Those departing included Peter Beardsley to Everton, David Speedie to Blackburn Rovers and Steve Staunton to Aston Villa, a transfer that Souness later admitted was a mistake.

There was an early-season switch in the boardroom too, as David Moores, the principal shareholder at the club, moved into the chairman's seat. A genuine Reds fan at heart, the affable new chairman was looking forward to maintaining Liverpool FC's position at the forefront of English football, as the club would enter its centenary year in 1992. His time in office would see a mixture of highs and lows on the field and controversy when the club was sold to American businessmen in 2007.

As Moores took up the reins in 1991, the look of Anfield itself was changing – the Anfield Road End had been made all-seater, and other projects were in process, including the reconstruction of the Kemlyn Road Stand and the transformation of the world-famous Kop from terracing to seats.

The Kop would say an emotional farewell to its original iconic look in April 1994, but not before more special afternoons and evenings would be enjoyed by its loyal inhabitants – standing, swaying and singing.

Domestic football was about go through a huge change too, with agreement having been reached between the FA and the Football League to make way for the start of the new Premier League from August 1992. That moment would also mark a major change in the balance of power in English football's top league, not least because a certain team from up the M62 were about to become market leaders on and off the pitch.

All that was a season away, and the race was on to be the final winners of the Football League Division One – to be the English champions – and this in Liverpool's special year. But it was a race Liverpool were never really in, confounded by early-season injury problems, the blame for which landed at both Souness and physio, ex-Liverpool player Phil Boersma's door. Their training regime was deemed too excessive by many of the first-team squad, and muscle injuries abounded early in the season.

To compensate for the many changes being made on and off the pitch in the English game, at Anfield there was a welcome return of an old friend – European football. After an enforced six-year break from European competition, Liverpool, four-time European Cup winners and with two UEFA Cup successes behind them, locked horns again with Continental opposition in the UEFA Cup.

I managed to secure the broadcast rights for the BBC to follow Liverpool's exploits in that season's competition, as the Reds made a low-key return to European football against Finland's Kuusysi Lahti. On a warm September evening, a small crowd of 17,131 turned up at Anfield, a match covered live on TV. The occasion was newsworthy for obvious reasons, but the game was something of a landslide victory for the Reds. They beat the Finns 6-1, with Dean Saunders scoring four times, including three goals in nine minutes, at the Kop end in a one-sided second half.

Bizarrely, Liverpool lost the second leg 1-0, and then lost 2-0 in the next round's first leg away against talented French side Auxerre. And it could have been more. What followed at Anfield in the second leg was a mini-classic. The Reds pulled back the two-goal deficit in the first half, but were struggling to get the all-important third goal when seven minutes from time Jan Mølby fed a through ball to new boy Mark Walters, and the ex-Aston Villa and Rangers man steered the ball home in front of a delighted Kop. Although the crowd was only 23,094, their roar as the ball hit the back of the net seemed to belong to many more thousand voices.

Next up were Swarovski Tirol, coached by an old adversary Ernst Happel, who had taken the Belgian side Bruges to two European finals against Liverpool, as well as the Dutch side to the 1978 World Cup Final. His Austrian side couldn't match those achievements, and a two-legged aggregate score of 6-0, including five goals from Dean Saunders, was not flattering to the Reds. I was quietly pleased the BBC were getting plenty of value for their investment in Liverpool's re-entry into European competition.

It was into March of the following year that the Reds picked up the threads of the UEFA Cup with a tricky tie against Italian side Genoa. This was the first time Liverpool had played an Italian side since that fateful night in Brussels in 1985. Restricted by competition rules and injuries, Souness had to field a relatively inexperienced side in the fiery cauldron of the Luigi Ferraris Stadium, and the home side took a 2-0 advantage to Anfield. This time there was to be no 'Auxerre' miracle, only Liverpool's fourth home European defeat, Genoa winning the match 2-1.

On the domestic front, the Reds finished a disappointing sixth in the league, and had slithered out of the League Cup in the last 16, losing away to Third Division underdogs Peterborough United 1-0 in the round's shock result.

The FA Cup was more promising. A John Barnes hat-trick helped Liverpool to a 4-0 win at Crewe Alexandra in the third round. Replays were needed to get past Bristol Rovers and Ipswich Town in the fourth and fifth rounds, respectively.

Michael Thomas, who had scored that famous goal for Arsenal against Liverpool in 1989, had recently signed for Liverpool when he scored the only goal of the Reds' quarter-final tie against Aston Villa at Anfield. The semi-final draw pitched Souness's men against Second Division Portsmouth at Highbury. Pompey gave Liverpool a very tough afternoon and were ahead 1-0 in extra time before Ronnie Whelan squared the game late on (the Reds would win the replay on penalties).

A short time after the Highbury game, Souness was admitted to hospital to have a triple heart bypass operation, which he was aware he was going to have to face ahead of the Highbury semi-final. Souness initially got through the prearranged operation safely, but a nasty infection set in and the Liverpool boss became very unwell and his stay in hospital lasted for 28 days.

During that period *The Sun* carried an exclusive interview with the Liverpool manager during his convalescence and a picture also appeared in the paper on the day of the Hillsborough anniversary. It is believed to have been held over one day because Liverpool's replay with Portsmouth had gone to extra time and penalties. It soured Souness's relationship with the Liverpool supporters – he subsequently recognised he had made a regrettable mistake. Indeed, in his 2017 autobiography he said he should have resigned there and then.

Souness had only been out of hospital a few days when to show solidarity with the club, its players and supporters, he attended the FA Cup Final against Sunderland at a rainy Wembley Stadium. I remember going to their St Albans base the day before the cup final and having a few words with the Liverpool manager. He looked tired and drawn as anybody who had been through his medical ordeal would have done.

On the big day he emerged from the Wembley tunnel, flanked by club doctor Dr Bill Reid and Liverpool physio Paul Chadwick. And he sat down on the bench, looking frail, with a tracksuit and then a heavy coat draped around his shoulders, caretaker boss Ronnie Moran having been given the honour of leading the team out on another big day for the club.

The final was no classic – not many are – but a spectacular goal from Michael Thomas and Ian Rush's almost routine Wembley goal secured the famous old trophy for Liverpool for the fifth time, and in their centenary year too.

The Premier League was just around the corner, but the FA Cup Final still enjoyed glamour and prestige the world over – often the one live TV game everybody made it their business to watch – and its annual winners were guaranteed a place in football folklore. It was a silver lining on an otherwise difficult season for Liverpool Football Club and the man at its managerial helm.

Kop That – *England full-back Rob Jones in 1992 went one better than his grandfather Bill, whose Cup Final appearance saw the Reds lose to Arsenal in 1950.*

1992/93 – FORM DIPS
AND ROYAL VIPS

LIVERPOOL FOOTBALL Club began its life on the pitch on 1 September 1892.

At a sparsely populated Anfield, the players, in their blue-and-white-quartered jerseys, met Rotherham Town in a friendly ahead of their first season in the Lancashire League. About 200 people turned up at 5.30pm on a Thursday evening to watch Liverpool president John Houlding's new venture get underway. Meanwhile, some 10,000 fans were preparing to visit Goodison Park the following day to see Everton's first game on their new ground. A row over rent had sent Everton to a new home less than a mile away, and Houlding decided he still had a stadium, and now needed a new team to play in it.

Liverpool Football Club was born. And John Houlding's premier place in the celebrated history of the club was secured.

Among the vast array of LFC memorabilia I have collected down the last six decades, I count the match programme from the club's very first match as the most precious item of the lot. It cost one penny in September 1892, and a rather lot more when I bought it from an antique dealer in the late 1990s. The four pages, still relatively robust I'm glad to say, included the team line-ups on the front page, and an explanation of the offside rule and a portrait of John Houlding on the centre pages.

Underneath his picture ran this eulogy of the founder of Liverpool Football Club: 'The above is a portrait of our esteemed president, Mr. John Houlding. To know him is to like him, though there are some who are hostile to him, because they never tried to know him. He is a man of energy, determination, and honesty of purpose, and under his Presidency the Liverpool Club is sure to prosper, in the same way as the Everton Club did.'

The back page of the club's first-ever programme gave a list of forthcoming fixtures in the Lancashire League and a large advertisement for Liver Salts, which the Rotherham Town players probably needed on the way back to South Yorkshire after being beaten 7-1 by this new band of brothers at Anfield. When there is a list of the great figures of Liverpool's illustrious past it is fair to think that the man who started it all should be at the very top – John Houlding.

On 1 September 1992, exactly a hundred years on from their first match, the Reds, having long since discarded their blue-and-white kit, hosted Southampton in a midweek FA Premier League match with a 7.30pm kick-off. Just over 30,000 people turned up to watch a 1-1 draw, which continued Liverpool's poor start to the season – one win in the opening six games.

Among those in the stadium that night was the UEFA president Lennart Johansson, at Anfield that evening to open the new Centenary Stand. Johansson had played a key part in returning English clubs to European competition and been a prime mover in bringing Euro 96 to England. Indeed, Anfield would host three group games and a quarter-final in that competition.

1992/93 was the first season for the FA Premier League, an elite, or elitist, competition, depending on your view, that had started as the brainchild of the 'Big Five' clubs of the time.

Liverpool's Noel White was joined by Everton's Phil Carter, Manchester United's Martin Edwards, Arsenal's David Dein and Tottenham Hotspur's Irving Scholar at a dinner hosted in London by ITV's Greg Dyke.

Over some fine dining, and, no doubt, a superior glass of wine or two, the plan was hatched to create a new league with its own management, commercial and creative initiatives and its own thumping-big broadcast deal.

The Premier League, with future Liverpool chief executive Rick Parry in the new organisation's senior executive role, was finally signed off in September 1991, after a series of meetings between the FA and the Football League. New kids on the block BSkyB controversially paid over £300m for exclusive live coverage of the competition for a five-year term.

Greg Dyke and ITV were 'blown out of the water' by the aggressive new boys in town and 'a whole new ball game' was upon us. Liverpool and Everton voted against the deal. Over the next 30 years, the broadcast rights fees, both domestically and globally for the competition, went through the roof – millions turned into billions.

The Premier League, which shook off their FA branding, became a broadcasting sensation the world over. The EPL, as it is known in foreign parts, delivered a slick, exciting style of football, enhanced by brilliant multi-camera coverage. Anywhere in the world I travel, the taxi driver taking me from the airport to my hotel will mention the EPL, and then explain why he supports whoever he supports. When I say I'm a Liverpool fan, that normally sends the conversation on to another level altogether as the taximeter merrily ticks away.

Anyway, whilst it is always important to remind people there was a football life before the creation of the Premier

League, it is important to register some of the elements that this new venture in our national game has led to – for good or ill.

As interest in it has grown, the Premier League has become a destination point for a legion of world-class players and the world's best coaches, helped finance the building of some of the world's finest stadiums and attracted plutocrats from across the globe to invest in our clubs. Not everything has suited the average fan. For some, our most influential league has become a 'brand' rather than a sport.

Some fans, or 'customers' as they now see themselves, feel a little disenfranchised – kick-off times spread over two or three days, expensive ticketing, the distancing of the players from their supporters, and some foreign owners who seem to be buying their clubs but not winning their hearts and minds.

All that was ahead of us when the Premier League's first season got underway. And once again, Liverpool were at the forefront of a new broadcasting adventure. The Reds' away game at Nottingham Forest was picked as BSkyB's first-ever live Premier League match. A 1-0 win for Brian Clough's men but another broadcast first for LFC.

The surprise transfer of Dean Saunders from Liverpool to Aston Villa in September had an immediate positive return for the Midlands club – within days of signing for his new team, he scored twice in a 4-2 win for Villa over his former team-mates. This the game when Ronnie Rosenthal missed one of the sitters of that or any other season.

By the end of September, the Reds were lying in 19th place in the brand-spanking-new Premier League, 14th then eighth at the ends of October and November, respectively, and by the end of the year they were lying 11th, and out of both the UEFA Cup Winners' Cup and the Football League Cup. January brought a shuddering blow too as Division Two promotion hopefuls Bolton Wanderers knocked Liverpool out in the FA Cup third round, 2-0 in a replay at Anfield.

The natives were getting restless. February's five games brought no wins. March started with a 2-1 defeat to Manchester United, leaving the Old Trafford team top of the Premier League and Liverpool a distant 15th. April began with a 4-1 defeat at Blackburn Rovers, managed by a certain Kenny Dalglish. A fightback ensued and they finished April in fifth place. A mix of results in May, including a 6-2 thrashing of Spurs, left them in sixth place for the second year running, but crucially out of the European places for the following season.

Manchester United went on to win the inaugural Premier League and the balance of power had suddenly switched from Merseyside to Manchester.

In a slightly surreal end to the Reds' disappointing season, my mood was lifted when I took a call from Reds' CEO Peter Robinson inviting me to represent the BBC on the day the Queen and the Duke of Edinburgh were due to visit Anfield as part of a wider visit to Merseyside. And so accordingly, I arrived at Anfield on 28 May 1993 for a unique occasion, along with 15,000 enthusiastic members of the public.

The royal couple seemed genuinely moved by the warmth of the welcome they received. They watched a display of football skills by a group of handicapped children, paid their respects at the Hillsborough Memorial and then went back inside the stadium to hear a moving rendition of 'You'll Never Walk Alone'.

On her arrival at Anfield, the Queen had been introduced to some of the club's famous players, past and present, and current manager Graeme Souness and former holders of that important post. ITV's Paul Doherty and I were also placed in the receiving line and were delighted when she stopped to have a brief conversation with us. She said she understood how much football meant to the city. Then she was whisked away for the rest of her Merseyside tour, and we were left with a unique memory and a few more bits and bobs for my memorabilia collection.

Kop That – *Teddy Sheringham scored the first 'live' goal in the Premier League on Sky Sports, against Liverpool.*

1993/94 – THE KOP'S LAST STAND

THE LIVERPOOL legends came out of the players' tunnel, one by one, cheered to the rafters by the adoring Anfield crowd. Great names from the past, heroes all – Albert Stubbins, Billy Liddell, Ian Callaghan, Tommy Smith, Steve Heighway, David Johnson, David Fairclough, Craig Johnston, ex-Kopite Phil Thompson and the greatest ever, Kenny Dalglish, who received an especially resounding welcome.

Then, to a standing ovation, former manager Joe Fagan emerged from the tunnel with a special lady on each arm – Mrs Nessie Shankly and Mrs Jessie Paisley – both there to represent their late husbands on this very special Anfield day.

Saturday, 30 April 1994 – the last home game of the season, and the emotional last stand of the world-famous Kop. The final time that fans would find their way to their favourite spot on a terrace as famous as the players it helped drive to victory, season in, season out. And the legends gathered at the centre circle, all facing the same direction, and clapping in unison to pay their respects to a sporting institution – the Kop.

Raucous, witty, wise, committed, fair-minded, packed, loud, proud and Red through and through. The Kop. The time had come for the most renowned terrace in football, and those sturdy metal barriers that went with it, to make way for seats. The sad events of April five years before was the catalyst for our stadiums to become safer places for people to watch their favourite sport.

Merseyside icon Gerry Marsden walked towards the Kop and led them in an unforgettable rendition of 'You'll Never Walk Alone', and we all joined in. It was an occasion not to miss.

And then the stage was left to that day's stars from Liverpool and Norwich City to play out the final act of an emotionally charged afternoon – the match itself.

The 1993/94 season had been another turbulent one at Anfield – inconsistent league form, a penalty shoot-out exit from the League Cup against Wimbledon and no European football. Then, in January, a shock exit from the FA Cup at the hands of Bristol City in a 2-1 defeat in front of nearly 37,000 fans at Anfield.

In the wake of that defeat, Graeme Souness resigned as manager, still, in truth, recovering and recuperating from the major operation he had undergone 22 months before. He would leave disappointed it hadn't worked out for him at Anfield. His dedication and commitment could not be challenged but some critical misjudgements in recruitment and retention, or otherwise, of players, and 'the photo blunder' undermined his time in charge. He remains a Liverpudlian at heart. Fondly remembered as a player, less so as a manager.

Boot Room stalwart, Scouser Roy Evans, a former player, was swiftly appointed to the Anfield hot seat and it seemed a logical choice. He had been at the club since he was 15. In an unusual move, Bill Shankly had asked Evans, a sturdy left-back, to take early retirement from playing in 1974, at the age of 25, and after only 11 senior appearances, to concentrate on a career in coaching – and through his super-successful work with the reserve team and then his move into coaching the first team, Roy Evans was time-served at Anfield. Now he was getting his chance to manage the 'big heads'.

So, a Scouser now in charge off the field, and a teenage Scouser, destined to become a legend of the club, making an instant impact on it. Robert Ryder was born in 1975, taking his mum's surname, until he started secondary school when he took up his dad's surname, Fowler. It became clear very quickly that young Fowler was a natural footballer and a supernatural goalscorer. An Evertonian as a boy, one of his heroes was top striker Graeme Sharp, but it was Liverpool who managed to land this supremely talented lad.

The coaching hierarchy at Liverpool knew he was special, and a lift home one rainy evening after schoolboy training from the Reds manager Kenny Dalglish didn't do any harm either. Under the careful eye of Liverpool's head of youth development Steve Heighway, Fowler's precocious scoring rate continued at reserve, A and B team level.

I was at Craven Cottage on the night Robbie Fowler made his first-team debut in a League Cup tie against Fulham. And sure enough, the 18-year-old everybody was raving about got his debut goal in a 3-1 win. 'Every player wished me well before the kick-off. They helped me to relax. And our captain Ian Rush guided me through the 90 minutes with advice whenever he could.'

A fortnight later Fowler got all five in a 5-0 second-leg romp against the Cottagers. In the same month, Fowler scored a league hat-trick against Southampton. He could notch every type of goal, especially via his deadly left foot. It would torment future opponents time and time over.

In what eventually turned out an ordinary season, Liverpool had unveiled an extraordinary player, and by the end of the campaign he had scored 18 goals, including a derby match winner, and he was still a teenager.

He would become one of Liverpool's finest – a goal machine – and, most importantly, he was one of our own. A real character who combined a touch of genius with a sense of mischief. And the Liverpool supporters loved him for both, and embraced his personality. He was a Scouser through and through, prepared to publicly support the dock workers in their strike action and, as he grew as a person and a Liverpool player, to fully understand 'the profound and lasting effect that Hillsborough had on the families, survivors and their loved ones'.

Back on the Kop's final curtain call on the last day of April 1994, Liverpool strove to put on a show, but typical of the type of campaign it had been, they fell short. The final goal scored at the Kop end came from Jeremy Goss of Norwich City. He had netted a famous goal against Bayern Munich earlier in the season, but this was almost as important a landmark goal. And a winner for the East Anglians.

For the record, the unlikely scorer of Liverpool's last goal at the Kop end had come three weeks earlier when Julian Dicks converted a penalty in a 1-0 win over Ipswich Town. The scenes at the end of Liverpool's last home game in front of the massed standing ranks of the Kop were emotional and lengthy. Not everybody had agreed with seating the Kop, but the original construction was given a splendid sign-off, bar a Liverpool win, of course.

First thing the following morning, I was in a TV production house in London putting the finishing touches to a video documentary John Motson and I had made telling the story of the world's most famous football terrace. We had completed most of it in the weeks leading up to the Kop's last hurrah but had left some space at the front and back of the film to add scenes from its final day. We delivered the finished article to BBC Enterprises the following day and by the end of the week

The Story of the Kop was on sale – a lovingly made tribute to a simply unique sporting institution.

One special elderly lady contacted me asking for a copy of the tape, and I sent one directly to her. I received this handwritten letter back:

Dear Mr Barwick,

Thank you so much for the tape – and the speed in which it was dispatched to me. As you say in your letter it brought back many fond memories – thank you so much again.

Yours sincerely, Mrs Nessie Shankly.

Kop That – *Only five players have scored five goals in a game for Liverpool. One of them, Ian Rush, was in the team when Robbie Fowler became the last of the five, in the defeat of Fulham.*

1994/95 – THE YOUNG ONES

WHEN ONE of the world's modern-day icons tells you that he supports your team, has followed its progress for nearly 30 years in extraordinary circumstances and then turns up unannounced to meet you in person, it is something incredibly special. When that man is Nelson Mandela, the newly inducted President of the South African Republic, the team he is talking about is Liverpool Football Club, and he explains how, for 27 years, he kept in touch with the Reds' games by listening to the radio while incarcerated in tiny cells on Robben Island and elsewhere, your respect is unbounding.

On Liverpool's post-season tour of South Africa in May 1994, Nelson Mandela surprised everybody when he entered the Reds' dressing room ahead of their friendly match against Aston Villa in Johannesburg. Having spoken privately with manager Roy Evans, he then requested a Liverpool shirt, took off his jacket and put the red jersey on before joining the players for a group photograph. It was an image reproduced on news media all over the globe. Mandela, who had led the fight against apartheid, had been made president of his country earlier that year and the Liverpool players there that day felt privileged to have met him in person.

Roy Evans's first full season in charge proved to be a distinct improvement on what had gone before in the previous two seasons. There was a freshness about their style, consistency of selection, a significant tactical change in defence and some youthful exuberance further up the field.

In Robbie Fowler and Steve McManaman, Evans had two local lads who played with a confident Scouse swagger – Jamie Redknapp was also becoming a fixture in midfield, Rob Jones had settled swiftly into the right-back berth and David James had now firmly taken over Bruce Grobbelaar's goalkeeping post. Allied to these talented young men was the vital experience of captain Ian Rush, John Barnes, Steve Nicol and Jan Mølby.

Roy Evans was also keen to play with three at the back. He already had Neil Ruddock, who could play the sweeper role, and having been publicly critical of Mark Wright's fitness and form, he acted decisively in the transfer market early in September and bought two expensive fellow defenders on consecutive days. Firstly, Irish international Phil Babb joined from Coventry City and 24 hours later Liverpool swooped to sign Wimbledon's stylish centre-back John Scales. Ruddock, Babb and Scales would play together for the lion's share of the season – not Hansen and Lawrenson perhaps but effective all the same.

In the opening game of the season at Crystal Palace, the Reds, in their away kit of dark green and white shirts and black shorts, were in scorching form, winning 6-1. The following Sunday Robbie Fowler's precocious talent came dramatically to the fore again when he scored a hat-trick against Arsenal at Anfield. But not just any hat-trick. He did it at double speed.

Three goals in the space of four minutes and 33 seconds was, at the time, the fastest hat-trick in Premier League history. Arsenal didn't know what had hit them. Ironically, future Liverpool star Sadio Mané would ultimately better Fowler's record time whilst playing for Southampton.

Liverpool's attendances were capped at 32,000 at the start of the season as the Kop was being reconstructed to an all-seater stand, and was increased as the building progressed. Spared of the injuries that had plagued his predecessor's reign as boss, Evans kept faith in the same players week in, week out. Over the season the Reds played 57 games in all competitions, and David James and Robbie Fowler played in all of them, both Jamie Redknapp and Steve McManaman in 55 of them, Neil Ruddock in 52, Ian Rush and John Barnes in 50, and new boys John Scales and Phil Babb 49 and 47, respectively.

Liverpool would finish fourth in the league table, only a late drop-off in form denying them a probable third place, they reached the FA Cup quarter-finals and the cherry on the cake was winning the Coca-Cola Cup Final, the latest incarnation of the Football League Cup. With that win came qualification for the UEFA Cup the following season.

On Sunday, 2 April and at a television-friendly kick-off time of 5pm, which annoyed both sets of fans travelling down by rail from the north, Liverpool and second tier Bolton Wanderers locked horns on a sunlit late afternoon at Wembley. Sir Stanley Matthews, a name synonymous with great Wembley finals, was the match's guest of honour, and both he and we were all treated to another English winger's masterclass, as Steve McManaman won the game for Liverpool.

Scoring two wonderful goals, and being a real handful throughout the 90 minutes, McManaman fittingly won the Man of the Match award in the Reds' 2-1 win. And equally fittingly, it was handed over to him by one of English football's all-time greats, Sir Stanley. Everybody was chuffed, especially the Boot Room colleagues of Roy Evans, Doug Livermore and Ronnie Moran, visibly delighted that the gaffer had got off the mark in the trophy-winning business.

And the Reds were involved in another significant trophy lift after their final home match of the season. In an extraordinary set of circumstances, Liverpool legend Kenny Dalglish was bringing his high-flying Blackburn Rovers side to Anfield knowing that if the Lancastrians won the game they would clinch the title – they would be Premier League champions, a remarkable feat from one of English football's oldest clubs.

Dalglish had taken Rovers out of the Second Division, and with help from Blackburn-born business tycoon Jack Walker's generous financial backing had built a team worthy of ending their 81-year wait for another title success.

However, in what had become a two-horse race, Manchester United could also win the title if Rovers faltered, and Sir Alex Ferguson's men won their game at West Ham. Rovers had a two-point lead over United that could be overhauled if they lost and United won.

Both games kicked off at the same time – Sunday 4pm – and the destination of the trophy was in doubt right until the very end of an intriguing afternoon. There was a strangely subdued atmosphere at Anfield as Liverpool fans knew a win for the Reds over Blackburn Rovers may well hand the Premier League title to their arch-rivals Manchester United. Rovers went ahead through a well-taken strike by Alan Shearer, but goals from Barnes and, late in the game, a tremendous shot by Redknapp won the game for the Reds.

Man United's game at Upton Park had ended 1-1 with Fergie's men pressing hard for victory and the title, and that familiar broad smile beaming across Kenny Dalglish's face told the whole story. Leeds United, Arsenal and now Blackburn Rovers had clinched a league title at Anfield, and the whole ground rose as one to acclaim one of their favourite sons, Kenny Dalglish.

Kop That – *Dalglish became only the second post-war manager to win the league with two different clubs. Brian Clough had been the first, doing so with Derby County and Nottingham Forest.*

1995/96 – ARMANI'S WHITE ARMY

AS THE 1995/96 season got underway, I was entering my final stretch as the editor of *Match of the Day*. It had been a privilege to oversee such a much-loved programme for seven years, its unmistakeable theme music once voted the most recognisable on British television. Desmond Lynam was in top form, Alan Hansen and Jimmy Hill would add their experienced eye, and in John Motson and Barry Davies we were blessed in having two top commentators – their styles differed but that was a bonus in many ways.

With Sky Sports building a significant bridgehead into people's consciousness with their coverage of live Premier League football, the fight to keep *Match of the Day* relevant was on.

Who needed highlights when you could watch the matches live? Well, seemingly millions of people did because the viewing figures were consistently high.

And, at the time, the BBC knew the value of the programme's prestige and its audience reach made it a key asset for the corporation. The BBC's director general at the time, John Birt, had written to me to say *Match of the Day* was his favourite TV programme. Useful to know that.

What was clear was that the football industry still knew the power of the *Match of the Day* message – a Saturday night institution – a programme that still carried weight and authority. It could clear up Saturday's big match controversies before the Sunday newspapers even hit the doormat. Which is why Alex Ferguson would occasionally call my office on Monday morning if he felt we had put a foot wrong with regards our programme's view on Manchester United's performance at the weekend, or even where we had placed their game in the programme's running order.

He was concerned about the make-up of the programme's experts and its boss. He felt there was a Liverpudlian bias, with Alan Hansen and latterly Mark Lawrenson as key influencers of public opinion on our team. And the editor of the show being known as a supporter of 'those other Reds'. The phone calls were always lively, and invariably short! I stood my ground and defended our show. Mind you, I never let Fergie know the man at the very top of the organisation, the director general, was also a Liverpool fan! In a begrudging way I admired Fergie's diligence and determination to not allow anything to get in the way of 'knocking Liverpool right off that ******* perch', even if we were innocent of any perceived bias.

Indeed, after taking one such call from Old Trafford, I opened two letters that had been left on my desk, one from a Liverpool supporter, and the other from a Manchester United fan. The Liverpool fan accused *Match of the Day* of being biased in favour of United every week, and the United fan thought we always favoured the Scousers. I felt like sending them each other's letters by dint of a reply, and then sending both letters to Fergie just to prove how professionally neutral we were – nobody liked us! I suppose it was all part of Fergie's famous 'mind games' – anything for a little marginal gain over his rivals.

I think Sky Sports putting Manchester United and Liverpool legends Gary Neville and Jamie Carragher together when they finished playing was a clever move, and in recent times, Graeme Souness and Roy Keane likewise. It just annoys everybody else now!

Manchester United and Liverpool met each other three times during the 1994/95 season. There were two compelling league matches and probably the dullest FA Cup Final since the war. The first league encounter, at Old Trafford, marked the return to competitive football of Manchester United icon Eric Cantona, some eight months after being suspended for his kung fu kick incident at Crystal Palace earlier in the year.

The Old Trafford crowd was at fever pitch for Cantona's return, and inevitably he stole the headlines. Inside two minutes the Frenchman had set up Nicky Butt for the opening goal. Cantona just stood still, nodding his head in admiration in a typically Gallic style. They had Cantona, but we had Robbie Fowler, and just before half-time he fizzed a shot past Peter Schmeichel at his near post. It was a tremendous goal, the best he had scored in his short career. Our 'God' was upstaging their 'Emperor' and sure enough Fowler added a second goal at the Stretford End early in the second half.

As is the way of these things, United got a soft penalty later in the half and, of course, Cantona stepped up and scored it. 2-2 the final score, and the Frenchman got all the headlines. But a belting game all the same.

In December, the teams met again, this time at Anfield, and Robbie Fowler once again was in top form, scoring twice as Liverpool beat United 2-0. This was the season when Newcastle United, under Liverpool former star Kevin Keegan's tutelage, were looking like potential champions. At one stage they were 12 points ahead of Manchester United, but their lead had been whittled away by the time the Geordies came to Anfield for a midweek match in April, which many still think was the game of the decade.

Any Kevin Keegan side puts attack ahead of defence, and even though results were beginning to turn against the long-time front runners, Newcastle United came to Anfield to attack, and win. What transpired was a simply fantastic game of football. All of us there marked it down as one of the best games they'd ever seen, and it is still worthy of the many reruns it gets on Sky Sports.

The story of the game? Liverpool went in front within two minutes, Fowler (of course) on target from a Stan Collymore cross, this time with a header. 1-0. Newcastle immediately hit back through Les Ferdinand and then went ahead when David Ginola hammered one home. The game was still inside the first quarter of an hour. 1-2. Into the second half and the Reds levelled the game, Robbie Fowler on the mark again in the 55th minute. 2-2.

Two minutes later, Colombian star Tino Asprilla, a recent acquisition for Newcastle, put the Geordies ahead. 3-2. The third goal in a magical 12-minute spell came from Liverpool, and their £8.5m summer signing from Nottingham Forest, Stan Collymore. Collymore scored a scorching winning goal against Sheffield Wednesday on his debut at Anfield in August, but had struggled with form, injury and controversy. But this was his night as he steered a Jason McAteer cross home. 3-3.

And so into the closing stages of a pulsating game, with Keegan and his sidekick, ex-Liverpool great Terry McDermott, urging their side, complete with ex-Red Peter Beardsley, to go for a winner. And his counterpart on the Liverpool bench, Roy Evans, was doing the same to the home side.

The game deserved a winning goal and it got one in injury time, old heads John Barnes and Ian Rush working an angle in the penalty area for Stan the Man to drive the ball home from close range. 4-3. An unbelievable match with a climax worthy of it. Evans punching the air and a devastated Keegan slumped over an advertising hoarding.

The game's other big winners were Manchester United – the result suited them most and they went on to win their third Premier League title. Could they do the double too? In front of them an FA Cup Final date with rivals Liverpool. It was a match-up that really caught the nation's imagination. Could *our* Reds stop *their* Reds from winning the double?

Against all expectation and huge build-up, the 1996 FA Cup Final turned out to be an absolute stinker of a game, eventually decided by a late goal from Eric Cantona – his resurrection complete.

The match also marked the final appearance of Ian Rush as a Liverpool player – a true great.

The other big talking point of the afternoon was the white Armani suits worn by the Liverpool team as they boarded their coach to Wembley from their hotel and then paraded around the famous pitch on the traditional prematch walkabout. Their outfits, and the 'shades' worn by some of them too, were several light years away from the more traditional club blazer and slacks, that's for sure.

The 'ice cream' suits gave critics another opportunity to build on the 'Spice Boys' tag that this young Liverpool side had started to get stuck with. Fairly, or unfairly, the lifestyles, fashions and 'cool' acquaintances of some of the players had lent themselves to a level of scrutiny and lads-mag interest they couldn't shake off.

Me? I couldn't care less what they wore ahead of the match. I'm a bit old school anyway, but my only view on the day was *if* you are going to wear those suits (and those shades!) you'd better win the game. And we didn't.

On a more sombre note, this season also marked the death of the great Bob Paisley. He passed away in February 1997, aged 77, a one-club man, player, trainer, assistant manager, manager, board director – modest, quietly spoken, warm and wise. His football knowledge helped guide Liverpool Football Club into a golden era of success.

Kop That *– Renowned for his FA Cup goals against Everton whilst at Anfield, Ian Rush's last goal in the competition came in his spell with Newcastle – that goal saw the Toon defeat ... Everton!*

1996/97 – THE MAGNIFICENT SEVEN

DELVING INTO the stack of books I have that celebrate the Reds' glorious history, I happened on a great photograph that captured a special period from Liverpool's past. It was a group of young players standing proudly together who had come through the club's youth development programme. Snapped in the late 1990s, the photo featured seven talented footballers, some of whom had already made their impact at Anfield, and a couple more whose footballing ability would make them world-famous sports stars.

In front of the logo 'Liverpool Football Club – The Academy' stood Steve McManaman and Robbie Fowler, two players who by 1996 were full internationals and key elements of the Liverpool first team; defender Dominic Matteo, with some senior appearances already to his name; three others, Jamie Carragher, Michael Owen and David Thompson, would make their first-team debuts in 1996/97; and completing the set was a younger-looking lad whose one-club career with the Reds would be the stuff of legend – Steven Gerrard. McManaman, Fowler, Matteo, Carragher, Owen, Thompson and Gerrard – what a roll call of young men, who between them would go on to make a remarkable 2,697 appearances for the Reds.

It is worth reflecting on the success of the School of Excellence and Academy programme back then at Anfield during this period, largely led by the drive and diligence of one of the Reds' heroes of the 1970s, Steve Heighway. His commitment to the cause, and to the young men for whom he was responsible, often meant he would come into conflict with the various managers of LFC who would pass through the club, and would look here and abroad for ready-made first-team players rather than closer to home and give youth a chance.

That was a consequence of the pressures attached with staying competitive in the Premier League and in European competitions, and was the route carried out at most clubs in English football's top league. But the Reds' seven captured together on camera would have forced any manager's hand.

A couple of weeks after Liverpool's miserable efforts in the 1996 FA Cup Final, their youth team went on to win the prestigious FA Youth Cup for the first time in the club's history. Jamie Carragher would describe it as one of the most important moments in his long and successful career.

The young Reds beat a strong West Ham United team, with future stars like Rio Ferdinand and Frank Lampard in their ranks. Winning 2-0 at Upton Park, the Reds finished the job with a 4-1 second-leg final victory in front of over 20,000 fans at Anfield. Many of those left the ground talking excitedly about the young talent they'd seen on show, especially a little striker whose turn of speed and eye for goal would take him to a World Cup within two years, where he would score a goal that would make him one of the most famous footballers on the planet.

Michael Owen, just 16, had scored a hat-trick in the FA Youth Cup quarter-final against holders Manchester United, a total of five goals in the two-legged semi-final against Crystal Palace and, having missed the first leg of the final against West

Ham, whilst scoring on England under-16 duty, came back to score a vital goal in the second leg of the final at Anfield. An FA Youth Cup winners' medal won, and five years later he would have a winners' medal from the FA Cup Final, in a match immortalised in his name.

In the summer of 1996, the nation had been transfixed with Euro 96, UEFA's European Championships, hosted by England. It caught the country's imagination. England, under Terry Venables, played exciting football and reached the semi-final before going out on penalties to eventual winners Germany at Wembley.

The highlight of England's tournament was their 4-1 drubbing of highly fancied Netherlands, a game in which Steve McManaman played his part. There was a real feel-good factor around the tournament, with Liverpool band The Lightning Seeds topping the charts with their invigorating 'Three Lions' song.

Anfield hosted four matches in the tournament, and I was there to see the Czech Republic's surprise win over Italy. The Czechs went on to make the final of the tournament. On duty for the Czechs that day was Patrik Berger, who scored a penalty in that final against Germany at Wembley. A 22-year-old attacking midfield player, Berger, who played for Borussia Dortmund, had attracted Liverpool's interest, and the Reds fan was Anfield-bound. He was an exciting player who described himself as best used in a deep attacking role. I saw him star in his first Anfield start when he scored two memorable goals in a 4-1 thrashing of Chelsea to add to the two he had notched at Leicester the previous week. The Kop welcomed a new hero.

Liverpool's season itself would disappoint. Still coming in for criticism for some of their lifestyle choices, the players couldn't deliver consistent performances and any title challenge fell away, ultimately finishing fourth behind champions Manchester United, Newcastle United and Arsenal.

In a bizarre repeat of the previous season's remarkable 4-3 Liverpool win over Newcastle, the equivalent fixture in this season at Anfield was another 'Magnificent Seven', and another 4-3 win to Liverpool. This time the Reds roared into a 3-0 half-time lead, before the Geordies, now under manager Kenny Dalglish, pulled it back to 3-3 in the second half. It was left to Robbie Fowler to score the seventh, and final, goal of the game in injury time.

In Europe things went better for the Reds, reaching the semi-final of the UEFA Cup Winners' Cup. On route they had played in an improbable tie against Swiss side Sion. Evans's side had won the away leg 2-1 and were no doubt expecting a comfortable return leg at Anfield. Well, it didn't turn out like that. Sion went 2-0 up early in the first half, before Steve McManaman struck for Liverpool and squared the tie.

In a six-goal thriller of a second half, Liverpool went behind on aggregate again to the resilient Swiss side, before putting on the afterburners and scoring five goals in 36 minutes to win the match 6-3 and go through on aggregate 8-4.

Liverpool's run in the competition ended in the semi-final when they went out to Paris Saint-Germain. A decisive 3-0 defeat in the French capital could not be rescued at Anfield in a nevertheless exciting 2-0 win for the Reds.

From this distance now, I recognise seeing Jamie Carragher score on his first start for the club, a close-range header, was one of my highlights of the season. The young Scouser was told the evening before that he would be playing in central defence against Aston Villa at Anfield as Liverpool's new signing Norwegian Bjørn Kvarme's international clearance hadn't come through. Overnight Kvarme was cleared to play but Patrik Berger had fallen ill. Carragher would be a starter in midfield.

I've got to know Jamie well over the years, both through his football and his broadcasting work, and I have a huge respect for him. 737 appearances for the Reds tell their own story, but even those impressive numbers can't really describe the level of commitment and craft he brought to his Liverpool career. A 'team of Carraghers' might not win the Premier League, but it would have the respect of everybody who watched them play.

His first league start could have been over very quickly. His enthusiasm and a late challenge on the experienced Andy Townsend brought him a yellow card just 20 seconds into the game. But his headed goal, from a corner at the Kop end, five minutes into the second half was followed by a suitably joyous celebration and an interview on *Match of the Day*. He watched it all back many times over.

My second highlight came at a late-season meeting between Wimbledon and Liverpool. The Reds needed to win to keep alive any slim chance of landing the title. Played at Selhurst Park because Wimbledon had moved out of their Plough Lane home, the match ended in a 2-1 win for the 'home' side, but Liverpool fans would remember it for the second-half introduction, off the substitutes bench, of 17-year-old Michael Owen, as he crossed the white line and kick-started his first-team career. I can still remember a real buzz of excitement from the vast army of Liverpool fans in the ground that evening.

I'd heard all the stories about this youngster, son of former Everton player Terry Owen and, like McManaman, Fowler and Carragher before him, an Evertonian turned Liverpool player. I just felt we might witness a little bit of LFC history that night. And sure enough, he came on and scored – the type of goal we'd get used to seeing him score – a confident close-range finish into the corner of the net. To that point in their history,

Michael Owen, at just 17 years and 144 days, had just become Liverpool's youngest-ever goalscorer.

Carragher and Owen became roommates when the Reds were on the road, and shared great moments as Liverpool players, but scoring their first goals for the senior side must have been right up there with the best of them.

And we enjoyed them too.

Kop That – *Before his 18th birthday, Michael Owen had become Liverpool's youngest scorer in Europe, the League Cup and the league. Shortly after that birthday he became England's youngest scorer.*

1997/98 – THE MACCA
AND MO SHOW

LIVERPOOL ENTERED the new season having had a busy time in the transfer market, securing four new names to try, yet again, to mount a serious challenge for the Premier League title.

In the controversial signing of ex-Manchester United midfield man Paul Ince from Inter Milan, Roy Evans was bypassing the traditional antithesis of players moving between those two bastions of English football, even if in Ince's case there was a stop-off in Italy for two years. Evans shrugged that off and made Ince his captain.

A Premier League title winner on board, shortly followed by a UEFA Champions League winner too, in Karl-Heinz Riedle, fresh from scoring two goals in Borussia Dortmund's final win over Juventus. Also recruited were Øyvind Leonhardsen from Wimbledon and a young Danny Murphy from Crewe Alexandra.

There were farewells to Stan Collymore, happy to settle back in the Midlands after an uneven time at Anfield, and the great John Barnes, who left on a free transfer after more than a marvellous decade's service to Liverpool. He headed up to Newcastle to join his old boss Kenny Dalglish.

As the season entered its early weeks, the shock news that Princess Diana had tragically died following a heavy car crash in Paris shook the nation and the world over. What followed was a week of nationwide grief for the popular princess, ahead of her funeral on the Saturday after her death. Like many other elements of British life, football went on the backburner, as the print and media coverage of the late princess swamped everything else.

As life slowly got back to normal, Liverpool were involved in a spectacular UEFA Cup tie with Celtic, renewing memories of their meetings in 1966. I went up to Parkhead for the first leg and was blown away by the incredible atmosphere in the stadium, especially when the whole of the ground joined together in an unforgettable rendition of 'You'll Never Walk Alone'.

The Celtic fans were up for it, and some. Michael Owen's sixth-minute goal quietened them down briefly, but the men in the green and white hoops had seized a 2-1 lead as the game entered its closing moments. That's when Steve McManaman struck with a late equaliser that has stayed long in the memory. Picking the ball up in his own half, he swerved past a retreating Celtic forward and gathered pace as he headed towards the Scottish team's goal. Leaving another opponent floundering in his wake, McManaman let fly with a low shot into the corner of the net, with five Celtic players trying to get to him.

It was a wonder goal. A game saver. And it underlined the qualities of the Liverpool forward, who would ultimately head off to Real Madrid in 1999 in an early example of a high-profile Bosman-style deal. It would split the Liverpool fans, some seeing it as a greedy move by McManaman, others recognising it as an opportunity he couldn't resist. But Liverpool had certainly missed out on a huge transfer fee when one of their prized assets left the club on essentially a free transfer.

Whilst writing this book I've reassessed my take on Steve McManaman's Anfield career. Firstly, he played lots of games for the Reds – 364 appearances in all. He was a goalscoring midfield player, from either out wide or through the middle; he was a scorer of 'great' goals – Aston Villa and Arsenal were on the end of two other belters in the same season he had weaved his magic at Celtic; he was a 'big-game' player, with match-winning performances in the 1992 FA Cup Final and the 1995 Coca-Cola Cup Final (and the 2000 Champions League Final for Real Madrid); and he made lots of goals for his team-mates, particularly his best mate Robbie Fowler.

On the field they were almost telepathic, and off the field lively Scouse companions. And McManaman scared the opposition. Sir Alex Ferguson was one manager who thought stopping McManaman was a crucial element in any plan constructed to beat the Reds. Yes, Macca was the real deal, literally. In July 1999, nine months after Barcelona pulled out of a plan to take him to the Camp Nou, and five months after his advisers and Real Madrid had shaken hands on a five-year contract, he arrived in Spain and would go on to win La Liga titles and Champions League finals.

Less dramatically, and minus the exotic locations, fanfare and fuss (and public interest!), I too had made a professional move that would get me heavily involved in world football's top club competition. The week after McManaman had scored that special goal at Parkhead in September 1997, I had been seriously thinking over a potential transfer from BBC to ITV. Heresy or opportunity?

After 18 years at the BBC, ITV's bosses had quietly approached me to become their new controller of sport, as well as launching their first new channel since 1955. I was even allowed to name it. ITV2. Negotiations went on for several weeks. I had loved my time at the BBC, but I knew I wanted a change of scene, and one of the draws was the commercial channel's five-star contract for the UEFA Champions League. Indeed, at the final meeting which sealed the deal, my would-be new colleagues and I spent most of the evening watching Newcastle beat Barcelona 3-2 in a classic Champions League encounter that was on ITV that night.

I left the BBC in November 1997 and joined ITV in February 1998 – a World Cup year. I had to sit out of the talks between the two broadcasters on which channel got which match in the tournament because, uniquely, I knew both their strategic objectives and the matches they would target!

The World Cup in France was ahead of us but Liverpool's 1997/98 season, despite some outstanding moments, again faltered. The Reds finished third in the league behind eventual champions Arsenal, and Manchester United, who were creating a new intense rivalry with the phlegmatic Frenchman Arsène Wenger, making successful changes on and off the field at Highbury and testing United's superiority, and their Scottish manager, to the limit.

Interestingly, Liverpool took maximum points off Arsenal, and and just one point from six against Manchester United in this season. However, the Anfield men slid out of the UEFA Cup against French side Strasbourg, having knocked Celtic out of the competition in the previous round. An FA Cup third round defeat at the hands of Coventry City and a run to the semi-finals of the Coca-Cola Cup, beaten over two legs by Middlesbrough, completed the season's headline statistics.

On an individual basis, Michael Owen, 'Mo', continued his remarkable introduction to top-class professional football. He scored 18 goals in 36 league games and won the Premier League's Player of the Year award as well as being elected the PFA's Young Player of the Year. Owen had also made his full England debut against Chile at Wembley Stadium at the tender age of 18 years and 59 days. He had scored on his debut at all other England levels –under-15s, 16s, 18s, 20s and 21s – but couldn't manage it this time in a game their stylish South American opponents won 2-0. Mind you, just to prove he hadn't lost his touch, in the league game immediately after his England debut, Owen scored a hat-trick against Sheffield Wednesday!

Liverpool contingent Owen, Paul Ince and Steve McManaman were selected in Glen Hoddle's squad for that summer's World Cup. England got off to a good start beating Tunisia, but then surprisingly lost their next game to Romania 2-1 – Owen was brought on as a substitute and scored within ten minutes of getting on the pitch. He was selected to start against Colombia, the final group game, that England won 2-0, and that set up a mega clash against Argentina in the tournament's last 16.

As ITV Sport's new boss, I couldn't have been more delighted. It was *our* game, we had it exclusively, the kick-off was at peak time on a Tuesday evening, and the whole country was talking about it. We knew it would be huge.

It turned out to be an epic contest which ebbed and flowed, and had more action, incidents and plot twists and turns than an episode of *Line of Duty*. David Beckham was famously red-carded, and the game was level at full time, 2-2. And in the penalty shoot-out, Ince, who had been colossal in the game itself, and David Batty had their spot kicks saved and England were out.

But the most memorable moment of the match had been when Michael Owen scored a first-half goal to put England 2-1 ahead. It was a goal in a million, and an average audience of 23.8 million watched it on ITV (over 27 million at its peak).

And just as Jonny Wilkinson's last-gasp winning drop-kick against Australia in the 2003 Rugby World Cup Final instantly made him a national hero, despite the actual result of the match, Owen's goal against Argentina was the defining moment of his career, and still at the tender age of just 18.

Receiving a pass just inside the Argentina half, he steered the ball away from a defender breathing down his neck and set off for goal. Owen got past another Argentinian defender, leaving him with only the goalkeeper to beat. He then noticed another England player out of the corner of his eye, Paul Scholes. In Owen's own words, 'I thought to myself, I've come this far – no one is going to score except me. And as the keeper came out, I lifted it over his head into the net.' And the watching nation went bonkers!

England went out of the tournament but Michael Owen's goal (and David Beckham's sending off) were the talk of the country in the days and weeks that followed.

That's Michael Owen of Liverpool and England.

Kop That – *Steve McManaman was joined by two future Liverpool players in the winning 2000 European Cup Final, team Fernando Morientes and Nicolas Anelka – whilst their opponents Valencia fielded Mauricio Pellegrino.*

1998/99 – BIENVENUE GÉRARD, ADIEU ROY

ON THE evening of 12 July 1998, I was lucky enough to be in the Stade de France in Paris watching hosts France put on an exhilarating display in beating Brazil 3-0 in the World Cup Final. The party that followed in the French capital was spectacular, and it lasted several days.

One of the men deservedly feted for his contribution to their success was former national coach, the French FA's technical director Gérard Houllier, who had assisted France's World Cup-winning coach, Aimé Jacquet. Houllier, presented with a World Cup winners' medal of his own by a grateful Jacquet, was credited with laying the foundations for France's summer triumph.

After such a heady time, Houllier was intent on securing the next step in a career that had already taken in roles as head coach at both Lens and Paris Saint-Germain. This time he was looking further afield, and Celtic, among others, were interested in bringing him to Scotland.

That's when Liverpool's executive vice-chairman Peter Robinson made his move. The two men knew each other through the many UEFA meetings they both attended.

Robinson inquired as to whether Houllier's move to Celtic was a done deal and when told it wasn't, he said to an inquisitive Houllier, 'Well, why not come to Anfield then?' Houllier liked the idea. He had lived in Liverpool for a year in the late 60s while completing his studies to become a school teacher. Indeed, in 1969, he had stood on the Kop on the evening the Reds thrashed Irish club Dundalk 10-0 in the European Fairs Cup.

Of course, Liverpool already had a manager in Roy Evans, but the long-time servant of the club was persuaded, reluctantly no doubt, that Houllier could bring some fresh thinking and support to the Liverpool boss.

Evans had already lost the services of Anfield stalwart Ronnie Moran, who at 64 had retired earlier that summer after nearly 50 years at the club, man and boy. Moran's contribution to Liverpool's success, both as player and coach could not be underestimated. He delivered tough love to players under his care. As sergeant major of Melwood he would demand discipline, concentration and commitment to the cause, and no room for complacency.

Robbie Fowler fondly remembers: 'After playing against Fulham, and scoring five goals, and pleased with myself, Ronnie came into the dressing room and said, "I don't know what you're looking so smug about. You should have scored seven."' Yes, Ronnie Moran would be missed.

Conversations took place between Evans and Houllier and with Peter Robinson's astute stewardship and quiet diplomacy, the pair were named as joint managers for the new season.

Sure enough, the newspapers carried preseason photos of the two smiling men together and seemingly up for the challenge.

But I wasn't the only person who asked Peter Robinson how it was going to work. 'Who picks the team? Who chooses the players to buy? Who decides the game plan? Who makes the substitutions? Who will the players actually think is their boss?' However well meaning, and however much both men compromised to allow the other some headroom, it seemed a coupling that was doomed to eventually fail, especially if results didn't go their way. And they didn't.

Houllier brought some early new ideas to training and tactics, and a new coach, Patrice Bergues. He also started to get the players thinking how they could better manage their diets and curb the excesses of their free time. His fellow countryman Arsène Wenger had set an equally lively Arsenal squad the same challenges with outstanding results.

Despite getting off to a reasonable start, including a memorable hat-trick from Michael Owen in a 4-1 win at Newcastle, Liverpool were labouring in 11th position in the Premier League and had just been knocked out of the Worthington Cup in a 3-1 fourth-round home defeat when, in early November, Roy Evans had 'joint managed' his last game.

Both men tried to make it work but, quite reasonably, they couldn't agree on everything. For instance, Roy Evans believed in the Liverpool philosophy of keeping a winning team together; Houllier was a fan of squad rotation. It was on a flight home from a European tie against Valencia that Evans decided he'd had enough.

The Valencia game had seen Liverpool, leading 2-1, have Ince and McManaman sent off in the closing minutes, along with the Spanish side's Carboni, for a silly touchline brawl. It was something and nothing. But the Spaniards equalised and nearly snatched the tie away from Liverpool.

In the dressing room after the game, Houllier picked up three discarded Liverpool shirts he said he had promised to give to the match officials. These, the same three match officials Evans and his players were furious about for the needless red cards which could have cost them the result. It was another clash of cultures.

After two quick-fire home defeats to Derby County and Tottenham Hotspur, Evans offered his resignation. The board, especially chairman David Moores, tried to persuade him to stay but for the proud one-club man there was no going back. Evans had been manager of Liverpool Football Club for 184 league games, and had won 87 of them, in the four seasons in charge – his Reds had finished fourth, third, fourth and third – and he had won the Coca-Cola Cup and reached an FA Cup Final and a European semi-final. For most clubs that would have represented a successful spell in charge but expectations at Liverpool were higher.

A thoroughly decent man, wholly dedicated to the club, Evans happened to be the Anfield boss when the Premier League was gathering pace and when clubs like Manchester United and Arsenal were delivering trophies on the field and earning vast commercial riches off it.

The north London side had won the double in 1998, and Manchester United went one better the following season, winning the treble, including a dramatic injury-time win against Bayern Munich at the UEFA Champions League Final in Barcelona.

Evans would leave Anfield frustrated and unfulfilled, but like his long-time colleague Ronnie Moran, he was one of the foundation stones behind the many years of glory the Reds had previously enjoyed. Some critics thought if Evans was going so should Houllier – joint managers, joint responsibility.

To try and retain an element of the unique Boot Room DNA, Houllier swiftly appointed Phil Thompson as his assistant manager. Thompson had been sacked as reserve team boss during Graeme Souness's time in charge, and six years on he was absolutely delighted to be back at Anfield.

Now in sole control, Houllier tackled discipline head on – use of mobile phones was banned the moment the players entered Melwood for training. Even as he was spelling out this new diktat to the group, David James's mobile phone rang. Message received loud and clear. Post-match drinking in the players' lounge was to be stopped. A firm position to take and one that was carried through in due course. He also decided the universal language at Melwood would be English – he was keen that the different nationalities at the club mixed with each other rather than stay in their own national groups. And training sessions were varied and stimulating, as Houllier outlined a five-year plan to take the club back to the top of the game.

On the field, with a disappointing seventh-place finish in the league, Houllier and Thompson knew going forward they would need to strengthen the defence as a priority, as well as move on some of the first-team stars who would struggle to buy into the Frenchman's philosophy.

And that philosophy was straightforward. You must give one hundred per cent commitment to the team. And he meant both on *and* off the pitch.

Kop That – *Michael Owen topped the Premier League scorers list on two occasions with 18 goals. In 1997/98 he did so with Dion Dublin and Chris Sutton, and the following campaign was joined by Dwight Yorke and Jimmy Floyd Hasselbaink.*

1999/2000 – OUT WITH OLD,
IN WITH THE NEW

AS WE entered the last summer of the 20th century, the transfer market was absolutely buzzing with the news that one major team's biggest and brightest star had jumped ship to join their arch-rivals. The news led all the TV and radio bulletins and filled the front pages of the national newspapers the following day.

No, not football this time. Television – big-time television. Desmond Lynam, the BBC's peerless sports broadcaster, was to join ITV to be the new presenter of their much-valued UEFA Champions League coverage. As the person leading the charge to get my former colleague to leave his super-secure home at the BBC and join me at ITV, it was the lure of fronting top-class live football (and a decent shift in salary!) that helped 'get my man'.

He, and me, would have to wait until the autumn of 2001 before Liverpool featured on ITV's Champions League coverage, but in 1999 his first outing on the commercial channel's midweek football feast was Chelsea v AC Milan. Big-time football.

And the Champions League was what Gérard Houllier and Liverpool Football Club were looking to get back into, as the Frenchman got busy in the transfer market in the close season, executing plans he had started to talk privately about with Peter Robinson and Phil Thompson around Christmas the previous year.

Houllier wanted to develop his own group of players, reduce the influence some seemed to have in the dressing room, freshen things up and improve key areas of the team. Some big names leaving the club in the summer of 1999 included the self-styled 'Guvnor' captain Paul Ince – he was off to Middlesbrough; goalkeeper David James to Aston Villa; Steve McManaman to Real Madrid; and Norwegians Kvarme and Leonhardsen, and German Karl-Heinze Riedle were also heading out of Anfield. So was South African Sean Dundee, the 'Crocodile' who had seemingly lost his 'snap'.

The new faces lining up at Melwood, and at the club's preseason training camp in Switzerland, were goalkeeper Sander Westerveld from Vitesse Arnhem; two talented central defenders, Sami Hyypiä and Stéphane Henchoz, from Willem II and Blackburn Rovers, respectively; and a striker, Titi Camara, from Marseille. Newcastle United midfielder Dietmar Hamann proved to be an inspired signing – Erik Meijer of Bayer Leverkusen less so. Like Hamann, the Czech Republic's Vladmír Šmicer, joining from Lens, would play a major role when Liverpool had their wonderful night in Istanbul six years further down the track.

Cameroon star Rigobert Song had joined Houllier's new Reds earlier in the year, and in February 2000 Liverpool would spend a record £11m signing Leicester City striker Emile Heskey. The French Revolution was truly underway – Houllier's new team of nations were recruited, and base camp was Anfield. In other key moves, Houllier promoted Jamie Redknapp to be the new Liverpool captain, and Robbie Fowler the vice-captain.

In Fowler and Michael Owen, Liverpool had two of the finest finishers in European football, but having them on the same pitch at the same time was proving difficult. Robbie Fowler's ankle injury and Owen's hamstring problems would lead Gérard Houllier to bemoan the fact the pair had spent just less than two hours together on the pitch at the same time in the first half of the new season. Indeed, in the 1999/2000 season the Reds' two great marksmen only made 30 Premier League starts between them.

Making Fowler vice-captain was probably an attempt by Houllier to give the brilliant, if challenging, star a greater sense of personal responsibility. In Houllier's first season at the club, he had lost his star striker for two avoidable misdemeanours which landed him a six-week suspension. He celebrated a goal in the derby match by simulating snorting cocaine on the white line of the penalty area in front of the Everton fans, who he felt had made false accusations of drug abuse. Another offence, making homophobic gestures at Chelsea's full-back Graeme Le Saux in a game at Stamford Bridge, quite rightly had also got him into trouble.

So, getting a fully fit Owen and Fowler on the pitch was one of the challenges that Houllier faced. There was, however, some good news – Liverpool had unveiled a young man who would become a legend at the club. Eighteen-year-old Steven Gerrard, another product of Liverpool's youth development system, had made his first appearance for the senior team as a 90th-minute substitute against Blackburn Rovers at Anfield on 29 November 1998.

'Keep the ball for us' had been Houllier's simple instruction to the young man shaking with anticipation on the touchline. In many ways Steven Gerrard spent the next 17 years keeping the ball for Liverpool, leading from the front, scoring vital goals time and again, making telling interceptions, passing with poise, winning games almost single-handed, resisting tempting offers to go elsewhere – a truly world-class player driving his beloved Liverpool on to domestic and European glory.

Captain ... our captain. And England captain too. Steven Gerrard.

Over the years I have got to know Steven. A good guy, serious about his football, understands the game inside out, approachable and polite. Surely, a future Liverpool manager in the making.

In the early stages of his first-team career, he suffered muscle injuries which were put down to the young man naturally growing into his skeletal frame. His wholehearted style of play was also a career-long contributory factor to any injuries he would suffer. He did, however, play a massive 710 games for the club, scoring 186 goals.

Gerrard made 13 appearances in the 1998/99 season, but featured far more in the new season, pairing up with new captain Jamie Redknapp in midfield. He came on as substitute in the season's first derby match with Everton at Anfield. Both sides were already down to ten men when in the 90th minute Gerrard got sent off for a rash tackle on Kevin Campbell. Following a three-match suspension, Gerrard was put back in the side and would later score his first senior goal against Sheffield Wednesday at Anfield. In all he would feature in 31 matches for Liverpool in his second season. He had made a hugely impressive start at Anfield but the following campaign would really stamp his name on the wider game.

One of the outstanding performers for the Reds in this campaign was new centre-back Finnish international Sami Hyypiä. For me, from the off, he looked the part. Strong, tall, athletic and reliable. And fit. He played in all 38 Premier League games for Liverpool that season, the only ever-present, and in late November, with injuries to both Jamie Redknapp and Robbie Fowler, Houllier looked to Hyypiä to captain his side in a match against West Ham United.

It was a short-term fix that actually lasted well into the spring of 2000. And his Premier League colleagues made him one of the nominees for their Player of the Year – the only defender on the list.

Ron Yeats, legendary centre-half in Liverpool's past, gave him the nod of approval. Liverpool had found their new 'Colossus'. And Hyypiä's ten years' service and 464 games for the club underlines just how much value they got for the transfer fee of just £2.6m.

Liverpool's new-look side was taking shape. But Champions League qualification, now available for the top three places in the Premier League, eluded them again after taking just two points from their last five matches of the season.

Disappointing. But things were about to get better. A lot better.

Kop That – *Three players scored on their opening day Premier League debuts for Liverpool in the 1990s, with their surnames all beginning with the letter C. Nigel Clough, Stan Collymore and Titi Camara strangely all did so against the same club – Sheffield Wednesday.*

2000/01 – TIME FOR A TREBLE!

*'Aim for the moon and maybe
you land among the stars.'*

LIVERPOOL'S VERY own French romantic, Gérard Houllier, was looking back lyrically on the first football season of the new millennium, which had started fitfully and ended fantastically for his Red high-flyers. Three major trophies, and arguably one even bigger prize was the glorious booty of the Reds' bloated, yet ultimately hugely successful, 2000/01 campaign of 63 matches spread across four tough competitions.

Heady times then for the club and its fans. Supporters from up the M62 might have questioned the relative weight of Liverpool's treble compared with that of their own two years before. But here's a thing: we didn't care – and still don't. Theirs was theirs and ours was ours, with all the special memories that go with it. Three major finals – each with its own extraordinary narrative – all won by Liverpool Football Club, and all won inside 90 days.

As Liverpool started this momentous season, Houllier was still moving his pieces around the chessboard – moving players on, and moving players in. In the departure lounge were Bjørnebye, Babb, Thompson, Matteo, Friedel, Song, Staunton, Meijer and Camara. Inward bound Markus Babbel from Bayern Munich, Pegguy Arphexad from Leicester City,

Bernard Diomède, a World Cup winner (if you blinked, you missed his time at Anfield), Nick Barmby from Everton … hold on … from Everton?!? Yes, a rare if not unique transfer between our two Merseyside giants.

German international Christian Ziege joined Houllier's men from Middlesbrough and by late autumn two further imports arrived – Igor Bišćan from Dynamo Zagreb and Grégory Vignal from Montpellier. One intriguing incoming free transfer was that of Gary McAllister from Coventry City. The bald 35-year-old Scotsman was certainly deep into the autumn of his career, but Houllier obviously saw something in him that we didn't.

In truth, the fans weren't sure on what trajectory Houllier was sending the club. The moon certainly looked well out of reach … and we weren't sure he had bought many stars either. The club was going through changes off the field too. Peter Robinson, the hugely influential figure around Anfield, had retired, somewhat reluctantly, after 35 years' service to the club.

Rick Parry, late of the Premier League, had shadowed PBR's work in the role of chief executive for nearly three years, and had waited somewhat frustratingly to get his hands on the tiller. A Liverpool lad, decent amateur goalkeeper, and like his predecessor, a quiet, serious and well-connected football administrator, Parry had some work to do to catch up with the likes of Manchester United on and off the field.

As the Premier League was growing in stature, both domestically and internationally, heavyweight commercial companies were looking to invest in big-time football. Companies such as Granada Television, a British broadcasting powerhouse, the creator of the nation's favourite soap opera *Coronation Street*, and the regional channel that aired the first-ever TV interview with unknown new group called The Beatles way back in 1962.

Now they wanted to break bread with another iconic Liverpool brand, Liverpool Football Club, buying a 9.9 per cent equity stake in the club for £22m. It looked a good bit of business for the Reds and Rick Parry, adding to their transfer fund, although Granada subsequently bought a 4.9 per cent stake in Arsenal for £40m – the value of the London pound I suspect.

Liverpool had an uneven start to the new season and by the time they went to Old Trafford in mid-December were lying in sixth place in the league. It was Houllier's 100th match in sole charge and Danny Murphy's marvellous free-kick winner proved to be the perfect way to mark the manager's anniversary. Following it up with a 4-0 Anfield win over Arsenal meant the Reds went into the second half of the season with a little bit of momentum, and the rest as they say is history.

In the first week of the new year Houllier added a genuine world-class player to Liverpool's ranks when Finnish star Jari Litmanen joined from Barcelona. A Champions League Final winner with Ajax, Litmanen had all the right credentials, including having been a Liverpool fan since a young boy, but injuries would cast a shadow over his one-and-a-half-year stay at Anfield.

And so, to those three famous finals that landed Liverpool with a very special treble.

Sunday, 25 February – the Worthington Cup Final

After five seasons without any silverware, Liverpool were finally able to unlock the trophy cabinet, with a dramatic penalty shoot-out win over Birmingham City at the Millennium Stadium in Cardiff. With Wembley Stadium closed and under reconstruction it was to the Welsh capital they went – the Reds would travel to Cardiff three times in 2001, and each time leave with a trophy.

Robbie Fowler, captaining the side in the Worthington Cup Final, put Liverpool ahead in the 30th minute with a superb left-foot rocket. It was a goal worthy of winning any cup final, but it didn't win this one. First Division Birmingham's Darren Purse deservedly scored a last-gasp penalty equaliser after a rash challenge by Stéphane Henchoz.

Indeed, the Blues might have been awarded a second penalty in extra time when Liverpool's Swiss defender repeated his recklessness, but this time the referee, David Elleray, waved play on. Lucky Liverpool. It all came down to a dramatic penalty shoot-out, and Liverpool's hero of the hour was goalkeeper Sander Westerveld who made two great saves from the spot. Robbie Fowler lifted the trophy and took home the Man of the Match award too.

Houllier's first orbit around Cardiff was mission accomplished – just.

Saturday, 12 May – the FA Cup Final

Three things stand out for me about the 2001 FA Cup Final between Liverpool and Arsenal. Firstly, it was boiling hot in Cardiff that afternoon. Secondly, Liverpool got away with highway robbery, winning a match they should have lost four or five times over. And thirdly, we were all privileged to be at a game that was so fundamentally turned on its head by one individual. The final will always be remembered in his name.

Now, I have watched football all over the world – and in all types of weather and many different climates – but I can rarely remember being as hot as I was that afternoon in the Millennium Stadium in Cardiff.

ITV were broadcasting the final live and, as their representative, I was invited to the formal prematch luncheon hosted by the FA – all very jacket and tie. When we went to our seats shortly before the game it quickly became obvious that we were in direct line of the hot afternoon sun and without cover. By half-time, I was in trouble, and going back into the tearoom I glanced at a mirror and saw my reflection – a bright red bald head.

Now, I drive a red car and clean my teeth with a red toothbrush, but I didn't really want to walk among football's great and good looking like an unused matchstick. Help came from an unlikely source – a very kind lady approached me and said, 'I've been watching you getting redder and redder as the first half has gone on, and I've got three things for you – here's a bottle of cold water, a small tube of sun lotion which I always carry around in my handbag and a baseball cap which I found under my seat. Please have them.' I couldn't thank her enough.

I can't remember what the cap was advertising (but checked it wasn't Arsenal!) and on my head it went, my face now smothered in 'Factor 30' and a cold drink in my hand – I was back in business. Barwick 1 Sunstroke 0.

Ah, the game itself? One-way traffic. Arsenal dominated proceedings; the Gunners missed some genuinely good opportunities. Stéphane Henchoz got away with a certain handball on the goal line. His defensive partner, Sammy Hyypiä, majored in second-half goal-line clearances.

When Arsenal finally went ahead in the 72nd minute through Freddie Ljungberg it all looked done and dusted. With all three substitutes, McAllister, Fowler and Berger, now on, the Reds were left chasing an unlikely equaliser. Then, in the 83rd minute, a McAllister free kick was not cleared properly by the Arsenal defence and Michael Owen flashed the ball into the corner of the net.

And he wasn't done yet. Five minutes later he chased down a brilliant long ball from Berger, outpaced both Adams and Dixon, before shooting low past Seaman. It was a simply stunning goal. Cue pandemonium in the stands behind the

Arsenal goal as the massed ranks of Liverpool fans went bananas. We had all just watched the 'Michael Owen final' – a most unlikely comeback – and the stars were beginning to align for Gérard Houllier.

Wednesday, 16 May – the UEFA Cup Final

The Westfalenstadion is home to Borussia Dortmund, a fantastic stadium for atmosphere, especially when the fans sing 'You'll Never Walk Alone' before their home games. It was the venue for one of the most extraordinary games ever played in the final of any European club competition.

Liverpool had reached the final with aggregate wins over Rapid Bucharest, Slovan Liberec, Olympiakos, Roma, Porto and Barcelona – a fair spread of Continental big and not so big shots.

Roma ran Liverpool close – having been beaten 2-0 in the Olympic Stadium (a Michael Owen double) they ran the Reds ragged at Anfield in the second leg.

They were leading 1-0 in the second leg when they seemed certain to have won a penalty at the Kop end. The referee seemed to point his arm towards the spot before inexplicably redirecting it towards the corner flag. The Kop roared their approval.

Several years later, I accompanied Fabio Capello, the then England coach, to Anfield for a match between Liverpool and Real Madrid, another of his former clubs. He looked towards the Kop and just uttered 'Roma, Roma' ... and slowly shook his head!

Barcelona were beaten in the semi-final with the only goal in the tie being scored from the penalty spot by Gary McAllister in the second leg at Anfield. McAllister was in glorious form as the season was drawing to a close, popping up with goals and assists in seemingly every game, including, most famously, an injury-time winner at Goodison Park that was a magical mixture of craft and cunning. McAllister would also be a key figure in the UEFA Cup Final, where Liverpool were pitted against unfancied Spanish opponents Deportivo Alavés.

Alavés is not a town – the 80-year-old club is based in Vitoria, capital of the largest Basque province Álava. 'This is the biggest day in Vitoria's history since 1812,' announced their club president Gonzalo Antón. 1812? That year, the town was the stage for the Duke of Wellington's victory over the French in the Peninsula War. No pressure then on the plucky Spanish side, making their debut in European competition, with gates of just 11,000 and a squad assembled at the cost of £11.8m.

It turned out to be a quite extraordinary match, with Liverpool racing ahead with two goals from Markus Babbel and Steven Gerrard. The Spaniards got one back before the Reds were awarded a penalty, which Gary McAllister duly converted. 3-1 at half-time.

The Spaniards would not lie down and squared the game at 3-3. When substitute Robbie Fowler scored in the 72nd minute to make it 4-3, the huge army of Liverpool fans thought the Reds were finally over the line. But back came Alavés – two minutes from time Jordi Cruyff, son of Johan Cruyff, headed home a corner to make it 4-4. Full time.

Into dreaded 'golden goal' territory. Alavés had two men sent off, before man of the match Gary McAllister, Liverpool's late-season talisman, floated a free kick into the Spanish penalty area where it was headed beyond his keeper by Alavés defender Geli. 5-4.

An amazing match and Liverpool had another trophy – and the post-match scenes were memorable as the Liverpool players and coaches put their arms around the next person's shoulders and joined the Liverpool fans in an emotional rendition of 'You'll Never Walk Alone'.

A great moment which captured the mood on a great night. One of my favourite games.

Saturday, 19 May – Charlton Athletic v Liverpool.

The Reds' final match of a marathon campaign and the prize for victory a place in the UEFA Champions League. Reputationally, and commercially, it was possibly the biggest game of the season for the Reds, and Gérard Houllier had made qualification for club football's senior competition his major target.

Liverpool were as flat as flukes in the first half but got it together in the second, and final, 45 minutes of the season with two goals from Robbie Fowler, and a goal apiece from Danny Murphy and Michael Owen. Job done, and star-bound Houllier could send a message back to Mission Control at Anfield ... 'the Champions League has landed'.

Kop That – *Liverpool played every game possible in the competitions they entered that season, having reached three cup finals. Of the 63 games played, Sander Westerveld missed just two.*

2001/02 – A SENSE OF PERSPECTIVE

I SETTLED into my seat on the train from Euston Station taking me up to Liverpool for their UEFA Champions League group opener against Boavista of Portugal.

Liverpool had comfortably got through the qualifying round against Haka of Finland, and I'd been in Monte Carlo to see the Reds pick up the UEFA Super Cup, beating Bayern Munich 3-2 in the austere surroundings of the tiny Stade Louis II Stadium in Monaco. Strange place for a major game.

Now it was time for the real thing – Liverpool back at European football's top table. The draw for the group stages of the various UEFA competitions had also taken place in the Principality. As we rattled past Watford, the train manager came over to check my ticket, and as he moved on, he turned and said, 'I've just heard on the radio there's been a big plane crash in New York – many people killed.'

The date – 11 September 2001. Liverpool played out a feisty 1-1 draw with their Portuguese opponents, but it was impossible not to think it mattered little against the carnage of what turned out to be an unprecedented terrorist attack on the World Trade Center in New York and other strategic targets in the USA. Thousands died and the Twin Towers collapsed to the ground in a mountain of rubble and dust. The images of those moments that were sent around the globe made us all draw for breath. And the world was never quite the same again.

Liverpool had already won the FA Charity Shield with a 2-1 win against Manchester United – their third successive win over their arch-rivals – then they beat Bayern Munich and took their trophy tally up to five in seven months. And Liverpool, sorry England, beat Germany 5-1 in a memorable victory in Munich.

When England won the World Cup in 1966, West Ham fans cheekily claimed themselves as world champions, with Hammers team-mates Geoff Hurst scoring a hat-trick and Martin Peters also on target in the final against West Germany, and club captain Bobby Moore famously lifting the Jules Rimet trophy.

In Munich, 35 years later, England won a vital World Cup qualifier against Germany in stunning fashion with a hat-trick from Liverpool's Michael Owen, and a goal each for fellow Reds Steven Gerrard and Emile Heskey. Nick Barmby and substitute Jamie Carragher also played their part too. This time it was Liverpool fans who could bask in the glory and claim ownership of a famous victory.

An early-season momentous win for England in Germany, and a small piece of TV sports history as well, as ITV launched *The Premiership*, the Saturday evening highlights programme that would be broadcast at peak time at 7pm, presented by Desmond Lynam. When ITV had beaten the BBC in the broadcast rights battle for Premier League Saturday night highlights, one tabloid newspaper ran a front-page headline – 'ITV 1 BBC 0' ... and, fittingly, Liverpool's opening home game of the season against West Ham United was chosen as the new programme's first main game.

The Reds had completed another treble – first to appear in BBC's *Match of the Day* in 1964, first to appear in colour in

1969, and now involved in the first match to appear in ITV's new exciting football venture. Liverpool duly won the game 2-1 with a double strike from Michael Owen.

The weekly programme was not a runaway ratings success, not least because on its first three Saturdays the weather was stunning, and people were still enjoying the sunshine and not home to watch it – and it wasn't *Match of the Day*.

As one of the guys who had come up with the idea of an early evening start time, I began to think I might have to perform a rain dance every Saturday evening to give the viewing figures a boost. About eight weeks into the run, *The Premiership* was moved back into the traditional late Saturday evening slot and replaced in peak time by *Blind Date*. This time the same newspaper ran a front-page headline of CILLA 1 DES 0 ...

Back at Anfield there was an unusual dip into the transfer market when on 31 August Gérard Houllier bought two goalkeepers on the same day. And neither knew the other was coming! Having made the firm decision that Sander Westerveld wasn't to be his long-term goalkeeping option, he bought Polish custodian Jerzy Dudek from Feyenoord as well as Coventry City's Chris Kirkland. What is it they say about waiting for buses ...?

Westerveld was off to Real Sociedad, and with Pegguy Arphexad also making a couple of appearances for the Reds, Houllier would have used four different goalkeepers between the sticks by the end of this campaign.

Liverpool's home game with Leeds United mid-October took on a whole different perspective when, at half-time, Reds boss Gérard Houllier fell ill and didn't emerge in the dugout for the second half. He was already in an ambulance racing at top speed to Broadgreen Hospital, where he underwent an emergency operation which lasted several hours. The doctors in the hospital's cardiothoracic centre repaired an 'acute dissection of the aorta'. To all intents and purposes, it had been a life-saving operation.

Houllier was known to be a workaholic – he lived and breathed football, and laboured 16 hours a day, day in, day out. Something was bound to give in the end. The Frenchman was in hospital for three weeks, but rarely off the phone to assistant manager Phil Thompson and Liverpool CEO Rick Parry. And both he and the club knew his recuperation from such a serious operation would take several months. Indeed, there were those who thought he may never return, but they didn't know Gérard Houllier, a man completely wedded to the game.

Another key member of the Anfield club, Markus Babbel, had also been hospitalised suffering from Guillian-Barre syndrome, a rare serious illness that hit the nervous system which in turn led to debilitation. It left him wheelchair bound for a time. His season finished in late August 2001. A year later he came on as a substitute in the Community Shield and his first start and next game was a League Cup tie against Southampton in the autumn in a Liverpool career that sadly tailed off.

Phil Thompson had taken over the managerial reins in Houllier's absence, and did so in some style. He reined back his sometimes highly emotional matchday style and became a dignified, measured leader, impressive but always impressing on everybody that he was only keeping the seat warm for Houllier. Thompson had been involved in a bust-up with Robbie Fowler during a preseason training session at Melwood when the striker had fired a ball at full pelt which hit the Liverpool assistant manager on the back of the head.

Thompson was not happy, believing it had been fired at him deliberately – Fowler said it hadn't.

Houllier insisted the Liverpool striker apologised, an instruction he resisted. Eventually, after further conversations,

Fowler backed down and he and Thompson were photographed shaking hands as if nothing was untoward.

Liverpool's goalscoring magician, who'd also had his share of injury problems, felt a victim of Houllier's rotation policy, that saw him pitching for a first-team place alongside Owen, Heskey, Litmanen and new signing, young Czech international Milan Baroš.

In November, in a move that surprised us all, Robbie Fowler left Liverpool to join Leeds United. The Anfield faithful were dismayed by this turn of events, losing one of their own to their fellow title hopefuls at Elland Road. A subsequent move that surprised us even more was the loan signing in December of Nicolas Anelka from Paris Saint-Germain. Nobody saw that coming. Anelka had been a huge success at Arsenal but had an image of being a surly, temperamental character and something of a loner, a notion that people I talked to, who had actually worked with him, dismissed.

I was at Anfield on the night Gérard Houllier made his public return to Anfield on the evening of the vital Champions League clash with Roma in March. There were rumours he would be in attendance and, sure enough, five minutes before the kick-off he emerged from the tunnel, and the capacity crowd gave him a huge welcome home.

The Reds finished runners-up behind Arsenal in the Premier League and reached the Champions League quarter-finals. They had won the FA Charity Shield and the UEFA Super Cup and had extended their winning run against Manchester United to five matches, their Anfield league clash including the goal of the season from John Arne Riise.

The Norwegian had already scored in a Merseyside derby but his thunderous strike against Manchester United from 26 yards, reaching speeds of 112km per hour, roared past his former Monaco team-mate Fabien Barthez in the United goal.

For many seasons onwards, the cry would come up from the Kop:

Joooooooohn Arne Riise!

Oohh! Aaah!

I wanna know-ow-how

ow you scored that goal!'

Bloody quickly would be the answer!

Kop That – *Riise scored seven goals in his debut season, with his first goal helping the Reds win the Super Cup at his former abode Monaco.*

2002/03 – THE FRENCH CONNECTION

WHEN THE 2001/02 domestic season ended, Gérard Houllier deservedly became the subject of a prestigious treble of his own, as influential local and international organisations lined up to mark his sporting achievements and positive effect on his 'adopted' city. The University of Liverpool made him an honorary Doctor of Law, whilst Liverpool John Moores University awarded him an Honorary Fellowship.

In between receiving those two awards Houllier travelled to the French Embassy in London, and in front of his family, friends and colleagues from Liverpool FC, he received the Chevalier de la Légion d'Honneur, the highest award available to any French citizen. He described it as the 'proudest personal honour I have ever received'.

In the summer of 2002, the football business decamped and headed off to the Far East for the FIFA World Cup in Japan and South Korea. One notable absentee was Gérard Houllier himself, who was persuaded that the close season would give him a proper extended chance to further recuperate from the naturally expected issues that followed the major operation which had saved his life in the previous October.

Houllier was always an ever-present at all key FIFA and UEFA events, much-loved and much-respected, but his wife Isabelle and assistant manager Phil Thompson, among others, urged him to rest up and watch the tournament on television. The Liverpool manager heeded people's advice and settled for the settee in his lounge rather than the VIP seats in the stadium.

He may have spotted injured England star Gary Neville making his early strides as a studio pundit after I persuaded the Manchester United star to work with us on our World Cup coverage at ITV.

Being British-based didn't stop Gérard Houllier from being busy in the transfer market, and everything he touched seemed to have some type of French connection. Firstly, he decided against extending the stay of Nicolas Anelka, a move that surprised colleagues at Anfield and further afield. Anelka had done well in his half-season at Anfield, his team-mates liked him and the Liverpool fans also had taken to him. But Houllier, having set up a deal to make Anelka's move to Liverpool permanent, changed his mind at the last moment.

Whether it was Anelka's brothers, always known as troublesome and who were now based in Liverpool, or the player himself, something made Houllier pull out of the deal. The former Arsenal man would end up at Manchester City.

One of the reasons may have been that Houllier had his eyes on Djibril Cissé of Auxerre as a young and powerful addition to the squad. But Cissé's club wanted him to stick around for another season, so nothing could be done. He would sign for Liverpool in July 2004.

In what seemed to be a classic 'under the radar' transfer coup, Houllier bought two stars of the Senegal team that would do so well in the World Cup. Striker El Hadji Diouf and midfielder Salif Diao were signed from French clubs Lens and Sedan, respectively. And they were both bought before the tournament got underway. Indeed, Diouf signed his contract on the morning of the opening game of the 2002 World Cup between holders France and Senegal.

And the African Player of the Year starred in his country's surprise win over a French team who ultimately took an early plane home from the tournament. Salif Diao scored one of the goals of the tournament against Denmark, and then got sent off in the same game.

A third new face at Anfield would be 24-year-old left-sided midfield player Bruno Cheyrou. Rather grandly described by Houllier as the 'next Zidane', Cheyrou was signed from Lille. His promise was never fully realised at Anfield. Indeed, all three of those purchases, amounting to about £20m, failed to live up to expectations.

Diao was bought as cover, and more, in central midfield, but local lads Gerrard and Carragher soon recognised the Senegalese star was going to come up short. Same for Bruno Cheyrou, a talented midfield player, yes, but equipped to play in the rough and tumble of the Premier League, no. He ended up playing on the flanks, when he wasn't injured that was.

El Hadji Diuof had a great World Cup but was not a success at Anfield, as Jamie Carragher pointed out: 'Do you remember being at school and picking sides for a game of football? We do this at Liverpool for the five-a-sides. Diouf was "last pick" within a few weeks.' Diouf, Diao and Cheyrou: three Houllier signings that promised to be the next step in Liverpool regaining their title-winning status both here and in Europe. And it simply didn't happen.

The season itself saw the Reds get off to a stunning start in the Premier League – unbeaten going into November with nine wins and three draws in their first 12 games. Then, with a remarkable turn in form and fortune, Houllier's men did not win any of their next 11 matches – six defeats and five draws.

A win at Southampton in January stopped the rot, and the following 14 games brought a record of eight wins, two draws and four defeats, including those against Manchester City and Chelsea in the last two games of the season, Steven Gerrard being dismissed for two bookable offences at Stamford Bridge. It all added up to a disappointing fifth place in the league table, and out of the following season's Champions League slots.

Their 2002/03 Champions League challenge had itself been a disappointment, with an exit at the group stage. They had lost their opening game at Valencia and failed to beat Basle in the final game. I was there in Switzerland on a night when the Reds conceded three goals without reply in the first half an hour of the match.

They saved face with three goals of their own in the second half, but it wasn't enough. They dropped into the UEFA Cup but went out to Celtic in the quarter-finals after two torrid matches, the first at Parkhead sadly best remembered for El Hadji Diouf spitting at a Celtic fan after the game, and the Scots winning 2-0 at Anfield with goals from an Englishman and a Welshman.

In the domestic cup competitions there were contrasting fortunes, with a fourth round Anfield replay exit from the FA Cup at the hands of Crystal Palace. In the Worthington Cup things went much better. A penalty shoot-out win at Anfield over Ipswich in the fourth round was followed up by an exciting 4-3 victory at Aston Villa, Danny Murphy scoring two goals, including the winner in the 90th minute. Sheffield United were dispatched in the two-legged semi-final and the Reds were off to Cardiff again to play Manchester United, this time in the Worthington Cup Final.

It was to be Liverpool's afternoon with goals from Steven Gerrard, a first-half strike deflected by David Beckham beyond Fabien Barthez in the United goal, and Michael Owen (who else?) sealing a famous win in the 86th minute. 2-0 and Liverpool's seventh win in this particular domestic cup competition.

Another piece of silverware for the Reds ... but the pressure was building on Gérard Houllier to deliver the big prize – the Premier League title.

Kop That – *Emile Heskey played in six League Cup Finals – with Leicester (won two of three), Liverpool (won two) and Aston Villa, where he finished on the losing side in 2010.*

2003/04 – GÉRARD AND GERRARD

LIVERPOOL FANS come in all shapes and sizes, but one outstanding Reds supporter stood above most of those around him, and not just because of his height. At 6ft 7in tall, England rugby union captain Martin Johnson was more than a big long-time Red – he was also a World Cup winner. On Saturday, 22 November, Johnson led his England team to a famous victory against Australia in the 2003 Rugby World Cup Final in Sydney. Jonny Wilkinson may have landed the last-minute iconic drop-kick that secured an extra-time triumph against the tournament's hosts, but it was Johnson who drove his men forward to the sweet spot from where the winning kick soared. I was privileged to be in the stadium in Australia that evening, but back in the UK a record daytime audience of 14.5m ITV viewers had got up early on this Saturday morning to cheer their heroes on from their armchairs. It was Johnson who both lifted the spirits of the England side and the golden William Webb Ellis trophy itself. Captain Johnson and fellow World Cup winner Ben Kay, both devoted Liverpool fans, enjoyed the acclaim of a nation when they landed back in the UK. For Johnson, a CBE in the 2004 New Year Honours list, and second place in the BBC Sports Personality of the Year award, behind winner Jonny Wilkinson.

Captaincy. Important or not important? Can a skipper be the 'X factor' for a team once it crosses the white line? I believe so, and watching Jordan Henderson pushing himself, and his team-mates, to greater efforts and greater heights has been a key constituent part of Liverpool's huge success under manager Jürgen Klopp. The understanding and respect between Klopp and Henderson are there for all to see – they share the same work ethic, belief in hard graft and never-say-die attitude. In the autumn of 2003, Gérard Houllier was looking to change things around. A sluggish start to the new season was not encouraging for Liverpool fans, and his new signings, Steve Finnan and Harry Kewell, were still settling down at the club, as were the young French pair Florent Sinama Pongolle and Anthony Le Tallec. Houllier, supported by his staff, decided it was time to make his best player his new captain as well. Steven Gerrard was still only 23 years old, but he would actually captain England too before the end of the 2003/04 season.

Moving Steven Gerrard into the captain's role was no sleight on the existing skipper Sami Hyypiä, who had given sterling service in the role as Houllier pointed out. 'Sami has been a good and successful captain for Liverpool Football Club. I must say that Sami's reaction (to my decision) has been nothing short of fantastic, both on and off the field, which illustrates what a great professional he is.' After checking Sami was alright with the change, Steven Gerrard relished the opportunity to be captain of Liverpool Football Club. 'I can never thank Gérard Houllier enough. I owe Gérard so much. I'll always remember what Gérard did for my career.' The young kid from Huyton, with a boyhood dream of playing for his beloved Reds, had joined a very exclusive club of great Anfield captains which included Ron Yeats, Tommy Smith, Emlyn Hughes, Phil Thompson, Graeme Souness, Alan Hansen, Sami Hyypiä and now Steven George Gerrard. It was in Liverpool's UEFA Cup first round second leg in October against the Slovenian side, Olimpija that Gerrard led the team out as their permanent captain. 'The Olimpija Ljubljana match was not my first experience as captain, but it was different. To get the armband and know I didn't have to give it back was a proud moment for me. I was thrilled to bits when I was given the job.' Gerrard would be captain of Liverpool Football Club for the next 12 years.

Captain issue sorted then, but Houllier was coming under increasing pressure to deliver the goods for the Anfield club. Whilst appreciating the achievements of his spell in charge it was difficult for Liverpool fans to watch Manchester United and Arsenal tussling it out for Premier League supremacy – and Chelsea were now under the ownership of super-rich Russian Roman Abramovich. And we know how supercharged the Stamford Bridge outfit became, with the new owner's wealth giving the London club a seismic change in its financial clout. And the self-acclaimed 'Special One', José Mourinho, was about to hit town. Off the pitch it was difficult for Liverpool to keep pace with the weight of money being invested into the game, a lot of it from a new breed of foreign owners. Some of them were genuinely interested in the club they were buying, and the sport they were playing, others were clearly not. On the pitch Liverpool's form was inconsistent, and Gérard Houllier's explanations why that was became increasingly inconsistent.

In the Premier League a decent late-season run-in, including a 1-0 away win against Manchester United – as usual Danny Murphy on target – garnered the Reds 11 points from a possible 15. Fourth place and a slot in the Champions League was secured. But they finished a massive 30 points behind the champions Arsenal, who didn't lose a single league game that season. 'The Invincibles', as they were dubbed, won 26 games and drew 12 – 90 points to Liverpool's 60. Both runs in the domestic cup competitions came up short, as did their trek across Europe in the UEFA Cup. Ties against Slovenian, Romanian and Bulgarian opposition were summarily dealt with. Then the Reds came up against Marseille, and a 1-1 draw at Anfield was followed up with a 2-1 defeat in France. A certain Didier Drogba was on target against the Reds – he would repeat the dose for Chelsea several times when his new club locked horns with the Reds in every type of competition in the immediate years that followed.

As the season closed there was wide speculation that the Houllier/Thompson reign was coming to an end. Fans largely thought it had run its course. And sure enough, in the midweek following Liverpool's last game of the season, the Anfield hierarchy parted company with their French boss. Although LFC were keen to keep Thompson involved at the club, it depended on the incoming manager, and, in due course, Thompson, too, left the club he remains in love with.

Thompson would go on to have a highly successful time with Sky Sports, a regular fixture on their hugely popular *Soccer Saturday* show until 2020. Houllier would continue an involvement in football, including a short stint as the manager of Aston Villa. He was also used by UEFA and FIFA in all manner of ways – a deeply respected professional in the sport. I bumped into him all over the world, especially at tournaments. He was always charming, courteous and curious about where I was career-wise. I would often see him and his wife in the company of Arsenal supremo David Dein and wife Barbara at football junkets.

Gérard Houllier died in December 2020. Phil Thompson spoke warmly about him, as did many of his former Liverpool players. Steven Gerrard and Jamie Carragher talked about how he had shaped them both as footballers and people. In his time at Anfield he had developed a new sense of professionalism and personal discipline for the players. He was an advocate of a proper diet more befitting of athletic demands, and considered alcohol as simply a career shortener. Gérard cared passionately about Liverpool Football Club, and it showed. And he delivered six trophies to Anfield and gave us back a little of our lost self-respect. He was a good football manager and a good man.

Kop That – *Gérard Houllier is the only Frenchman to manage an English club to European competition success.*

2004/05 – LIFT OFF!

IT HAS been the subject of tens of thousands of words, a Brazilian rainforest of newsprint, compelling and captivating literature, epic and emotional prose, witty and pithy plays and films. And, most importantly, the stuff of a million magical memories. And, all of the above are lovingly captured in one simple word: ISTANBUL. The UEFA Champions League Final between Liverpool and AC Milan at the Atatürk Stadium in Istanbul on Wednesday, 25 May 2005 was one of the most remarkable sporting comeback stories of all time. A game that defied belief, the greatest of its type, an iconic tale of heroic heart-stopping moments with a remarkable finish. And we were all there to witness it on that sultry Turkish night in a brand-new stadium seemingly built in the middle of nowhere. But it was the only place to be that night.

Yes, *we were there* when our stylish Italian opponents, AC Milan, coached by maestro Carlo Ancelotti, ran rings around the Reds in the first half; when our club's inspirational anthem was belted out by supporters at half-time; we watched captain Steven Gerrard typically grab the game by the scruff of the neck, Šmicer score from outside the box, Alonso ram home a penalty rebound, while substitute Didi Hamann calmly settled things down in midfield. We suffered with cramp-ridden Jamie Carragher as he gallantly refused to leave his post; we saw Jerzy

Dudek complete a double save that defied astronomical physics; watched a global superstar, Andriy Shevchenko, buckle under the pressure of a penalty shoot-out; and roared on the delirious Liverpool players, a famous and unlikely victory secured, as they made a beeline for their Polish goalkeeper at a speed only Usain Bolt could have matched. And when Steven Gerrard lifted that wonderful trophy, Liverpool's for keeps, we knew we had witnessed something extraordinary. An unforgettable Turkish magic-carpet ride.

The night before the game, Liverpool coach Rafa Benítez had spent part of the evening playing host to some Spanish friends in the Liverpool team's hotel, and as he walked over to the lifts and waited for one of them to descend, open and take him back up to his room, Benítez pointed very specifically to one of the ground floor's four lifts and said to his friends, 'If this one comes down first we'll win the final by penalties tomorrow.' It did. And they did.

Eleven months earlier, Benítez, the coach of Valencia, was named as the new manager of Liverpool Football Club. The first Spanish manager in English football. With a recent record of two La Liga titles, taming the giants of Real Madrid and Barcelona, and a UEFA Cup Final win over Marseille (conquerors of Liverpool) under his belt, 44-year-old Benítez was a hot property. Despite the fans of Valencia having a huge emotional respect for their studious, clinical coach, Benítez seemed to be at loggerheads with the hierarchy of the Spanish club. We would recognise a similar trait at Anfield in due course. Benítez decided it was time to 'vamos' from Valencia and Liverpool moved in to secure their man – the Reds' CEO Rick Parry said he was their number one target. One of Benítez's first acts as Liverpool boss was to get permission from England coach Sven-Göran Eriksson to fly to Portugal and have a private meeting with the Reds' three most influential players, Steven Gerrard, Jamie Carragher and Michael Owen, who were in the England camp for the Euro 2004 tournament.

The upshot? Gerrard and Carragher excited by the future possibilities for the Reds under Benítez, but Michael Owen a little concerned about the new manager's plans for him. Owen had been struggling with the dilemma of wishing to spread his footballing wings and potentially play abroad at one of the great Continental clubs or continue his career at Anfield, his spiritual home. Real Madrid had expressed a strong desire to take the brilliant Liverpool goal machine to the Spanish capital, and when Benítez kept Owen on the bench for the UEFA Champions League qualifier with Grazer AK, the die was cast. Owen wasn't to be 'cup tied', and soon he was on a flight out to Madrid to join fellow England international David Beckham and an army of 'Galacticos'. He admits he cried on the plane to Spain – his time at Liverpool had been studded with some magnificent moments and some mentally sapping injuries. But, without doubt, at his best Michael Owen was world class. From being Houllier's rendezvous for French footballers, Anfield now became 'El Casa' for Benítez's countrymen.

After concluding the already-established transfer of Djibril Cissé from Auxerre, it was Rafa's Spanish Armada that sailed up the River Mersey. Benítez's top picks, the brilliant Xabi Alonso from Real Sociedad and diminutive Luis García from Barcelona led the fleet, with Real Madrid's Fernando Morientes whistled on board at Anfield in early January 2005. By the end of that month, Liverpool had already reached the Carling Cup Final, and qualified for the knockout stages of the UEFA Champions League via the first of the two major comebacks in the competition that would ultimately lead them to European glory. 1-0 down at half-time to Olympiakos in a final pre-Christmas group game that Liverpool needed to win by two clear goals, another special 'Anfield European night' was about to unfold. The Reds' first two goals in the comeback came from unlikely sources, two substitutes, Florent Sinama Pongolle and Neil Mellor, before once again Steven Gerrard rode to the club's ultimate rescue with a blinding 86th-minute goal. 'You Beauty!!!' Sky Sports Andy Gray's famous commentary line hit the airwaves as Gerrard's bullet burst into the Greek team's net. Even Benítez, always presenting himself as a cool, calm, calculating coach, must have been elated inside. Liverpool would enter the new year with a chance to progress in European football's five-star competition, but they would be set some real tough challenges on that particular journey.

Ah, real tough challenges! That's what I'd just set myself with a significant change in direction in my career, having applied for, and subsequently been appointed as, the Football Association's new chief executive. In November 2004 I had found myself filling in an application form for the high-profile vacancy in one of the most senior roles in British sport. I had loved my 25-year career in top-class sports broadcasting and achieved everything, and more than I could have possibly expected in it. I considered myself privileged to have had the opportunities presented to me at both BBC TV and ITV – working on the big sporting events, dealing with the major stars, fighting for major contracts, helping deliver huge TV audiences, the travel, the excitement and sheer chutzpah of knowing on certain occasions that nearly half of the nation were tuned in to a programme that we were broadcasting. But now I had a chance to get directly involved in a sport I truly loved, felt I had a great working knowledge of, and was well known by many people in its own special world. It was also considered a poisoned chalice! I started as the FA's new chief executive on the last day of January 2005 and spent the best part of the next four years in a role that was challenging, impossible, inspiring, intellectually stimulating and very public, and occasionally all

SIXTY YEARS A RED ... AND COUNTING!

on the same afternoon! One thing I knew was that I would be watched carefully on my neutrality and objectivity when dealing with issues at the very top of the sport.

In a way all those years in TV had helped prepare me well for those potentially tricky moments.

For example, in the UEFA Champions League, I made it my business to go to Stamford Bridge, Highbury and Old Trafford as often as I did Anfield. I also made sure I was at Goodison Park for Everton's Champions League qualifier with Villarreal. And I made it clear that I wanted all our English clubs to succeed, not just the one I was most associated with. Mind you, I can't escape the fact that during my four-year spell in charge at the FA, Liverpool FC reached two UEFA Champions League Finals, a European Super Cup, a World Club Championship Final, an FA Cup Final, a Carling Cup Final, a FA Community Shield match and a couple of FA Youth Cup Finals! And they won most of them! I enjoyed my dealings with the other home associations, and the powerbrokers at FIFA and UEFA. And it was with the latter I made an early sortie into the heavyweight world of football politics.

Liverpool were making great progress in the knockout stages of the 2004/05 Champions League with Bayer Leverkusen beaten 3-1 in both legs of their round of 16 tie. Juventus were up next, and a 2-1 home win at Anfield was followed up with a goalless draw in Turin. Liverpool were now in the competition's semi-finals against José Mourinho's Chelsea, who had beaten the Reds in both of that season's Premier League tussles and the Carling Cup Final. An own goal from Steven Gerrard, seemingly a transfer target for Chelsea, helped Mourinho's men back into the game they eventually won 3-2 after extra time. One thing I had noticed was that Everton were bombing along well in the Premier League and Liverpool weren't looking like they would catch them.

Why was this a problem? Here's why. I had alerted UEFA in person, and then by email, that at the end of the season there could be a situation where Everton could finish fourth in the Premier League and therefore qualify for the next season's Champions League, whilst their city rivals Liverpool could finish fifth ... but win the Champions League. I told UEFA it would be impossible and totally inappropriate to replace Everton, who would have finished above Liverpool on merit, and replace them with the European Cup-winning Reds in the following season's Champions League competition. And surely it was only right that the champions should be allowed to defend their crown. 'Your problem, not ours,' UEFA seemed to suggest. 'England has four representatives in next season's Champions League, not five. It is up to the FA to decide which four.' They also told me that it was one of those football conundrums that would resolve itself on the field as is often the way of things. Sure enough, Everton did finish fourth, and having got past formidable German and Italian opposition, Liverpool were still on course for a place in the Champions League Final, but first they had to find a way past Mourinho's men.

The first leg at Stamford Bridge ended goalless. The second leg at Anfield was tumultuous. The noise inside the stadium that night was unbelievable. The place was absolutely rocking. The Liverpool fans had got there early, and as the Chelsea players warmed up you could sense, experienced as many of them were, that they were genuinely affected by the sheer volume of the noise being made by the Liverpool fans. When the game got underway, the Reds scored early through Luis García. The Spaniard had beaten Chelsea goalkeeper Petr Čech to a ball and sent it goalward. It was cleared as it crossed the line and the Londoners complained that García's opportunistic strike had not actually crossed the line, but in the days before goal-line technology or VAR, the goal stood. Fifty-odd thousand Liverpool fans believed it had, and most importantly so did Slovakian referee, Ľuboš Micheľ. It was a very tense match – my 'objectivity' was being stretched to the limit – and when Chelsea's Eiður Guðjohnsen had a clear chance in the last few moments of the game, the Kop held its breath ... and watched his shot slip past the post. Liverpool were in the 2005 UEFA Champions League Final. The Anfield crowd was ecstatic, and I was dutifully phlegmatic outwardly ... but absolutely buzzing inside! In defeat, Mourinho was in awe of the Liverpool crowd. 'I felt the power. It was magnificent.'

As our Football Association was providing one of the finalists for UEFA's big night, myself and senior colleagues were given VIP status. I did reflect as we took off from Heathrow Airport for the four-hour direct flight to Istanbul that 28 years previously I had set off by train from Lime Street Station on Monday teatime to get to Rome by Wednesday morning, watched the 1977 European Cup Final, returning to Liverpool on Friday evening – homemade sandwiches, flasks of coffee and warm beer on the way out – and next to nothing on the way back. In Istanbul, the official UEFA Champions League celebration party on the eve of the final treated us to a five-course meal of a Turkish 'meze' platter, mixed seasonal salad, beef medallions with eggplant, cherry compote and ice cream, rounded off with tea, coffee and petit fours. Bon appétit ... or *Afiyet olsun*, as the locals would say.

The following evening, we were treated marvellously, and I had one of the best seats in the stadium. Mind you it didn't make the first half any easier to watch. 3-0 down and seemingly out of the contest. At half-time, former French superstar and UEFA council member Michel Platini wandered over to me and rather apologetically said, 'So, Brian what happens next?' 'Well,' I said, 'we are either going to witness the heaviest defeat in European Cup history ... or the greatest comeback.' I didn't tell him Rafa Benítez had picked the right hotel lift the previous evening, so everything was already sorted. The match would be going to extra time and the Reds would win on penalties! Which, of course, they did.

Kop That – *Since 1962, AC Milan are the only side to score more than once in a European Cup/Champions League Final and still finish as losing finalists.*

2005/06 – FOOTBALL ROYALTY

'WELL DONE – what a game, what a comeback, fantastic …
but now we have a problem, yes?'

Michel Platini was right on all counts, but he duly swilled
down his glass of white wine and disappeared into the throng
of football's great and good, busy congratulating Liverpool
FC's jubilant top brass in the post-match fervour. It would be
left to others to work out what would happen next. The media
were on the case too. Thursday morning's sports pages would
be crammed full of reports on the glory of one of the greatest
games in modern times. Friday's newspaper columns would
still be reliving the drama of that night in Istanbul and the
club's fantastic welcome home the following evening. Their
fresh news angle though had turned to whether the Liverpool
team, who had triumphed against all the odds, would be
allowed to defend their title in Europe next season.

As the FA chief executive, I was liberally quoted across the
media on the matter, always insisting that any positive news for
Liverpool would not be at the expense of neighbours Everton.
Rick Parry, Liverpool's CEO, threw the problem the FA's and
UEFA's way, and so influential people at Soho Square began
a set of time-sensitive talks with the key people in Geneva. I
think there was always a little bit of resistance to what UEFA,
and others, perceived as English football's frequent requests to

be the exception rather than the rule. I was learning quickly that what happened off the pitch was as important at times as what happened on it. For Liverpool FC this was one of those occasions. We kept up the pressure, with trips to UEFA headquarters, phone calls and emails – and on 10 June, they announced that Liverpool FC would be allowed to defend the title in an 'historic' one-off decision which would allow five English clubs to enter the following season's Champions League. Victory in Europe for the Reds (and the FA!) came with one caveat – they had to start their defence of the competition at the very start of the competition – the first qualifying round. And that's why Liverpool had to play Welsh part-timers TNS in early July, with Wimbledon, the Open Golf Championship and a riveting Ashes series significantly more on the radar of the country's sports fans.

That didn't stop over 44,000 fans turning up at Anfield to watch the reigning champions of European football beat the minnows from Llansantffraid 3-0 in the first leg of the new season's Champions League first qualifying round. Fittingly, it was Steven Gerrard who scored a hat-trick that night, just days after finally signing a contract to secure his long-term future at Anfield, Chelsea's aspirations to secure the services of Liverpool's iconic star finally laid to rest. The Reds added the UEFA Super Cup to their collection with a 3-1 win over CSKA Moscow, the night after the Liverpool fans' unquenchable backing of their team in Istanbul was formally recognised by UEFA at a gala dinner held in Monaco. Liverpool's defence of their title would end in the round of 16, Benfica victorious in both legs. Everton would go out of the competition at the final qualifying round stage. And the Reds latest venture in FIFA's World Club Cup came up short. I went over to Yokohama in Japan to see the European champions beat Saprissa of Costa Rica, only to lose in the final against São Paulo of Brazil. I felt then, and still do now, that the event is a poor relation to the UEFA Champions League, and probably always will be. But, on the other hand, try qualifying for it!

Rafa Benítez's 'second season' squad had even more of a Spanish feel to it. Despite his heroics in Istanbul, Jerzy Dudek was to be displaced in goal by Pepe Reina, who arrived from Villarreal. His La Liga team-mate, Dutchman Jan Kromkamp, and Valencia midfielder Mohamed Sissoko headed to Anfield too, as did Danish international defender Daniel Agger. Also on board was lanky English striker Peter Crouch, a £7m buy from Southampton, who after a barren run in the early months of his Liverpool career finally got off the mark on the first Saturday of December, with a double strike against Wigan Athletic in front of a hugely appreciative Kop. A likeable guy, his height made him a menace in the air, but he was also no mug on the floor. Crouch made 49 appearances that season, scoring 13 goals. It earned him a place in England's 2006 World Cup squad. And he was honoured with a lovely Kop chant all of his own. 'He's big, he's a Red, his feet stick out the bed, Peter Crouch, Peter Crouch!!'

From a former Saint to a living 'God', Benítez's most newsworthy acquisition was the mid-season move of Robbie Fowler from Manchester City back to his spiritual home at Liverpool. The January transfer caught the imagination of the general public and was raucously cheered by the Kop. Fowler himself described being back at Anfield to be 'like a kid waking up on Christmas morning every day'. Given he was lovingly nicknamed 'God' by the fans, Fowler's Christmas analogy seems quite fitting! He scored his first goal on his much-feted return against Fulham in March, the first of five he notched in what remained of the campaign. In May 2006, he was offered a new one-year contract with the club and duly celebrated by scoring in the Reds' 3-1 win at Portsmouth in their last game of the season. The Reds finished third in the Premier League but went on an impressive run in the FA Cup. It started at Kenilworth Road where Liverpool ended up beating Luton Town in a dramatic FA Cup third-round tie 5-3, despite having trailed 3-1 as the live televised game entered its final half hour. Sinama-Pongolle scored twice, as did Xabi Alonso, one of them from his own half! Four goals between the two men to rescue the Reds' FA Cup adventure before it nearly had a very premature end. Portsmouth were put to the sword in the fourth round, and the fifth round pitted the Reds against Manchester United in a monster of a match at Anfield. Peter Crouch scored the only goal of the game.

Mind you, I had been a little distracted around this period as the *News of the World* had run a front-page story (and another ten pages!) about Sven-Göran Eriksson, and what he had said on certain football matters whilst on a midweek trip to Dubai. It turned out to be the latest 'sting', orchestrated by the now-defunct newspaper's reporter, the 'Fake Sheikh', but it was damaging for the England coach, and made for an exceedingly difficult few weeks at the FA, with Sven agreeing to step down after that summer's 2006 FIFA World Cup in Germany. The procedure to replace him proved a challenge as well – too long, too public and too many people getting involved in the decision-making process. We were heavily criticised at the time – fairly on my reflection.

One pleasant distraction during this difficult period was when England played one of their World Cup warm-up games at Anfield. While Wembley was being rebuilt, the England team played home matches all over the country and on 1 March 2006 their international friendly against Uruguay was staged in front of the Kop. I was proud to be the FA CEO that night, and my all-areas pass was hardly needed as I knew every inch of the stadium, indoors and outdoors. Before the kick-off

I was on the Anfield pitch, with the FA and Uruguayan FA top brass, carrying out the formal duty of 'meeting the teams' – then it was back in the stand to enjoy the action. England won 2-1, with Anfield's own Peter Crouch equalising Uruguay's opening goal, and future Red Joe Cole scoring a late winner.

Now, on occasions, it could be a little awkward being the boss of the FA when invited to attend a big match by the hosting club, be welcomed warmly, treated to generous hospitality, sense their great anticipation, and then watch their heroes get clobbered on their own home turf. Good example? 21 March 2006. FA Cup sixth round – St Andrew's – Birmingham City 0 Liverpool 7. Sami Hyypiä scored for the Reds in the opening minute, Peter Crouch in the fifth and 38th minutes – 0-3 at half-time. Small talk in the boardroom just a little strained. Morientes, 59th minute, Riise, 70th minute, a Birmingham City own goal, 77th minute and Cissé on 89 minutes – four second-half goals in 30 minutes. Final score: 7-0 to the visitors. Small talk in the boardroom at the end of the game just got a little bit smaller. In desperation, I did remind the Blues' directors they had handed out Liverpool's record away defeat, 9-1, back in 1954. A fact that seemed of little comfort on the night, and my FA colleague and I slipped away quietly into the night. The FA Cup semi-final was the latest titanic struggle between Liverpool and Chelsea – their fifth meeting of the season. Chelsea had won both Premier League matches, and two Champions League group games had ended in goalless draws. At Old Trafford's semi-final, in a pulsating match, Liverpool came through 2-1 winners.

The 2006 FA Cup Final at the Millennium Stadium in Cardiff proved to be one of *the* special days of a lifetime of my supporting the Reds. The appointment of Prince William as president of the Football Association had been seen as a positive move and the FA Cup Final was to be his first public outing in his new role. I took him down in the lift into the bowels of the stadium and we watched as the two teams, Liverpool and West Ham United, emerged from their respective dressing rooms. Prince William briefly exchanged glances with Liverpool captain Steven Gerrard, who broke into a broad smile, shyly returned by our Royal guest. Walking along the two sets of players with our new president was a memorable personal experience. I had watched on black-and-white TV in 1965 when Prince Philip, the Duke of Edinburgh, had been introduced to the Liverpool and Leeds United teams ahead of the final at Wembley. Fifty-one years later I was accompanying his grandson on the same prematch protocol, before settling back to watch my team play in the FA Cup Final. As I made my way along the West Ham players, I made it my business to be strenuously fair-minded, but I am sure there was just a little bit extra oomph in my handshakes with the Liverpool team. Anyway, to the TV viewers, any illusions of neutrality went out of the window when the BBC commentator, John Motson, said, 'Brian Barwick there, a staunch Liverpudlian who has supported the team all his life!'

The match itself was an absolute thriller. The Hammers went 1-0 up through a Jamie Carragher own goal, and Dean Ashton added a second. Four minutes later Gerrard played a magnificent ball through to Cissé, who finished with typical French flair. Into the second half and Gerrard (who else?) pulled Liverpool level. 2-2. But West Ham weren't done and full-back Paul Konchesky lofted a cross into the Reds' box which Pepe Reina misread. 3-2 to West Ham. I had made sure that my FA colleague and Hammers legend Trevor Brooking was sitting near me, and Prince William enjoyed watching our constrained joy or disappointment as either of our teams scored or conceded a goal. The game was in injury time and the FA Cup was heading off to the East End of London, when Steven

Gerrard pulled it out of the fire again for Liverpool with one of the FA Cup Final's greatest goals. His 35-yard screamer burst the Hammers' bubbles, and I admit to briefly showing my true colours in front of our Royal guest, who reacted with a warm smile. After all, as a football fan it is in the blood – red or blue.

Liverpool went on to win the final on penalties, Reina saving three of West Ham's spot kicks – Liverpool's successful penalty kicks taken by Hamann, Riise and Gerrard (of course!). And Prince William handed the priceless piece of sporting silverware to Steven Gerrard – Liverpool's very own football royalty. A memorable day.

Kop That – *Steven Gerrard is the only player to score a goal in the finals of the FA Cup, League Cup, UEFA Cup and European Cup/Champions League.*

2006/07 – THE WILD WEST

THE 2006 FIFA World Cup was my 12th as a committed football lover. I'd watched the World Cup as a football nut from 1962 onwards, attended my first World Cup match at Goodison Park in 1966, loved Carlos Alberto's wonderful goal for Brazil in 1970, and had worked on those much-anticipated four-yearly tournaments professionally since 1982 – four times for BBC TV Sport, including Italia 90 – 'Nessun Dorma' and all that – two for ITV with its record audiences, and now in 2006 I was on the plane that was leaving Luton Airport carrying the England squad to Germany for that summer's big event. 'You're living the dream!' a pal texted me, as the plane landed in Germany, all live on TV. Probably true. But, ultimately, a major disappointment too as we set off home for England a week earlier than we had hoped, and without that much sought-after piece of special golden cargo – the World Cup itself.

Our time in Germany had been an experience of relative highs, including two wins and a draw, guaranteeing a safe, if unspectacular, passage through the group stage; Liverpool pair Crouch and Gerrard both on target against Trinidad and Tobago; then a narrow 1-0 win against Ecuador in the round of 16, before enduring the despair of going out on penalties against Portugal in the quarter-finals. A match in which the

England team finally played some of its best football. And for Jamie Carragher, and Steven Gerrard, who would play in three World Cups for his country, along with Frank Lampard, there was the the pain of missing their spot kicks in that shoot-out, as Sven-Göran Eriksson's reign as England coach was over.

Six weeks later, Carragher and Crouch started the Community Shield match in Cardiff for Liverpool against Chelsea, and Gerrard came on as a substitute after an hour. The football business never closes. John Arne Riise opened the scoring for the Reds, but an old adversary and new big-money Chelsea purchase, Andriy Shevchenko, pulled the Premier League champions level. Peter Crouch secured another trophy for the Reds, scoring ten minutes from time, and yet another marker was put down on what was becoming a long-running saga with the Londoners. For Liverpool Football Club, the 2006/07 season would be a bumpy ride on and off the pitch. They still couldn't nail a much-anticipated league title win, ultimately finishing third in the Premier League behind champions Manchester United and Chelsea, and were knocked out of the two domestic cup competitions by Arsenal within three days of each other, both home ties at Anfield.

The first was the most attractive tie of the 2006/07 FA Cup third round, and I headed up to Liverpool to watch it having taken in the Tamworth v Norwich City match on my way up the M1. When I got to Anfield that evening, Rick Parry asked whether I minded being introduced to representatives of Dubai International Capital who were at Anfield and whom it had been suggested may be looking to buy the club. Times were changing it seemed. As the FA chief executive, and a Liverpool fan, I was probably the perfect guy for the Liverpool officials to parade in front of their Middle Eastern guests. I left Anfield that night believing my club was heading for foreign ownership, and, incidentally, we were also out of the FA Cup as Arsenal put Liverpool to the sword, 3-1. Three days later, the Gunners were back at Anfield for a Carling Cup quarter-final and took part in a topsy-turvy game which ended in a bizarre 6-3 victory for the visitors. Not to dwell exclusively on defeats by Arsenal, mention must be made of a Liverpool win over Arsène Wenger's men, 4-1 in their Premier League encounter at Anfield in March, most memorable for a superb hat-trick by Peter Crouch.

By this time Liverpool were under foreign ownership, but not from the east but from the west. And what turned out to be the Wild West. An American consortium of two quite different characters, in both style and stature, had rode into town and taken up the reins at Anfield. Tom Hicks and George Gillett, old-time friends but not business partners, had joined together to buy Liverpool Football Club. They both were involved in major sport franchises in US sport and ran other commercial and investment businesses, but what became clear is they didn't have any proper working knowledge about English football. Texan Hicks, had been involved in Major League Baseball and National League Hockey franchises, Wisconsin-born Gillett with an NHL franchise, the Montreal Canadiens, and NASCAR motor sport. They split the shareholding of Liverpool Football Club 50/50 and made all the right noises on their arrival at the club in February 2007. 'Liverpool is a fantastic club with a remarkable history. We fully acknowledge and appreciate this unique heritage and intend to respect it in the future.'

I went to the Reds' round of 16 Champions League match against Barcelona the following month and was introduced to the two new owners as 'the chief executive of the Football Association and a lifelong Liverpool fan'. Hicks and Gillett almost stood to attention – football 'top brass', the game's 'commissioner', as they saw it. I took the opportunity to explain to them what I felt, both professionally and personally – that they had a genuine responsibility to the club and its supporters. I told them they were now the guardians of something more than a brand, more than an asset, more than a name on a balance sheet, more than a part of a foreign investment portfolio. That they were involved in something that was at the very heartbeat of tens of thousands of people's lives. Something that was uniquely part of Liverpool's life. Indeed, part of my own personal history. They nodded in all the right places, but I doubted whether they really 'got' it. Indeed, at the end of the game, I turned around to them and explained the Anfield crowd were going mad because we had just knocked Barcelona out of the competition. They looked confused as we had lost the match 1-0. 'Away goals,' I said. Their mutual look of bemusement told me this was going to be a long and painful journey.

At one match I was approached in the Liverpool boardroom by one of our Texan visitors. 'Sir, I believe you know a lot about this club. Tell me more.'

'Well,' I said, 'a man called Bill Shankly came to the club in 1959 and with personality, drive and commitment, he created the Liverpool you see today.'

'Wow! And is he still alive?'

'No, he sadly passed away many years ago. When he had retired, his role as manager was taken over by a quietly spoken, one-club man called Bob Paisley and he turned Liverpool into European champions.

'Wow! And is he still alive?'

'No, he died many years ago too. And, when he retired, he was replaced by a local man, Joe Fagan, who won the treble in his first season in charge.'

'OK! Wow! And is Joe still alive?'

'No. And, before you ask, it was Kenny Dalglish – and he's over there having a glass of red wine!'

Another Champions League semi-final ... and another Champions League semi-final against Chelsea. And with a similar triumphant outcome for Liverpool. Joe Cole's goal secured victory for the Londoners in the first leg at Stamford Bridge and a Daniel Agger strike squared things at Anfield. Extra time couldn't split these increasingly familiar adversaries and so to another penalty shoot-out. A decisive 4-1 advantage in the spot kicks, the clincher scored by the popular, hard-working Dutchman Dirk Kuyt.

The UEFA Champions League Final in Athens proved to be something of an anticlimax for the vast army of Reds supporters who travelled across to Greece for Liverpool's seventh tilt at European football's top prize. Interestingly, only five players who had started the final in Istanbul two years before were on the field in Athens at kick-off time – Gerrard, Finnan, Carragher, Riise and Alonso being joined by Reina, Agger, Jermaine Pennant, Javier Mascherano, Boudewijn Zenden and Dirk Kuyt.

The game was no classic, and Liverpool weren't at their best, losing 2-1 to opponents AC Milan, who had a score to settle with the Merseysiders. Kuyt got a late consolation goal for the Reds.

There were problems in Athens, with plenty of people using fake tickets or forcing their way into the stadium at the expense and discomfort of those Liverpool fans who had travelled with genuine tickets. The scenes outside the stadium were chaotic and the organisation shambolic. Throughout the match I spotted Rick Parry looking worryingly at the 'Liverpool' end of the ground. It looked overcrowded to him, and me.

All in all, not a great night for the Reds – it was certainly no Istanbul. And in the immediate aftermath of the final, Rafa Benítez added a whole new layer of potential conflict. In his press conference on the morning after the game, he attacked

Liverpool's new American owners. 'They say they will support us, but now is not the time for talk but to take decisions. It's not just about new faces, it's about the structure of the club.' Benítez had lit the 'red' touchpaper and suddenly a sense of disharmony had spread across the club.

The wonderful aspects of that well-used phrase 'The Liverpool Way' were being blown away in the hot winds of the Greek capital. As Liverpool's famous ex-chairman John Smith would say, 'We're a very, very modest club at Liverpool. We don't talk. We don't boast. But we're very professional.' And, whatever issues were being dealt with inside the club, a united front was always presented. Times *had* changed it seemed.

Kop That – *Dirk Kuyt was the first Liverpool player to score in every round of the Champions League including the qualifying round, with his first in the competition coming in the 2007 final itself.*

2007/08 – LIVERPOOL'S NUMBER NINE!

TO ASSIST with the painstaking research(!) for this book I have just sat down, large glass of Spanish white wine and a bowl of salted peanuts on hand, and watched *Fernando Torres: All the Goals* on LFCTV. It is a great reminder of just what a quality player this son of Madrid truly was. Every type of goal, from the classy to the crafty, the tremendous to the tap-in.

Many of those goals were made by his inspirational captain Steven Gerrard, who seemed to love having the Spanish striker up ahead of him to slot in or steer home his inch-perfect passes from midfield. Torres agreed. 'I always say the best player I played with was Steven Gerrard. He completed my game. I think my level got to a different dimension when I was on the pitch with him.'

Torres brought the whole package to LFC, especially in matches played at Anfield, including inspiring the hugely creative song (one of my own personal favourites) that followed him wherever and whenever he played with his Liverpool team-mates. The manner in which he joined Chelsea in the final hours of the last day of the January 2011 transfer window left Reds' supporters with something of a bitter taste, but as we've learned, in the modern era, very few players stick around forever, and so it is a case of enjoying them while you can.

And that was certainly the case with Torres – 65 goals in 102 games, including 33 in his first season. An instant payback of his big transfer fee from Atlético Madrid of £20m. The same transfer window also brought the likes of Yossi Benayoun, Ryan Babel to Anfield, as well as Lucas Leiva from Gremio, and what a servant he proved to be for Liverpool Football Club.

Still, despite this influx of talent, it seemed relationships between Rafa Benítez and the club's American owners continued to be strained, not helped when the deadly duo, Hicks and Gillett, decided to have a chat with USA-based German icon, player turned coach Jürgen Klinsmann. One of two chats it is believed. Whatever, Reds' fans became aware of it and remained staunchly behind Rafa, and typical of that pair of owners they proved to be ten years out in their timing.

'Jürgen K' did come to Anfield, and completely changed its destiny – Jürgen Klopp that is!

November 2007 proved to be a tough month for me, as England failed to qualify for the European Football Championship finals scheduled for Austria and Switzerland the following summer. Beaten by Croatia on a rainswept night at Wembley, England were out of the competition, coach Steve McClaren out of a job, and, as the FA's CEO, yours truly never out of the newspapers in the days that followed.

In the hunt for the new England coach, I took on board observations from previous respected holders of the post like Sir Bobby Robson and Terry Venables. I also listened to thoughts of a range of experienced football men, including Sir Alex Ferguson and Roy Hodgson. I also contacted England captain John Terry and Steven Gerrard to try and get a feel of it all from their perspective as current senior internationals.

As always, the search for the new England coach was very newsworthy and when, in December, we announced that proven coaching maestro Fabio Capello was to be the new man, it created a broadly positive response. And off we went again.

Back at Anfield, Liverpool were struggling to win games at home, and would finish fourth in the Premier League behind champions Manchester United, Chelsea and Arsenal. The Reds won just 21 of their 38 games – just 12 of their home matches – and drew 13 league matches overall in this season.

A bright spot? Torres scored 24 goals in 33 league appearances, including hat-tricks in successive home games, against Middlesbrough and West Ham United, respectively. Torres scored another hat-trick in a League Cup tie with Reading, but the Reds were eliminated by Chelsea in the competition's fifth round.

In the FA Cup, Liverpool were paired with Luton Town again and Gerrard bagged a hat-trick for himself in a 5-0 third-round replay win. Next up, non-league Conference South side Havant & Waterlooville – a pushover for the Reds surely?

As the FA CEO, I had been at the non-leaguers' third-round replay win over Swansea – a memorable night for the Hawks and their ecstatic fans, especially with a trip to Anfield booked in the FA Cup fourth round. The FA Cup at this stage of its life was beginning to struggle to compete with the juggernauts of Premier League and Champions League football. The most well-loved domestic cup competition in world football was fighting to stay attractive to fans and broadcasters alike.

Nobody gave Havant and Waterlooville a prayer at Anfield, so much so that the match wasn't even one of the live matches chosen by the broadcasters in the fourth round. 'No chance of an upset there' most likely the mindset. But the FA Cup sprang back into life on that Saturday afternoon, a traditional three o'clock kick-off and suddenly a potential old-fashioned giant-killing act underway – twice. The Hampshire side were 1-0 up inside the first ten minutes, and then unbelievably 2-1 ahead just after the half hour.

The Hawks' supporters, who had joined the Liverpool faithful in a full-blooded rendering of 'You'll Never Walk Alone', were now in seventh heaven. And I must admit 'wearing' my FA CEO 'hat' I was beginning to think, 'What a story this is!'

Unthinkably, given my long-time allegiance to the Reds' cause, I was now of the view, if they are going lose this afternoon so be it. What a fillip it would be for a competition that needed a leg-up if the non-leaguers beat the mighty Reds – FA Cup Final winners only two years before.

Dream/nightmare dilemma over. Liverpool scored four goals without a response, with a hat-trick by Benayoun, to ultimately win the game 5-2, but not before they had been scared to death.

The papers were full of it the following day – the FA Cup had nearly delivered one of its great stories – but it only had to wait until the next round when the Reds went out the FA Cup in a surprise 2-1 defeat at the hands of Barnsley. Good old FA Cup!

It was in the UEFA Champions League again where Liverpool made their greatest impression.

Their home game in the competition's third qualifying round against Toulouse is best remembered for the emotional playing of Everton's *Z Cars* theme tune ahead of the game at Anfield as a mark of unity and support following the murder of 11-year-old Rhys Jones, an avid young Blues fan, whose untimely death had brought the city together in its disgust and sympathy. Rhys's mum, dad and brother proudly wore their Everton colours on the Anfield touchline as the crowd loudly clapped both them and the famous Everton theme. I was there at Anfield that evening and like everybody else was touched by the bravery of Rhys's family. Some things are bigger than local football rivalries, as was proved that night.

Having sailed through the competition's third qualifying round with a 5-0 aggregate win over Toulouse, They suffered two unexpected early defeats in Group stage games against Marseille at Anfield, and Besiktas in Turkey. The return match with the Turkish side put things back in order – and some. I was at Anfield as Liverpool created a group stage record winning 8-0 with a hat-trick from Benayoun. A 4-1 home win over Porto and a 4-0 away win in Marseille confirmed second place in the Group.

A brilliant round of 16 win, home and away, over old adversaries Inter Milan set up a quarter-final against fellow English qualifiers Arsenal. Their two Premier League matches had both ended in 1-1 draws, as did the first leg of their quarter-final at The Emirates.

The second leg at Anfield was a cracker. The Gunners led 1-0, and then pulled level at 2-2 with just six minutes left. But in those closing moments, Gerrard and Babel pulled the Reds clear to win 4-2.

Next up. You've guessed it. Chelsea! Their third Champions League semi-final in four years. Liverpool had won both the previous dramatic encounters and were heading for a solid 1-0 lead in the first leg of their latest tussle. Dirk Kuyt's first-half goal looked to be enough when four minutes into injury time, John Arne Riise inexplicably headed the ball into his own net. It was a remarkable own goal in both its execution and its impact on the tie. The Kop went from fevered excitement to a shocked silence that was as loud as a roar.

And, in his refreshingly honest autobiography, Riise explained how he felt. 'The next day my face was plastered on every newspaper in England, and it didn't stop there. The whole world seemed to be writing about my insane own goal. My name was on everybody's lips. I didn't leave home for days. I didn't answer the phone. I couldn't go on the internet because of all the things that were written about me.'

Riise did play in the second leg which was another classic encounter between the Blues and the Reds. Drogba put Chelsea ahead after 33 minutes; Torres equalised on 64 minutes. Extra-time goals from Lampard (pen) and Drogba proved decisive despite Babel's late consolation.

Liverpool had two matches left to play against Manchester City and Tottenham, and before them Rafa Benítez asked Riise to come to his office. 'I think it's time we go our separate ways. You could benefit from new challenges, and we've bought a new left-back that we intend to rely on.'

With 348 appearances under his belt, the shocked Norwegian asked whether he could be chosen for the last two games to take his final tally for the Reds up to 350. Rafa Benítez just shook his head.

Contrast that with Liverpool's star 'number nine' Fernando Torres, who scored the only goal against Manchester City and the final goal of Liverpool's season in a 2-0 win at Tottenham. And I was in the Ernst Happel Stadion in Vienna on the June evening Torres scored the only goal in Spain's European Championship Final win over Germany. He was later awarded the UEFA Man of the Match award.

Two very different sides of the football fame game.

Kop That – Torres *became the most prolific scorer in a debut season in Liverpool's post-war history, averaging a goal every 1.4 games (46 games, 33 goals), whilst his 24 league goals saw him become the most prolific foreigner in a first Premier League season.*

2008/09 – OH,
NOT CHELSEA AGAIN!?!

BY THE start of the 2008/09 season Liverpool had not won the title for 18 years – unimaginable given the Reds' dominance of English football in the previous two decades.

As we know, the painful wait for Premier League glory would go on for some time longer – another 12 years. Equally unimaginable. During those title-barren years, there were seasons when the spell should have finally been broken. 2008/09 should have been one of those.

Firstly, get a positive return on the matches against your closest rivals. Tick. Secondly, minimise the number of games you lose. Tick. Thirdly, deliver the best goal difference – often worth an extra point. Tick. Fourthly, put pressure on the chasing pack by being top of the division going into the new year. Tick.

Liverpool delivered on all four of the above indices, but came up short again. The Reds return from the season's big games was impressive. Home and away wins against Manchester United and Chelsea, four points from the derby clashes with Everton and two draws with Arsenal – 18 points from a possible 24. They only lost two league matches all season, against Tottenham Hotspur and Middlesbrough.

And they outscored all their closest rivals – 77 goals in their opponents' nets.

And yet, despite a stunning start to the season – eight wins and two draws in the first ten games of the campaign – and an even better climax to their title tilt – ten wins and a draw in their last 11 games – it wasn't enough, as Manchester United topped the Reds' total of 86 points by four points.

How come? Well, between a sparkling opening and spectacular closing to their season's work, Liverpool dropped too many points against teams that by right they should have beaten.

In the other 17 matches, Liverpool won just seven, drew eight and lost two. A return of just 29 points from those matches. Significantly, Liverpool drew 11 games in all, seven of them at Anfield, including three goalless games against Stoke City, Fulham and West Ham United.

Another very frustrating season for the Anfield faithful, who had become an increasingly disillusioned set of supporters given their quickly fractured relationship with the new American owners. It seemed Hicks and Gillett were spiralling the club into debt. They promised a brand-new stadium project on Stanley Park – undelivered. And they had lost the confidence of the fans, and seemingly with each other. It was already a total mess.

Back on the pitch, Liverpool exited the FA Cup in a fourth-round replay against Everton at Goodison Park, a match possibly best remembered for the Blues' extra-time winner from Dan Gosling being unseen by millions of ITV viewers as the broadcaster mistakenly cut to an advert break mid-action. Up came an advert for the mint sweet Tic Tacs, and by the time ITV cut back live to the game, Everton players were celebrating the 'phantom' goal! Tic Tacs or mischievous 'Tactics' perhaps.

Once again it was in the UEFA Champions League that they made a great impression – they squeezed through a qualifying round against Standard Liège and topped their group ahead of Atlético Madrid, Marseille and PSV Eindhoven. The round of 16 pitched them against Spanish giants Real Madrid. A Benayoun goal clinched a 1-0 win in the Bernabéu and then, on another stunning Anfield evening, the Reds dismantled their famous rivals 4-0, with Steven Gerrard on target twice.

The Liverpool captain had come through a difficult personal issue having been charged with assault and affray after an incident in an upmarket bar in Southport. It was obviously very newsworthy and had followed Liverpool's 5-1 win at Newcastle United in which Gerrard had starred and scored twice. He was ultimately cleared of all charges with the jury unanimously in his favour, but it must have been an unsettling episode for Liverpool's highest profile player.

The quarter-final of the 2008/09 Champions League competition paired Liverpool with Chelsea again. It continued a remarkable series of matches between the two clubs. Since Rafa Benítez had started at the club in the summer of 2004, Liverpool played Chelsea no less than 22 times – eight times in the Champions League, including three semi-finals, ten times in the Premier League, one FA Cup semi-final, two Football League Cup games, including the 2005 final, and one FA Community Shield.

During this period Chelsea had employed four coaches: José Mourinho, Avram Grant, Luis-Felipe Scolari and Guus Hiddink. Ray Wilkins had also briefly been caretaker manager. And looking ahead, our own Rafa Benítez would go through the revolving door at Stamford Bridge to be their temporary boss between November 2012 and May 2013.

Back in 2008/09, Chelsea took a decisive 3-1 lead at Anfield in the quarter-final despite Torres giving the Reds an early lead.

It looked an uphill task for Liverpool in the second leg, but the Reds gave it their all and goals from Aurélio and Alonso levelled the tie at 3-3 in the first half at Stamford Bridge.

It was game on, a view I shared with Steven Gerrard at half-time in the Chelsea boardroom. Having just failed to make the game through a troublesome groin injury, the Liverpool captain was upbeat about our chances after the Reds' first-half display.

The second half was spellbinding stuff. Chelsea got themselves back ahead on aggregate with goals by Drogba (who else!), Alex and Lampard. This time it did look like job done but the Reds scored two late goals through Lucas and Kuyt – another goal would have taken Liverpool through on away goals. In a frantic finish there was one more goal and it went to Chelsea's Frank Lampard. 4-4 on the night – 7-5 to Hiddink's men.

They went out in the semi-finals to Lionel Messi's Barcelona, who beat Manchester United in that year's final. The 2008/09 season saw some ins and outs around the Anfield scene and wider.

I formally stepped down from my role as FA chief executive in December 2008, having effectively left the post four months earlier. I was at Wembley at England's August friendly international against the Czech Republic when at half-time on Sky Sports it was 'breaking news' that I was leaving the FA. It certainly made the tea and biscuits go down quicker as fellow Wembley goers looked for some reaction from me.

The FA were going to announce it the following day but in time-honoured fashion somebody had leaked it to the media. I did tell my mate Andy, who was my guest in the Royal Box that evening, that it was no time to pick his nose as I'm sure as the evening progressed the odd close-up of yours truly would pop on screen and he would be in shot too.

A new independent chairman had come into the FA and wanted to change the way the organisation ran its affairs – and that meant new people and a new chief executive. So be it. I had been in one of sport's top jobs and been proud to do it. A remarkable opportunity for somebody who was a football fan at heart, something I think the general public understood, even if they didn't understand every decision we made.

One of the first calls I took the following morning was from Rick Parry just checking I was okay. Once we had established all was fine, he asked me which match I was going to at the weekend.

'I don't know – as you can imagine I haven't looked at the fixtures yet,' I said. 'Well, I do. You are coming home to Anfield.'

A lovely gesture which I appreciated. And, sure enough, I watched Liverpool beat Middlesbrough 2-1 that Saturday afternoon. Rick himself left Liverpool Football Club as its CEO the following spring. Some fans saw him and former chairman David Moores to blame for Hicks and Gillett being at the club. I can only speak as I find, and throughout my dealings with both Rick and David, I always found them genuinely passionate about the club, good to work with and to be around.

Two other comings and goings caught the eye. Benítez had bought Irish striker Robbie Keane from Tottenham Hotspur in July 2008 for over £12m. Keane never really settled at Anfield, felt he was being played out of position and in a bizarre turn of events was transferred back to White Hart Lane on 2 February 2009 for £16m.

One significantly longer-serving Liverpool great, Sami Hyypiä, bade farewell to the club after representing it magnificently for ten seasons. In the final home game of the 2008/09 season, against Spurs, Hyypiä was brought off the bench by Benítez, rather belatedly the Anfield crowd thought, and was given a hero's welcome and a hero's farewell. One of the club's most astute signings. The story goes that a TV cameraman who worked in football across Europe gave his name to Peter Robinson.

Chief scout Ron Yeats picked it up and Gérard Houllier landed this outstanding player for just £2.5m from Willem II. He went on to play 464 games for Liverpool. A genuine Anfield legend.

Kop That – *Andrea Dossena scored two goals in his brief Anfield career, but both came in memorable games – the 4-0 Anfield defeat of Real Madrid and four days later the 4-1 demolition of Manchester United at Old Trafford.*

2009/10 – ALL HAT, NO CATTLE

THE FINAL full season of the first decade of the new millennium for Liverpool Football Club was a toxic mixture of rancid disharmony off the pitch and a significant downturn in performance on it.

The tectonic plates were moving rapidly at Anfield. Americans Tom Hicks and George Gillett were becoming persona non grata at their own club. And so were their relatives too. Unacceptable levels of debt were being piled on the club, the blueprint for the new stadium was gathering dust and the pair's infrequent visits to Anfield had to be handled like a military operation.

Hollow sound bites and unfulfilled promises had infuriated Liverpool fans, who could see the prestigious heritage of their much-loved club going up in smoke. Reds' supporters really feared one of the most famous clubs in world football was heading for a financial meltdown, and even the ignominy of a spell in administration.

And the fans made 'big on talk, poor on delivery' Hicks and Gillett aware, in no uncertain terms, that the two US businessmen were not welcome at Anfield. To use a Texan phrase, the fans thought the American duo were 'all hat, no cattle …' Although the Liverpool fans said it in rather more direct language!

New men were brought in at the helm. Christian Purslow came in as the club's managing director, and Ian Ayre was settling into his role as commercial director. And in April 2010, the owners stepped down as joint chairmen and essentially put the club up for sale.

It wasn't just the *Footy Echo* now that was a vital 'pink' newspaper read on Merseyside. *The Financial Times* had almost become just as important for the committed Liverpool fan as they scanned the pages for any breaking news story on the economic welfare of their club. Everybody who cared about the future of LFC was trying to digest the league tables on a Monday morning and the business pages every other morning.

Perhaps it was an appropriate time to have returned to my home city as a Visiting Professor of Strategic Leadership in the Management School at the University of Liverpool, at the invitation of the football-mad vice-chancellor (and Derby County season ticket holder) Sir Howard Newby.

For me it was a simple case of wanting to give back something to the city that had given me so much in return. I ended up working part-time at my old university for nine years, much of it on the Football Industries MBA course, which had been created by long-time Liverpool fan and champion for supporters Rogan Taylor. Rogan and I would talk economics in the lecture theatre and Liverpool FC's latest fortunes in the canteen.

And another member of the FIMBA team was former Liverpool captain Phil Thompson who had become an established member of Sky Sports's very popular *Soccer Saturday* programme.

Back at Anfield, Martin Broughton, chairman of British Airways and Chelsea season ticket holder, was brought in as chairman of Liverpool Football Club to lead on the sale of the club.

Both Purslow and Broughton actually dropped into my office in Twickenham, ostensibly on other business, but the conversation soon got around to the complicated situation at Anfield.

Rafa Benítez also seemed increasingly unsettled at LFC, and it was no real surprise when at the end of the season he packed his bags and left by mutual consent. The Spanish coach had been at the club for six seasons and delivered major European and domestic honours, and would continue to be successful when he left Anfield, but his final campaign in charge of the Reds proved his poorest in terms of on-field achievement.

The Reds finished a very average seventh in the Premier League, having been runners-up the previous season. It was their lowest finish in 11 years, and with Steven Gerrard, by his own high standards, having an average season, and star striker Fernando Torres missing a substantial number of games through injury, the Reds managed only 18 wins and nine draws in Rafa Benítez's last season with the club.

In the close season, Sami Hyypiä and Xabi Alonso had left the club and the big-name buys were Alberto Aquilani from Roma and Glen Johnson from Portsmouth. Johnson would chalk up 200 appearances for Liverpool, Aquilani, a very talented ball player but recuperating from a serious ankle injury, failed to do himself justice at Anfield, and looked an expensive mistake by Benítez at over £17m. Indeed, Roma only sold him to Liverpool because they had financial problems of their own. Aquilani would end up returning to Italy on loan to Juventus the following season.

Liverpool's first eight games of the 2009/10 campaign were a mixture of five wins (including a hat-trick for Torres against Hull City) and three defeats. In their next game, at the Stadium of Light, the Reds lost to a freak goal scored by Sunderland's Darren Bent. Bent's shot was heading harmlessly towards Pepe Reina in the Liverpool goal when it struck a fully blown-up beachball, which had been thrown on by fans behind Reina's goal. The goal, in fact, where the Liverpool fans were stationed. What an own goal!

Indifferent league form in the autumn put Benítez under pressure, but important wins over Manchester United and Everton gave him some breathing space. A mid-December defeat against bottom-of-the-table Portsmouth was poorly received by the Anfield faithful, and the Reds' last match of the year at Aston Villa was a mid-season tussle for fourth place, won by a Torres goal in the third minute of stoppage time.

Liverpool completed the double over Everton in February, but in the home straight of the season, the Reds won just four of the last ten games.

No Champions League football for the Reds in the following season, and very nearly no European football at all. Finishing seventh they were out of the qualification slots for the Europa League as well, but Portsmouth, FA Cup Final runners-up, had failed to apply for a UEFA licence and Liverpool, as the best-placed team not qualified for the European competitions, took their place. In through the back door.

Early exits in the two 2009/10 domestic cup competitions were compounded by a poor performance in that season's Champions League, finishing third in the group stage, meaning, post-Christmas, they dropped into the last 32 of the Europa League. Wins against little-known Unirea of Romania, Lille and Benfica, lined them up against Atlético Madrid in the semi-final.

The Spaniards won the first leg 1-0, and then lost the second leg after extra time 2-1 but went through on away goals – both Madrid goals in the tie had been scored by an old adversary of Liverpool, ex-Manchester United striker Diego Forlan. He would score twice in the final too.

Aquilani had scored the goal to level the tie in only his 11th start for the Reds, and still rues the missed opportunity Liverpool endured that night.

'If we had won, we would have played Fulham in the final and so had a big chance of winning the Europa League. It would have been a first trophy for me and changed my luck – my life – at Liverpool.'

Aquilani would head off back to Italy on a year-long loan spell at Juventus. Fulham lost to Atlético Madrid in the Europa League Final, ex-Red Danny Murphy, a star of the Londoners' unlikely European adventure, captained the side, and for their experienced manager Roy Hodgson, Fulham's heroics had opened up a very unlikely opportunity.

Kop That – *Dirk Kuyt became the first overseas Liverpool player to score in both winning Merseyside derbies in a Premier League season. Sadio Mané was the second in 2016/17.*

2010/11 – HIGH NOON
AND HI KENNY!

THURSDAY, 14 October 2010 was a genuine red-letter day for Liverpool Football Club. In a vital decision that was the lead item on BBC TV's *10 o'clock News*, the High Court ended Hicks and Gillett's fractured ownership of a sporting institution formed some 118 years earlier, and that had been in real danger of being damaged beyond repair the longer those two Americans stayed on board.

Having received two excellent bids for the club, one from Asia and the other from the USA, the board, including Anfield executives Christian Purslow and Ian Ayre, had been given the task of selling the club and were keen to progress affairs with New England Sports Ventures.

And the High Court's ruling against Hicks and Gillett essentially allowed them to do just that. Hicks and Gillett gained a restraining order in a Texas court, but to no avail – the High Court in London ruled it ineffective.

NESV principal owner John W. Henry expressed his pride in their being confirmed as the new owners of Liverpool FC. 'We are committed first and foremost to winning. We have a history of winning and today we want LFC supporters to know that this approach is what we intend to bring to the club.'

The transaction valued the club at £300m and eliminated all the acquisition debt placed on LFC by its previous owners, reducing the club's annual debt servicing obligations from £25m–£30m to £2m–£3m. Liverpool chairman Martin Broughton, who had been brought in to lead the sale of the club, thought the new owners were the right fit. 'This is a good deal which comprehensively resolves the pressing issue of the club's debt and gives staff, players and fans great confidence regarding the future of Liverpool FC.' Tom Hicks later called the sale an 'epic swindle' but their time at the club was over, and Kopites cautiously welcomed the new owner.

NESV, through its Fenway Sports Group, could point to one of their country's own famous clubs, Major League Baseball's Boston Red Sox, as an example of how they had restored a club to its previous legendary status. The Red Sox's famous name had travelled around the world, but they hadn't won the Major League title since 1918 when the Fenway Sports Group bought the organisation in 2001.

In 2004, after a wait of some 86 years, the hoodoo was finally broken amid wild scenes of celebration in Boston, Massachusetts. The Red Sox have gone on to win it three more times since.

Liverpool fans hoped their new American owners could provide the spark to end Liverpool's seemingly endless hunt for the Premier League title – a mere 20 years when John Henry and co. first came on board. The journey with the Fenway Sports Group was underway, and they made a good early impression. And over the next decade Liverpool Football Club would enjoy some very special moments.

But, in time, they too would have some very awkward issues with their misunderstanding of what English football, the Premier League, and the unique football pyramid that lies below it, means to the people who play it, watch it, and read or view every aspect of it. And, above all that, love it. Harsh lessons would be learned in late April 2021. But that conflict was some years ahead. The new American owners' first taste of English football life was attending the Merseyside derby at Goodison Park just a couple of days after having acquired the club.

The Reds, under the new manager, Roy Hodgson, were struggling in the league, and so were Everton – something had to give. It would be fair to say the new Liverpool owners got a traditional warm welcome (!) from those Evertonians sitting near the directors' box. One prominent Evertonian, former local politician Derek Hatton, sitting to the left of the directors' box, handed out some choice advice to the new Americans.

I was sitting just a few seats from Hatton, a rabid Blue, who I had lived close to when we were both growing up in Liverpool. It would be fair to say he enjoyed his afternoon more than I did.

It was Everton's day – they won 2-0, and Hodgson's Reds were well beaten, although the Liverpool manager begged to differ in his after-match comments. 'I watched the performance and the second half was as good as I saw a Liverpool team play under my management, that's for sure.'

The Liverpool fans didn't agree. The clamour for the return to the manager's chair of Anfield hero Kenny Dalglish was building momentum. Second from bottom in the Premier League, the experienced and likeable Hodgson now owned the worst record of any Liverpool manager after eight league games since George Patterson in 1928.

And Liverpool were also already out of the Carling Cup, sent packing on a rainswept September evening at Anfield, losing on penalties to League Two side Northampton Town.

I had seen the Cobblers play the Reds in the First Division at Anfield back in 1965 – a 5-0 trouncing to Shankly's men that day (St John, Stevenson, Hunt, Callaghan and Thompson the scorers) – 45 years on finally came Northampton Town's revenge.

Just over 22,000 fans, many from Northampton, were there to witness the big cup upset, and interested spectators included Kenny Dalglish, then working as one of LFC's ambassadors and in and around the LFC Academy. I happened to be sitting next to him on the night. As the Reds struggled against their lower-league opponents, the familiar 'Dalglish' chants ringing out from the Kop, the great man's awkwardness was palpable. He was conscious that however well-meaning the chants were, they would not be missed by the current Liverpool manager having a tough night.

Throughout his short time at the club, Hodgson would cut a frustrated figure on the touchline at Anfield. Results were disappointing and, whilst he had a strong CV to fall back on, he never made a real connection with the fans, and, in the end, a dismal away defeat at Blackburn Rovers in the first week of January brought the curtain down on a disappointing six-month spell for Roy Hodgson at LFC. He would go on to manage England in the 2014 World Cup and do good things at West Brom and Crystal Palace.

Liverpool made an urgent call to a cruise ship in the Middle East to invite club legend Kenny Dalglish to help them out of a deep hole and take the manager's role on a temporary basis until the end of the season.

The proud Scotsman would have swum all the way home to take up the invitation, but a jet plane proved the more practical option. He was on the touchline at Old Trafford as Liverpool went down 1-0 in their FA Cup third-round tie with Alex Ferguson's Manchester United, captain Steven

Gerrard getting a red card for a dangerous tackle in the hard-fought match.

On the final day of the January transfer window all hell broke loose at Anfield. Fernando Torres moved to Chelsea in a £50m move to the London club, which the Spanish player had been pushing for in the months that preceded it. His touch and his temperament seemingly at odds with his proven ability, it was an unsatisfactory end to his Liverpool career.

Liverpool didn't let the enormous cheque burn in their pockets. On the same evening they signed Uruguayan striker Luis Suárez from Ajax for £22.8 m and then surprised the game's observers with a £35m capture of promising centre-forward Andy Carroll. The Reds had effectively got two for the price of one, and, in time, one would become a legendary figure at the club, and the other seemingly over-priced and injury prone.

Dalglish's influence, assisted by Steve Clarke, saw the Reds rise to a respectable sixth place in the Premier League, but without qualifying for European football the following season. It was a season when, amid managerial changes and high-stakes transfer activity, some of the lesser lights on the playing staff did some of the heavy lifting.

Players like Portuguese midfield man Raul Meireles; tough-tackling Greek defender Sotirios Kyrgiakos; Brazilian Lucas, whose slow start at Anfield would blossom into a ten-year career; and Argentine Maxi Rodríguez, a skilful forward who scored a hat-trick in a late-season thrashing of Fulham on a warm May evening at Craven Cottage. And as always, Dirk Kuyt put in a substantial shift and finished as the club's top scorer with 15 goals.

After the 2010/11 campaign drew to a close, Dalglish was offered a three-year contract as the club's permanent boss. What a season it had been. Liverpool now had new owners, a new chairman, a new CEO, a new manager and an expensive new strike force. It was a whole new dawn – optimism was high, but there was still one big nagging problem to solve.

How do you win the Premier League?

Kop That – *Liverpool's last game of the season saw them oppose Gary McAllister's Aston Villa, where Stewart Downing scored the only goal of the game. Downing's next league game was with the Reds on the opening day of the following season.*

2011/12 – THE FLAWED
LITTLE GENIUS

I FIRST saw Luis Suárez live in action in the 2010 World Cup in South Africa. He was playing for Uruguay in their quarter-final against Ghana in Soccer City, Johannesburg. It was the first time football's premier competition had taken place on the continent of Africa. The indigenous people had excitedly embraced their selection as hosts, and now an African team looked like going further in the competition than any other had before.

We had loved the freshness of the Cameroon sides in previous World Cups, but this time on African soil, Ghana looked capable of doing great things. They had successfully come through a tough group, and then knocked USA out in the round of 16. Their quarter-final with Uruguay was 1-1 when in the final moments of extra time a Ghanaian free kick was launched into the South Americans' penalty area. Suárez, on the line, blocked a first effort but then blatantly stopped the rebounding header from Ghana's Dominic Adiyiah with his hands.

A certain goal illegally prevented. An immediate red card for Suárez. And then Ghana dramatically missed the penalty – the last kick of the game – that would have taken them into the semi-finals of the World Cup. Uruguay would ultimately win the tie on penalties. Suárez was captured celebrating Asamoah Gyan's last-gasp missed penalty. Back in Uruguay, the nation celebrated with him. In South Africa he was labelled a 'cheat and a villain'. In the summer of 2011, Suárez would be named as the 'player of the tournament' as Uruguay won the Copa América.

Luis Alberto Suárez Díaz was born in the Uruguayan city of Salto in January 1987. He played for Nacional in Uruguay, and then moved to the Netherlands and played for Groningen before moving to Dutch giants Ajax. He amassed a century of goals for the club, was made club captain and named Dutch Footballer of the Year in 2010. A biting incident against PSV Eindhoven's Otman Bakal cost Suárez a seven-match ban, which meant when he arrived at Anfield in January 2011, he wasn't fully match fit.

Still, just two days after signing for Liverpool, Kenny Dalglish named him as a substitute in a home game against Stoke City. He came on in the 63rd minute and scored 16 minutes later. A clever goal, and the Anfield crowd took to him straight away.

It was the first of 82 goals in just 133 games, goals that would take your breath away – he would score in ones, twos, threes and even fours, and by the time he left Anfield in July 2014, certain clubs were sick of the sight of him. Ask Norwich City fans!

He was a genius. He would chase down impossible passes and emerge with the ball; his subtle movement would send not just his opponents the wrong way, but the crowd as well. And when he scored, his celebrations always included pointing to the provider, invariably Steven Gerrard.

He was a one-off. Popular with his team-mates and feared by his opponents. He would miss too many matches through lengthy suspensions but would rarely miss a game through injury, and he would get off a plane from international duty in South America and be ready to play for the Reds from the moment the aircraft touched down in England.

Where does Luis Suárez fit in the Reds' all-time greats? Right up there for me for his talent, although serious on-field indiscretions, and the relative shortness of his stay at Anfield, would count against him. Mind you, when he left Anfield in 2014, he was going to Barcelona to team up with Lionel Messi!

Liverpool's 2011/12 Premier League season started with a home draw against Sunderland – Suárez scored the Reds' goal, having previously missed a penalty which he himself had won after being brought down in the box.

That home game marked the debuts of summer signings Charlie Adam, Stewart Downing, José Enrique, and a certain Jordan Henderson. His place in Anfield folklore lay in the future.

The first half of the season brought a reasonable return of 34 points, including away wins at Arsenal, Everton and Chelsea.

Their 1-1 home draw against Manchester United was marred by the accusation that Luis Suárez had racially abused United full-back Patrice Evra. Suárez argued that his use of a racially unacceptable term meant something different in Spanish than it would in English. Liverpool defended him fiercely. Too fiercely for many. It dominated the media for several weeks, and the club's reputation, and that of his supportive manager, took a hit. Despite declaring his innocence Suárez was eventually given a stiff eight-match suspension, the thorough final report on the case running to 115 pages.

When the two teams met later in the season there was huge interest as to whether the two players would shake each other's hands as per the Premier League prematch protocols. They didn't, and Suárez was blamed for not offering his hand. And his manager Kenny Dalglish's support for his player was seen as condoning his actions. Both Liverpool men subsequently apologised for their part in an unsavoury episode.

If the first half of the season had been acceptable, Liverpool's Premier League form from January onwards dipped alarmingly. The Reds won only five of their 19 league fixtures in the second half of the season. And, in one damaging sequence, they won just one of nine matches. Mind you, that was against Everton – it completed a double over their Merseyside rivals, and included a hat-trick from captain Steven Gerrard.

A week later I was at Loftus Road and watched the Reds squander a 2-0 lead by letting relegation-threatened QPR score three in the last 13 minutes of the game. A late-season victory included a hat-trick for Suárez in a 3-0 win at Norwich City, and not his last against the East Anglian side.

In the final match of the 2010/11 season, they would lose 1-0 at Swansea. It told the story of Liverpool's uneven league campaign. And taking only 18 points from the second half of the campaign left them lying in eighth at the end of the season, their joint-lowest Premier League finish since finishing in the same position in 1994.

Now, one of the things that frustrated me most around this time was that Liverpool had still to make their debut in the new Wembley Stadium. They had played that often at the old stadium between 1970 and 2000 that it was lovingly dubbed 'Anfield South' by Liverpool fans. I had been to many of those occasions, and there was something special about the Reds going about their business underneath the Twin Towers. The country's best team playing in the country's biggest stadium. It was the right fit.

It had been on my shift as FA CEO that the new stadium was finally finished and opened by the FA president Prince

William ahead of the 2007 FA Cup Final between Manchester United and Chelsea. I admit to feeling very proud on that day accompanying our royal guest on to the Wembley pitch to make his short address and formally open the stadium.

I then waited over four and half seasons to see 'my lot' play there. By which time all sorts of teams had made their 'new' Wembley bow – from the biggest to some of the smallest – England, Brazil, Tottenham Hotspur, Aston Villa, Everton, Portsmouth, Cardiff City, Manchester City, Stoke City, Ebbsfleet, Stevenage Borough, Dagenham and Redbridge, Barrow, Whitley Bay, Glossop North End, Coalville Town ...

And St Helens, Wigan Warriors, Leeds Rhinos and Warrington Wolves from rugby league. The Miami Dolphins hosted the New York Giants at Wembley Stadium in NFL action in October 2007. And new F1 champion Lewis Hamilton drove his title-winning McLaren Mercedes around a figure of eight track set up in the stadium. The Wembley groundsman needed a sedative after seeing what that particular event had done to his beloved Wembley turf!

Even Muse, George Michael, Metallica and Take That beat Liverpool to playing at the new Wembley.

It was time for the Reds to regain their squatting rights. And it finally came in triplicate with three appearances in 70 days in the early part of 2012. On Sunday, 26 February the Reds faced Cardiff City in the Carling Cup Final. It was the Welsh team's fourth visit to the new Wembley Stadium. The Reds were about to play in their 11th Football League Cup Final. Their last win? In Cardiff.

It proved to be a tough match for Kenny Dalglish's men. They went 1-0 down in the first half and equalised through Škrtel on the hour. 1-1 at full time, and in extra time substitute Dirk Kuyt put the Reds in front, only for the Welsh team to pull things level in the game's final moments.

A penalty shoot-out for Liverpool under the arch at the new Wembley. Steven Gerrard missed the Reds' first penalty, and spot-kick expert Charlie Adam their second. Kuyt, Stewart Downing and Glen Johnson all notched for Liverpool and Anthony Gerrard, Steven's cousin, crucially missed Cardiff's fifth penalty. For the eighth time, the Reds had won the League Cup, their first piece of silverware for six years.

On Saturday, 14 April, Liverpool met Everton at the new Wembley Stadium. David Moyes's Blues fancied their chances – the Reds' early-spring form had been disappointing. Everton's fans were up for it, and went wild when their team took the lead through Jelavić in the 24th minute. If ever there was a match for Everton to press home their advantage, this was it, but Moyes went safety first and a goal from Luis Suárez in the 62nd minute squared the game, and left both sets of supporters knowing there would only be one outcome.

And, sure enough, a header from Andy Carroll three minutes from time sealed the deal for the Reds.

Saturday, 5 May – the FA Cup Final – Chelsea v Liverpool.

An unpopular 5.15pm kick-off gave Reds followers problems on return rail journeys, and Didier Drogba was on target again, adding a second Chelsea goal after half-time. Ramires had scored their first in the 11th minute.

The 54th-minute substitution of Andy Carroll for midfielder Jay Spearing gave Liverpool a bit more menace up front. The big man pulled one goal back after 64 minutes, and then with a towering header seemed to have equalised. Petr Čech made a brilliant save, but was the ball over the line? From where I was sitting it looked like it was, but with no goal-line technology nobody could be sure other than referee Phil Dowd, who waved play on. Gutting.

Liverpool would beat the Londoners 4-1 at Anfield in the Premier League three days after their Wembley clash, and

Roberto Di Matteo's men would end the season as European champions for the first time with a win over Bayern Munich.

And on 16 May Kenny Dalglish lost his job as Liverpool's manager. His legendary status at Anfield was already secure, and, indeed, the depth of that respect would be most positively illustrated in years to come.

Kop That – *Although Ian Rush holds the record of scoring the most FA Cup goals with five, Didier Drogba's goal in the 2012 final saw him become the first player to score in four different finals.*

2012/13 – AMBITIONS REALISED!

'BARWICK SIGNS FOR LIVERPOOL!'

YES, THE headline that I had spent most of my childhood days, teenage years, 20s, 30s (and even 40s and 50s) dreaming of finally landed in 2012.

Don't panic. I wasn't being asked to join Liverpool's new manager Brendan Rodgers's first-team squad – nobody was that desperate. Although, just in case, I did dive into the garden shed to find my old white Hummel boots (the ones Everton's Alan Ball made famous, but more importantly for me, Tommy Smith also wore for a while – and nobody was going to tell him he looked a bit odd in them!).

No, my playing days were officially well and truly over (some critics would say they never actually started), and I was not in the running to replace Kenny Dalglish as the Reds' next manager either. Swansea's Brendan Rogers was about to take over the managerial reins at Anfield, for what would be an exciting few years.

What Liverpool Football Club's new chairman Tom Werner and LFC CEO Ian Ayre signed me and my company Barwick Media and Sport up to do was to study their fledgling club channel LFCTV for three months, and advise them on what I felt worked, what didn't and what was needed to take the enterprise to the next level in terms of content and style.

Werner was a hugely successful American broadcast figure in his own right but was still getting used to the life and times of Liverpool Football Club. For me, it was falling back on my 25 years of sports broadcasting experience, my in-depth knowledge of the 'Liverpool FC story' and knowing where some of the best unseen archive material still could be found. It was a labour of love and I have the final report in front of me right now. It is grandly entitled, 'LFC Media – The Way Forward' and runs to 47 pages. Its key message seems to have been to get the channel in shipshape order ready to make a connection with the club's growing global fan base online.

And so, they did. I still watch LFCTV regularly and it has matured into a very watchable channel, serving up the club's news, action, analysis, interviews with current players and legends of the past, and some expertly made documentaries.

If 'signing' for Liverpool was one ambition realised, another one came along at the same time. I was approached by the *Liverpool Echo*'s sports editor John Thompson to write a regular full-page column in *The Post*, their new weekly edition of their former morning paper *The Daily Post*. I was delighted to accept. Not least because I was given the freedom to write about the breadth of the sporting world, not just the two local juggernauts, Liverpool and Everton. And also, because the offer of this new role came some 35 years after my enthusiastic letter to the *Liverpool Echo* applying for a vacancy as a junior reporter had been returned with the usual two-sentence rejection.

I ended up writing a fortnightly column across a mixture of the *Echo*'s titles for nearly ten years, and enjoyed doing it enormously. And it kept me firmly in touch with my home town, and the life and times of all things Anfield.

Mind you, in the summer of 2012, all eyes were on the capital itself as London staged the Olympic Games. From a spectacular opening ceremony through to the Olympic flame being extinguished 16 days later, the country was transfixed with the world's greatest sports stars and performing at their peak in their chosen discipline. And for Team GB, it was a resounding success. They finished third behind the USA and China with 65 medals, including a post-war record of 29 golds.

Day eight, 4 August, would be immortalised as 'Super Saturday' with six gold medals for the Brits, including a remarkable three athletics gold medals in just 46 minutes in the Olympic Stadium, with Jessica Ennis in the heptathlon, Greg Rutherford in the men's long jump and Mo Farah in the men's 10,000 metres creating sporting history.

Along with millions of other keen sports fans I had sent my ticket wish list into the ballot, and ended up with a good mix of events, including boxing at the Copper Box Arena, where I witnessed the rise and rise of British heavyweight Anthony Joshua; weightlifting, football, a couple of evenings at the athletics and the closing ceremony itself.

The closest I got to the action came for free as the men's cycling road race literally sped past us at the bottom of our road in Twickenham. And boy, do those guys go fast. One of the stars of the Games, Bradley Wiggins, won the men's time trial just ten days after winning that summer's Tour de France. It was a feat felt to be impossible but not to Wiggins, who became one of *the* stories of the Games. Wiggins, uniquely landed both yellow and gold that summer but had a very strong penchant for Red as a devoted Liverpool fan with two season tickets in the Kop.

He got many good luck messages ahead of his Olympic exertions, but the one he said he treasured the most was from 'God' – Robbie Fowler – who sent Wiggins his best wishes for

London 2012 having been captivated by the Kopite's victory in the Tour de France. Wiggins was knighted in the New Year Honours list.

Brendan Rodgers had been named as Liverpool's new manager on 1 June 2012. His work at Swansea City had got him noticed, the Welsh side performing with a real swagger, playing the ball out from the back, promoting a passing game and keeping the ball on the deck. Andy Carroll would be an early casualty of that change of style.

If Kenny Dalglish had been relatively short on words to the media, Rodgers was the complete opposite. In fact, it ultimately worked against him. Liverpool also were filmed 'up close and personal' for a documentary series – a risk worth taking? Perhaps. And now something that has become the norm. But back then it did carry the odd risk.

Two of the more memorable images in the series were the full-size portrait of Rodgers on his own lounge wall, and of CEO Ian Ayre enjoying a bit of R and R whilst riding his sparkling Harley-Davidson motorcycle in front of the River Mersey. One player who took warmly to Brendan Rodgers was Luis Suárez, who liked what he heard when the man from Northern Ireland explained his coaching philosophy, in fluent Spanish.

Rodgers's first season in charge was actually a bit of a curate's egg of a campaign. No wins in his first five league games until up popped Suárez with a hat-trick in a 5-2 away win at Norwich City. For the Canaries goalkeeper John Ruddy, it was a case of déjà vu, and he took it in good heart. 'Always you! Hey, next time, don't worry about turning up, alright.' When Suárez left for Barcelona, Ruddy joked on Twitter that he surely deserved a cut of the transfer fee.

Never far from the back-page headlines, Suárez would be sent off for biting the arm of Chelsea's Branislav Ivanović at

Anfield in April 2013. His latest extraordinary transgression landed him a ten-game ban that ended up being spread across the end of the 2012/13 season and the beginning of the one that followed it.

Liverpool finished seventh in the table, out of the European places, went out in the round of 32 in the Europa League and were sensationally knocked out of the FA Cup by League One side Oldham Athletic, 3-2, Suárez being made captain for Liverpool that match. And Rodgers's former club Swansea City took care of the Reds in a fourth-round League Cup tie at Anfield. Much to work on then for the likeable new Liverpool boss, but activity in the transfer market offered signs of a positive future ahead for LFC.

In the January 2013 transfer window Liverpool signed Daniel Sturridge and Philippe Coutinho. If the Kopites knew all about Sturridge, they knew a lot less about the little 20-year-old Brazilian Coutinho, who was signed from Inter Milan for £8.5m.

Coutinho would become a hero at Anfield, the scorer and maker of great goals. When he left in 2018, he would cost his new club Barcelona £140m all in, a transfer fee that helped Jürgen Klopp fund key world-class building blocks to his developing Reds side in ace defender Virgil van Dijk and goalkeeper supreme Alisson.

One player who said goodbye to his playing days at Anfield at the end of the 2012/13 season was Jamie Carragher, a special Liverpool player, and one whose 737 appearances for the Reds leave him in second place in Liverpool's all-time appearances charts behind the great Ian Callaghan (857 apps).

Carragher, the Bootle Boy made good, was held in the highest esteem by the knowledgeable Liverpool crowd. They knew a player when they saw one, and in the modern era of players from all over the world, dropping in to play a few seasons before moving on, there was something reassuring in having local boys Carragher and Gerrard giving it their absolute all *on* the pitch, and *off* it too, making it clear to team-mates in the dressing room what was expected of them as Liverpool players as they prepared to go into battle.

Carragher summed up his philosophy to the game when he said, 'I've trained every day as if it was a match and disciplined myself to make sure that every training session and every game counts.'

A total football nut, team-mate Steven Gerrard would say, 'Carra is a student of the game. He is always reading books about football. Conversations with Carra are 90 per cent football. Ask Carra any football question and he'll answer before you've finished!'

Jamie's 737th and final game for Liverpool was against QPR at Anfield on 19 May 2013, and he very nearly rounded off his splendid career with a spectacular goal from long distance.

A true Anfield great who has become a leading football pundit on Sky Sports, where he uses his experience and know-how to help illuminate their coverage – and his on-screen banter with once-sworn enemy Gary Neville makes very entertaining television.

Kop That – *Daniel Sturridge, by scoring against Mansfield Town, Manchester United and Norwich became the first player to score in his first three games for the club since Ray Kennedy in 1974.*

2013/14 – MANY A SLIP

IF YOU have ever doubted whether world-class footballers actually care about their work, given the fame and remarkable fortune that is now guaranteed to go with it, I suggest you read a section from Steven Gerrard's autobiography *My Story*.

It tells you about his troubled build-up to one of the most important matches he ever played in for Liverpool. He then goes on to explain, in detail, the moment in time when his accidental 'slip' put paid to the Reds' chances of landing that elusive first Premier League title.

And it takes you inside the immediate aftermath, torment and torture the Liverpool captain went through reliving the 'moment', and how he still finds that split second of misfortune a recurring nightmare. This from a player that truly graced Anfield, led from the front, pulled rabbits out of hats time and again for the Reds, and stayed loyal to the cause despite lucrative offers to ply his trade elsewhere.

We will return to *that* match, *that* slip, *that* moment in time – 27 April 2014 – Liverpool v Chelsea – in due course.

Steven Gerrard had spent most of the previous summer concentrating on one objective – to keep the mercurial Luis Suárez at Anfield. The Uruguayan wanted away. And he felt Liverpool had promised he could leave at the end of the

2012/13 season if the Reds hadn't qualified for the Champions League. And they hadn't.

He was also completely fed up with the level of media interest in his daily life, on and off the pitch. And how he had been portrayed. He wanted out.

The Liverpool hierarchy, including owner John W. Henry and manager Brendan Rodgers, were standing firm – their star player was under contract and not going to be sold. And certainly not to Premier League rivals Arsenal, who put a cheeky bid exactly one pound above the £40m transfer threshold that was believed to be in Suárez's contract.

This strong-willed position by the Fenway Sports Group was somewhat driven by how American sport dealt with its major assets – its star players. But this was a five-star stand-off which involved Suárez not being allowed to train with the first-team squad, or indeed be at Melwood at the same time they were there. And to add a further complication, Suárez was still only halfway through the ten-match ban he had received for biting Chelsea's Branislav Ivanović in the previous season.

Steven Gerrard took on the role of peacemaker, or at least tried to persuade Luis Suárez to give LFC one more season, if he was still hell-bent on leaving Anfield. And it was an uphill battle – Suárez was furious with the club, and the imposed splendid isolation from his team-mates.

Gerrard had been tempted to leave Anfield at one stage of his career but made the right call for both himself and the club that he loved. And, against the odds, he now helped manage to find a way to keep Suárez on board at Anfield, and at relative peace with the club.

Why did Steven Gerrard work so hard with his South American team-mate, part Merlin, part menace? Well, partly self-interest – he knew a Liverpool team with Suárez in it was a force to be reckoned with – without him just a decent outfit.

The answer may also lie on a framed Liverpool shirt that is fixed to the lounge wall in Luis Suárez's home back in Uruguay. It is signed by Steven Gerrard with the simple message to Suárez. 'The best I ever played with.'

The 2013/14 season was the high watermark of Brendan Rodgers's time in the hot seat at Anfield. Without European football and relatively early exits from the two domestic cup competitions, the Reds could genuinely 'concentrate on the league', and did so to great effect.

They played with great flair and scored goals for fun – 101 league goals in 38 matches. Luis Suárez won the Premier League's Golden Boot with 31 strikes, whilst Daniel Sturridge was the league's second-highest scorer with 21 goals.

Suárez would also be named Footballer of the Year by both the FWA and the PFA. This was the Liverpool of Suárez, Sturridge, Sterling, Coutinho and Gerrard all on the front foot, Jordan Henderson, developing as a midfield player, and a new goalkeeper between the posts. Simon Mignolet followed Henderson from Sunderland to Liverpool and in his Premier League debut saved a penalty to guarantee maximum points in the season's opener against Stoke City at Anfield.

Two further wins away at Aston Villa and at home against Manchester United gave the Reds a solid start to the season – and Luis Suárez rejoined the party in late September with a two-goal burst at Sunderland. He followed it up with the opening goal against Crystal Palace at Anfield and then a hat-trick against West Brom. His strike partner, Sturridge, was also regularly on the scoresheet.

A lively 3-3 draw at Goodison Park was followed by a surprise defeat at Hull City. The Reds' response was electric – four wins on the bounce, scoring 17 goals in the process. Norwich City were beaten 5-1 (four more for Suárez), West Ham United 4-1 (two for Suárez), a remarkable 5-0 win at

Spurs (Suárez two) and finally a 3-1 home win over Cardiff City (Suárez two).

Two back-to-back defeats over the Christmas period, to title rivals Manchester City and Chelsea, halted the runaway Red train. But as Liverpool went into the new year, they went on a run of league form that made them favourites to win the Premier League title.

Fourteen wins and two draws in 16 matches. The football they played was the among the best we had seen for years. There was a 4-0 Anfield demolition of Everton in January, and a pulsating 5-1 home win over Arsenal. A Saturday lunchtime kick-off, it was a great day to be at Anfield watching in awe as Liverpool were four goals to the good within the first 20 minutes.

Into March, and Liverpool went to Old Trafford and hammered the home side 3-0. This time, Steven Gerrard converting two penalties.

A week later it was to Wales, and a 6-3 win at Cardiff and yet another hat-trick for Suárez. With 31 matches played, Chelsea were top with 69 points, Liverpool had one point less and Manchester City were third on 66 points but with two games in hand.

On Saturday, 29 March, things turned in Liverpool's favour. Chelsea surprisingly lost 1-0 to Crystal Palace and Manchester City were held to a 1-1 draw with Arsenal at the Emirates. It was now clear if Liverpool won all of their remaining seven matches, the Premier League title would be won. And there was a real sense that it was 'on'. The level of expectation was growing by the minute, and the remarkable matchday scenes as the Liverpool team coach made its slow progress to Anfield ahead of these closing games of the season graphically told its own story.

Flags, banners, flares, chants and songs – all aimed at giving the players the signal that 'we believe' so you guys should too. Tottenham were blown away 4-0, and an away trip to West Ham delivered another three points.

For the next home game – Manchester City – the prematch raucous welcome was there again for the Liverpool team coach. However, complete and utter silence was observed immediately ahead of the game as the crowd showed their respects for the 96 victims of the Hillsborough disaster, just two days away from the 25th anniversary of that dreadful event. The silence was profound.

In bright sunshine, the match itself was dramatic. An early goal by Sterling, followed by a header from Škrtel gave the Reds a 2-0 lead at half-time.

City bounced back to level the game just after the hour, before Liverpool's little magician, Coutinho, guided the winner home at the Anfield Road End. 3-2.

Cue pandemonium. The crowd were ecstatic, and the captain had a heady mixture of excitement and emotion. He pulled the team together in a huddle and drilled his message home. 'We go to Norwich. And we do exactly the same. We go again. COME ON.'

Two days later, it was another beautiful afternoon at Anfield, and this time the complete centre of attention were the 96 who had lost their lives at Hillsborough. 24,000 people attended the annual Hillsborough Memorial Service, and once again the dignity and courage of those most intimately affected by those tragic events shone through. 'Justice ... for the 96' rang out around Anfield. Sustained and supported by all there.

Heading to Norwich the league table looked rosy Red. Liverpool 34 games/77 points, Chelsea 35/75 and Manchester City 33/71. The Reds were two up in 11 minutes at Carrow Road, Sterling scoring on four minutes and Suárez seven minutes later. His now routine goal against the Canaries. Liverpool left East Anglia 3-2 winners and now seemingly nailed on for the title, but one team, and one man, could still spoil the party – Chelsea and José Mourinho.

Chelsea were unlikely to actually win the Premier League, and the fixture fell between their two-legged Champions League semi-final with Atlético Madrid, but Mourinho always seemed to have scores to settle with Liverpool, and here was another chance to do just that. Steven Gerrard knew all about Mourinho, and knew he would have a plan. The Liverpool captain had dual concerns – firstly his back was playing up. He was in agony, and it was keeping him awake. It is the stuff us fans never hear about. He ultimately needed an injection to get him over the line.

Secondly, Gerrard felt the Liverpool boss Brendan Rodgers was just a little over-confident that his team would do to the Londoners what they had to Manchester City and Norwich City. Gerrard had his reservations. They were also without the suspended Jordan Henderson.

Mourinho picked a strong team and gave them their instructions – slow the game down and waste as much time as possible.

I had been at all the Anfield games in this dramatic title run-in and just sensed a more tense atmosphere in the stadium that afternoon. Upbeat, for sure, but tense all the same. No goals and into first-half injury time, the game-changing moment, the season-changing moment.

Coutinho passed to Sakho. Sakho aimed a pass in Gerrard's direction. Just a run-of-the-mill pass, nothing out of the ordinary. Gerrard went to trap the ball, but it slid under his right foot – his concentration more on Chelsea's Demba Ba. He turned to correct himself, and slipped. And went down.

Ba, seeing the ball go free, chased in from the centre circle and took control of the ball, heading towards the Liverpool goal at the Kop end. Time seemed to freeze. In truth, it was just all over in seconds, as Ba confidently put the ball past Mignolet. 0-1. Gerrard devastated.

Chelsea saw out the second half much as they had the first 45 minutes. Then to rub it in, former Liverpool hero Fernando Torres teed up Willian to score a late second goal. Mourinho was ecstatic.

Steven Gerrard was inconsolable, driven home in tears. He, his wife Alex and a close friend flew out of the country for a couple of days to try and clear his mind. That slip, just a moment in time, looms as large in Gerrard's memory as any of his outstanding achievements for his beloved Reds. It says as much about him as a person as it does a world-class sportsman. A man who cares, who is committed, and who is harder on himself than others.

Liverpool went to Crystal Palace still with an outside chance of the title, and in blowing a 3-0 lead left London with a point.

The final game of the season was a home win over Newcastle United – but Reds fans' transistor radios were held to their ears much more in hope than expectation. Manchester City duly secured the result that won them the title. Liverpool had finished runners-up.

Kop That – *Mo Salah's first game at Anfield was in the decisive Anfield defeat to Chelsea in April 2014. Three years later he scored on his Liverpool debut in a 3-3 draw at Watford.*

2014/15 – ONE OF A KIND

IF STEVEN Gerrard thought Luis Suárez was 'the best he had ever played with', the 2014 World Cup in Brazil gave him an unwelcome taste of what it was like 'to play against him'.

Roy Hodgson's England had travelled to Brazil with the usual mass media party in tow – as always, our hopes outstripped the likelihood of success. But we watched the matches on TV in our tens of millions, often from behind the settee, such was the nerve-shredding experience of willing on our heroes to great things whilst preparing ourselves for the worst.

England's draw in the 2014 World Cup saw a tough opening group game against Italy to be played in the heart of the Amazon rainforest, followed by a potentially explosive tussle with Uruguay, with Suárez and Cavani up front for the South Americans. Costa Rica would have seemed to be the makeweight in the group, but it didn't prove the case.

Gerrard was the England captain, and proud to be it. And another four Liverpool players, Glen Johnson, Jordan Henderson, Raheem Sterling and Daniel Sturridge, made the starting line-up against the Italians. Soaked in sweat even whilst singing the national anthem, England went behind to a goal from Marchisio, but before half-time Sturridge had levelled it up for England following a move involving Sterling and Wayne Rooney.

Hodgson's men sensed they could actually win the game, despite the well-proven maxim that not losing the opening group game in a tournament is a very acceptable outcome. And England did lose the match to a Mario Balotelli header – Balotelli's next goal in top-class football would be for Liverpool. Get your head around that.

Uruguay had lost their first group match too – a surprise 3-1 win for Costa Rica. So, the stakes were really high when 'Gerrard met Suárez' in the Arena de São Paulo five days on from England's cloudburst in the Brazilian rainforest. This time in a city teeming with people, the little Uruguayan would have his day. A brilliant Suárez header from a Cavani cross put his team ahead.

Rooney would equalise for England 15 minutes from full time – once again a 1-1 draw looked a decent result, and once again England blew it. Five minutes from time, the Uruguayan goalkeeper Fernando Muslera launched a long kick over the halfway line. In trying to stem its progress, Steven Gerrard rose to head it – it skidded off the top of his head, and Suárez was the first to read its deflected trajectory, with England defenders nowhere in sight. He was on to it like a flash, let the ball bounce before hammering past Joe Hart in the England goal. 2-1.

On the final whistle, the two great Liverpool team-mates briefly acknowledged each other, and then moved on, one to the delight of victory, the other to the despair of defeat and elimination.

England's last game was a tedious goalless draw with Costa Rica but a sudden newsflash from ITV's match commentator Clive Tyldesley that Suárez had been involved in another biting episode in their final group game with Italy woke us all up from our slumbers.

'Bye everybody!' said an astute Mr Tyldesley as he knew we were all in the process of switching over to ITV4 to watch live coverage of *Carry on Chomping* or Uruguay v Italy as it was more formally called.

Gerrard was on his way home from Brazil, and Suárez, with another lengthy ban from all football activities, was on his way out of Anfield and off to Barcelona for £65m. He would score in the Champions League Final the following May as Barcelona beat Juventus 3-1.

Liverpool had got busy in the transfer market, spending £117m on no less than eight players. Rickie Lambert, Adam Lallana and Dejan Lovren came to Anfield from Southampton for a total of £49m, Lazar Marković from Benfica for £20m, Emre Can and Divock Origi for £10m apiece from Bayer Leverkusen and Lille, respectively, Alberto Moreno from Sevilla for £12m and, late in the 2014/15 summer transfer window, the complex character Mario Balotelli for £16m from AC Milan. Money well spent? Not all of it, that's for sure.

One signature that didn't appear on a new contract was that of club captain Steven Gerrard. Now 34, Gerrard knew his distinguished career as a player at Anfield was drawing to a close, but with one year left on his existing contract he was looking for a one-year extension. By the time an offer finally arrived, Gerrard's mindset was that it was probably time to look elsewhere, and an interesting new challenge presented itself at LA Galaxy in America's MLS.

Gerrard's final season was one of stops and starts, Rodgers trying to ease his captain through the season. For the Liverpool captain it proved frustrating. Sitting on the bench in the Champions League group game away at Real Madrid was a low point for Gerrard in his final season, a game in which Brendan Rodgers was fiercely criticised for not playing a full-strength side. He was resting some of his key players for the following weekend's home game with Chelsea, which they ended up losing anyway.

Rodgers's expectation that the Reds would pick up enough points in their two remaining Champions League group games for qualification to the knockout stages proved to be unfounded. Liverpool won only one of their six group games in total and were out of the Champions League. And their consolation of competing in the UEFA Europa League only lasted one round, going out on penalties to Turkish side Beşiktaş, a certain Demba Ba scoring for Beşiktaş in the shoot-out.

Gerrard was also sent off against Manchester United at Anfield just 38 seconds after coming on as a substitute at the start of the second half. United went on to win the game 2-1. The Reds ended the season in sixth position in the Premier League, having won just 18 of their games.

Liverpool's best form was reserved for the two domestic cup competitions, reaching the semi-finals in both. Aston Villa beat Rodgers's men in their FA Cup semi-final at Wembley. I happened to be on holiday in Dubai that week, but I soon got a sense of the magnitude of Villa's win from my son Joe. A fanatical Villa fan, he was whooping and hollering down the phone to me from Wembley. One very happy chap. He was quieter after Arsenal thrashed his favourites 4-0 in the FA Cup Final itself.

In the League Cup, the Reds were involved in a remarkable third-round tie with Middlesbrough. 2-2 after extra time, the teams were only split after a penalty shoot-out that lasted 30 spot kicks. 14-13 to Liverpool including successful conversions from the likes of Balotelli (twice), Lucas (twice), Lallana (twice) and Suso (twice). He had scored in extra time as well. Only Raheem Sterling missed for Liverpool. Liverpool came up short in a two-legged semi-final with Chelsea (who else!), losing 2-1 on aggregate.

Steven Gerrard's final games for Liverpool were memorable. Banners celebrated his unique contribution to the club. 'One of a Kind' proclaimed one set of fans' thanks. At an away game at Stamford Bridge Gerrard was given a standing ovation by the crowd, led by manager José Mourinho, as he was substituted in the second half. The mutual appreciation of those two major football figures is well known.

At his final home game, a 3-1 defeat to Crystal Palace could not dampen the occasion. Given a guard of honour on to the pitch, he was serenaded by the Kop throughout the game and after the final whistle, his playing colleagues emerged from the dressing room all wearing number eight shirts bearing Gerrard's name, as he took a lap of honour around Anfield.

Liverpool's final match of the season was a disastrous 6-1 defeat at Stoke City, Gerrard, of course, scoring the Reds' only goal of the game. A true legend of the club, and I was pleased to attend the Liverpool Players' Awards Evening, where he won an Outstanding Achievement Award. Surely the time will come when he takes his place as the manager of the club he has graced as a player over 700 times.

The loudest cheers on that awards evening were reserved for two former players, who were the foundation of Bill Shankly's Red revolution. Fifty years on from winning the FA Cup for the very first time, Ron Yeats, the captain, and Ian St John, scorer of the winning goal that day at Wembley back in 1965, were given a standing ovation.

Two elderly gentlemen who were the very backbone of the modern Liverpool Football Club.

Kop That – *In October 2014 Liverpool retained the Women's Super League title despite trailing Chelsea on the last day of the season. The Reds beat Bristol 3-0, and Chelsea lost at Manchester City, with Liverpool lifting the trophy on goal difference.*

2015/16 – THE PERFECT FIT

'WHAT WE can do is give people a distraction, make people happy ... I cannot do anything to improve the political circumstances, I can't change anything about the social reality – but we can give these people a moment of happiness.'

Sound familiar? The quote has echoes of the great Bill Shankly, and the wonderful ability he had to emotionally charge a willing and hungry public.

In fact, they were the words of a German football coach – Jürgen Klopp. In May 2011, Borussia Dortmund (BVB) had finally won their seventh German championship – their first Bundesliga title since 2002 – and the city in the heart of the Ruhr partied like never before. They were a proud German football club that had fallen on hard times – poor leadership and chronic financial mismanagement had sent them on a downward spiral.

Gone were the heady days of the UEFA Champions League and Intercontinental Cup victories of 1997, Bundesliga championships in 1995 and 1996, and UEFA Cup Final defeats in 1993 and 2002 – indeed, stretching back in time, of Borussia Dortmund beating Bill Shankly's Liverpool in Glasgow to win the European Cup Winners' Cup Final in 1966.

In 2008 Borussia Dortmund were a middle-of-the-table club – just. They had finished 13th in the league, were beaten in the DFB Cup Final by Bayern Munich, and coach Thomas Doll was shown the door. In came Jürgen Klopp, from coaching FSV Mainz 05, and with a promise of 'full-throttle football', Borussia Dortmund's adventure was underway.

And Klopp's love affair with the club's huge support at their Westfalenstadion was instant. 'The first few times you come to our stadium, and you see 80,000 fans there, you think: Wow! And it never becomes routine. You get the same rush every time you come here. It sends a shiver down your spine, every single time.'

The Dortmund fans took to Klopp and loved his style of all-action football. Klopp's achievements at Borussia Dortmund (BVB) were outstanding. Two Bundesliga titles (2011 and 2012), the DFB Cup winners (2012) and UEFA Champions League finalists 2013. When he announced he would be leaving, in the midst of a disappointing 2014/15 season, it was an emotional BVB sporting director Michael Zork who said, 'Over the last seven years we have written a modern football fairy tale, with Jürgen Klopp playing the main role.'

Klopp's farewell to the people at Dortmund's final league game of the season was equally emotional, the crowd loudly expressing their appreciation for his time at their club. 'It's never important what people think of someone when he arrives. What is important is what people think when he goes. I would like to thank everyone for what they think now. We will take that with us, pack it up. And regardless of where we'll land in the world, we'll never forget this.'

Jürgen Klopp was about to land in Merseyside, and quickly become the perfect fit for Liverpool Football Club, for the Anfield faithful, the city of Liverpool and the Premier League.

The man who had written a university thesis on 'Walking' as part of a sports science diploma while studying in Frankfurt had joined a football club where he would learn very quickly 'You Never Walk Alone'.

Liverpool had a fitful start to the 2015/16 season and, on 4 October, just one hour after a 1-1 draw in the season's first derby match at Goodison Park, Brendan Rodgers was sacked. The Reds were lying in tenth place after eight games, and four days after Rodgers's departure, Jürgen Klopp signed a three-year deal with Liverpool, and the new era was about to unfold.

Although it started with a 0-0 draw at Tottenham Hotspur, two impressive away wins at Chelsea and Manchester City, gave us Liverpool fans a sense of confidence in our new man at the top. But it was an unlikely episode in a league encounter against West Bromwich Albion at Anfield in mid-December that set Klopp apart from others.

The Reds had scrambled a point in a 2-2 draw with an equaliser deep in injury time from Divock Origi. Not really a result on which to push the boat out. By now, we were getting used to Jürgen Klopp's fist-pumping celebrations, and the odd celebratory dance down the touchline. And we enjoyed seeing it – sort of. And he certainly put all those elements together reacting to Origi's late, late strike against West Brom.

On the final whistle, he gathered his players together and they all joined hands, walking towards and ultimately saluting the Kop. Opposition fans ridiculed the Reds for celebrating an innocuous draw in a routine mid-December league match.

Klopp was totally unconcerned. The post-match gesture was to remind the players that they were playing for those fans, and for the fans to realise they were part of the team as well. 'I wanted to show we really are *one* unit; that means I am responsible for the performance, but the people are responsible for the atmosphere. It should be a win-win situation – when we play well it's easy to get the crowd going and when they don't play well, we need you to encourage us – get on your feet, tell us "COME ON" – you have to be the stars then.'

Klopp was building the emotional connection between the players and the supporters, which had worked so well for him at Mainz and Dortmund. And the Liverpool fans didn't need telling twice. Their leader was saying it as he saw it, and in perfect English, and his soon-to-be devoted followers totally bought into it.

One of the things that really struck me about Jürgen Klopp was his massive enthusiasm for his players, the fans and the club. But what was also apparent was an intelligent sense of perspective. Sport was sport – winning football matches was important, but other things mattered more.

And, in that context, one of the most important victories for all those associated with the Anfield club was achieved off the field of play. In April 2016, after years of fighting for the truth and justice for their lost loved ones who died in the Hillsborough disaster, a second set of inquests, held in a nondescript business park on the outskirts of Warrington, established that the 96 who perished were unlawfully killed, that the policing on the day had been negligent, and the fans were not to blame for any element of the disaster.

The city of Liverpool was united in celebrating that the truth was now accepted – the next step would be justice. The journey would continue from inquests to criminal courts for this remarkable set of people who had been determined to get both the truth and justice for the innocent victims of a disaster that could, and should, have been avoided.

Jürgen Klopp's first part-season with Liverpool ended with them finishing eighth in the Premier League, and out of the European qualification places. Leicester City had surprised all avid football watchers, and entranced the whole nation, by winning the Premier League. Fairy-tale stuff.

For Liverpool, the wait went on ...

An FA Cup fourth-round replay exit by West Ham United was disappointing. Now beginning to feel like a poor relation to the Premier League, Liverpool's form in the FA Cup would continue to falter down the seasons. It is 15 years and counting since Liverpool won the FA Cup, and nine years since we appeared in the final. Perhaps I'm a little old school but I still think the competition has real merit, not least giving the fans a great day out at Wembley.

Klopp's Reds did better in the League Cup, reaching the final where they met Manchester City. Liverpool had won two penalty shoot-outs on route to the final, firstly against lowly Carlisle at Anfield (3-2) having drawn the game 1-1.

And in the two-legged semi-final with Stoke City, the Reds won the away leg 1-0, and then lost the home leg by the same score. The penalty shoot-out that followed was won 6-5 by Klopp's men.

The final itself was won by Manchester City on penalties (3-1) after the two teams finished 1-1 after extra time, Coutinho having levelled for Liverpool late in normal time. Liverpool's exploits in the Europa League saw them top their group unbeaten, but with just two wins in the six games.

The post-Christmas knockout games included a double-header against Manchester United, which ended in a 3-1 aggregate win for Klopp's Reds. The Europa League quarter-final pitched Liverpool against the German coach's former club Borussia Dortmund. They were both emotionally charged occasions, the first leg in Dortmund ending 1-1.

The second leg at Anfield was another of those very special European nights, the very DNA of the club. Borussia Dortmund got two early goals and had seemingly put the tie beyond Liverpool – Origi scored early in the second half to briefly reduce the arrears. Dortmund scored again. Liverpool needed three goals to go through and only half an hour to do it. With the home crowd playing their part, as Klopp had demanded, goals by Coutinho, Sakho and an injury-time header from Lovren secured the most unlikely of victories in a stadium that was in raptures.

The final itself, in the St Jakob-Park, Basle, saw Liverpool facing Spanish side Seville. The Reds had beaten another Spanish side, Villarreal, in the semi-final but Seville were a different proposition altogether. They were chasing a hat-trick of Europa League wins, and a fifth in all.

Daniel Sturridge put the Reds ahead shortly before half-time, but a defensive error by Alberto Moreno (we all groaned) let in Gameiro and Coke, the Seville captain, followed it up with a brace of goals. Game, set and match to the Spaniards, and Liverpool's last route into the following season's European competitions had gone kaput!

A month later the UK decided we would all be out of Europe when the referendum to consider our future in the European Union narrowly voted for us to leave. Brexit was off and running (rather slowly)!

Kop That – *Sadio Mané was the first player to score a league goal against a Jürgen Klopp Liverpool side, doing so in a 1-1 draw with Southampton at Anfield. He would later score twice in a 3-2 defeat of the Reds at St Mary's, coming on at half-time, and also missed a penalty.*

Anfield's floral tribute to those who lost their lives at Hillsborough.

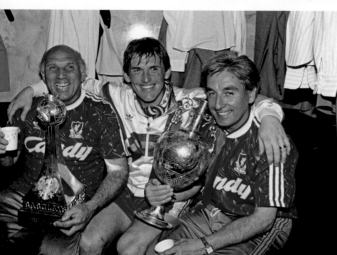

Enjoy it chaps … it will be another 30 years before we win the league again!

Steven Gerrard and Jamie Carragher in jubilant mood.

Jordan Henderson with the Champions League trophy – we've won it six times!

Liverpool's inspirational boss – Jürgen Klopp.

It is ours at last! Title win number 19 is secured!

Roger Hunt and Ray Wilson parade the World Cup around Goodison Park.

I have the honour of helping to unveil a statue of Barrow-born Emlyn Hughes.

Steven Gerrard and Fabio Capello in conversation – I listen in!

Gary Sprake own goal at Anfield – 'Careless Hands!'

I'm the man in the grey overcoat – keeping an eye on that number seven shirt.

Me and my best mate Andy Proudfoot with a very welcome new friend!

I always enjoy the company of Sir Kenny.

Pre-match chat with Ian Rush.

Best player, best team, bestseller!

An invitation to meet the Queen at Anfield.

The Magnificent Seven. Back row: Steve McManaman, Jamie Carragher, Dominic Matteo, Steven Gerrard. Front row: Michael Owen, David Thompson, Robbie Fowler – 2,697 Liverpool appearances between them!

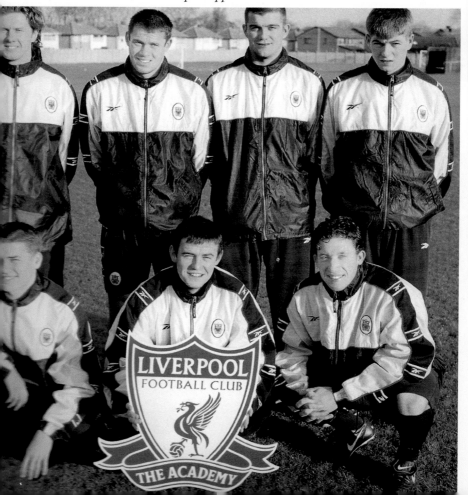

A special note from a special lady.

The pass that got me on the pitch … thankfully not to play for the Reds.

Liverpool training at Melwood – a half-term treat.

Two epic Champions League semi-finals.

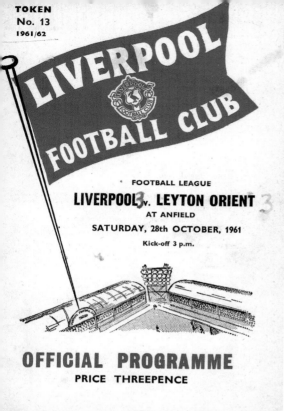

Liverpool v Leyton Orient, October 1961 – my first match.

Nelson Mandela proudly wearing his Liverpool shirt.

Liverpool FC set off for Iceland – the first steps on an incredible football journey for the Reds.

2016/17 – THIS IS ANFIELD

IN THE first week I started as CEO of the Football Association in February 2005, I was taken to a vast building site in north London – absolutely vast – and was told, 'This is your problem now!'

It had once been the home of the world's most famous football stadium, and now was the home of massive mechanical diggers, pile-drivers, pipes, drains, steel girders, hard hats by the thousands, and hard-luck stories by the millions of dollars. The hard-luck stories were all about why the completion of the new Wembley Stadium was heavily behind time and why the cost of the project was shooting up by the day.

On a slow news day, it would often pop up on the front page with headlines that made you shudder. I knew little or nothing about building stadiums – wouldn't trust myself to put up a set of shelves – but I did understand the simple mathematics of the numbers and there didn't seem to be a minus sign anywhere.

Eventually, we got the stadium built – the vast overspend was broadly the problem of the Australian construction company Multiplex – and the new Wembley Stadium, opened in April 2007, with its magical new arch, wowed people when they first visited it. With a capacity of 90,000 it became a destination point for many football fans from all over the world – you couldn't take 'Wembley' out of Wembley.

And Liverpool Football Club's new American owners recognised the same was true of Anfield, and set about extending, modernising and securing its future. This is who we are, and this is where we stay. The games, the goals, the legends, the noise, the wonderful history all captured in that original little stretch of land.

And fittingly, in the club's 125th year and its 55th consecutive season in the top flight of English football, the crowd capacity was increased, and its Main Stand was enlarged, towering above the pitch – an architectural masterpiece. The construction of the extended Main Stand started in December 2014 and was opened to the public on 9 September 2016, with the Reds hosting the new champions Leicester City in front of their biggest crowd since 1977.

The building work had taken the stadium capacity to 54,074 – a familiar size figure if you had watched Liverpool in the 1960s – with plans to extend the Anfield Road stand to take it up to 61,000.

Critically, Liverpool FC's future life looked guaranteed to stay on the same patch of land it had started out on way back in September 1892. Back then the team would have been 'over the moon' with an 7-1 win in their first-ever game, but they wouldn't have dreamed that man would have been actually walking on the moon some seven decades later. And that the club they helped kick-start would become a global sporting sensation.

As the sign says on the stairs leading down to the pitch, 'THIS IS ANFIELD', a message that inspired the home team for decades, and sent many an away team on to the pitch resigned to having a tough 90 minutes ahead of them. And long may that be the case.

Liverpool's preseason activity included participating in the International Champions Cup – another one of those 'cosmetic' tournaments that sound bigger than they really are.

My friends Andy and Ross Proudfoot built a holiday around the Reds' first two matches, played in the USA, against Chelsea and AC Milan.

And nearly 90,000 fans, myself included, turned up at Wembley Stadium to watch Liverpool play Barcelona on a hot Saturday afternoon in August. Whatever the relative status of the competition, it was fun to watch Liverpool, with their new £30m signing from Southampton, Sadio Mané, starring in a comprehensive 4-0 win. That scoreline against the Spanish giants has a familiar ring about it!

Mané opened the scoring, former Red Javier Mascherano put through his own goal a minute later, Origi added the third and Grujić completed the rout. You did get a sense that the Catalan maestros, including Lionel Messi and Luis Suárez, had just got off the sunbeds.

This had been a transfer window where Klopp began to build his squad. Mané, the influential Georgino Wijnaldum from Newcastle United for £23m, and free transfer Joël Matip came on board from Schalke 04, as did a goalkeeper from one of the German coach's old clubs, Mainz 05 – his name, Loris Karius. The biggest transfer out of the club was Christian Benteke, who left Anfield to join Crystal Palace for £27m after just one season. He would have his day in front of the Kop later that season.

With no European football on the Reds' menu, this was a season where Jürgen Klopp was able to bed in his culture and playing style with the group he had assembled. Roberto Firmino had arrived the previous summer, Sadio Mané was in, and Mo Salah would join the Reds in the summer of 2017, and that devastating three-pronged strike force would be complete. In his first season at Anfield, Sadio Mané, despite a late-season injury, made his mark as Liverpool's joint-leading scorer in the league with Philippe Coutinho – 13 apiece.

The Reds enjoyed remarkable success against their fellow top-six rivals during the 2016/17 season – five wins and five draws in ten matches – they also did the double over seventh-placed Everton, and won and lost against champions Leicester City. It was losing points against less-fancied opposition that held them back, possibly best illustrated by defeats to Burnley, Bournemouth and Hull City on the road, and to Swansea and Crystal Palace in front of the Kop.

On that day in April, Christian Benteke scored both goals for the Londoners, no doubt a sweet return to Anfield after his short unspectacular stay there. Too many draws and unexpected defeats cost Liverpool, but they qualified in fourth place for the following season's UEFA Champions League competition.

As usual the Reds dipped out early in the FA Cup, fielding their youngest-ever team up to that point in their third-round tie against Plymouth Argyle. The ploy backfired on Jürgen Klopp as a 0-0 draw meant another match in their fixture list, and a fair old distance to travel to play it. The replay was duly won but they went out in the next round to a 2-1 home defeat to Wolves.

The Reds fared better in the League Cup, reaching the semi-finals before being knocked out in the two-legged tie with Southampton. On route Ben Woodburn's goal against Leeds United made him the Reds' youngest-ever goalscorer at 17 years and 45 days. For Jürgen Klopp, it was a second and much fuller test of the English football scene, and it helped set him up for the seasons that followed.

And what seasons!! Strap yourselves in!

Kop That – *The home game with Leicester City saw Anfield record its highest league attendance (53,075) since the Reds drew with West Ham on 14 May 1977, when 55,675 saw the club clinch the title.*

2017/18 – SECOND IS NOWHERE

IN LATE spring 2017 I took a phone call from the Mayor of Liverpool's office. The ensuing conversation was both a complete surprise and a potentially exacting challenge. I was invited to be the chairman of the city's bid for the 2026 Commonwealth Games. No mean task but what a great privilege to do something so positive for my home town.

I had major experience across the competitive worlds of top-class sport and sports broadcasting, a strong network in the media and experience of how to put together bids of this nature. But the real appeal was to lead the bid on behalf of the city I was born and raised in, and to repay it for the many qualities it had embedded in me.

I said yes, and gathered a set of top professionals across the fields of activity we would need to put together a winning proposal. It became clear that Birmingham would be our main domestic rival for the Games.

To give our newly assembled team a sense of purpose and direction I held our first meeting in the Shankly Hotel in the city centre. I hoped a little bit of the great man's lustre would rub off on us all, and I think it did, although the odd Evertonian in our midst looked a bit sceptical.

Our bid – now for 2022, not 2026 – as Durban had defaulted on hosting the earlier date, was dynamic, exciting, original and used all the tick boxes a major event would benefit from by being held in Liverpool (with support from Manchester). Both our Premier League clubs got heavily involved – Everton's new stadium (if/when built) would host the athletics; Anfield would be the venue for the opening ceremony and the rugby sevens.

We took the Commonwealth Games decision-makers around Goodison Park (earmarked for the boxing competition) and Peter Moores, the new CEO at Anfield, gave our guests an extensive tour of LFC's legendary stadium, including the splendid new hospitality areas and the massive modern dressing rooms.

Over lunch in the main Anfield boardroom, with the walls laden with trophies and photos of the glory days, former Liverpool greats Robbie Fowler, Mark Lawrenson and Alan Kennedy popped in to say hello to the Commonwealth Games folk, and, in a short speech, I was able to joke with our staunch Evertonian mayor that if he didn't recognise the unusual smell in the room, it was silver polish!

In Liverpool's first home league game of the season against Crystal Palace, a large banner was unveiled in the centre circle asking everybody to 'Back Your Bid'. It had been a hectic few months, ones in which I truly re-engaged with the city and its unique appeal. And I thought we made a compelling case.

When the decision was made, Birmingham won the day. I was disappointed but proud of how the people of Liverpool had embraced the bid, and knew we had made a great impression and that major sporting bodies would now have their eye on Liverpool as a potential venue for their future events. As, indeed, has been the case, but for a few days it did feel that in a competition like that, as Bill Shankly once said, 'First is first, second is nowhere.'

That match against Crystal Palace did give me an early look at two of the new players Jürgen Klopp had brought to Anfield in the close season. Mohamed Salah had been signed from Roma for ultimately £43.9m. Salah had a short spell at Chelsea and had not made an impact there, but Liverpool's scouting team persuaded Klopp that he was the real deal. The rest is history.

Mo Salah would become a scoring sensation and his teaming up with fellow frontmen Roberto Firmino and Sadio Mané became simply irresistible to us Liverpool fans – unstoppable to our opponents.

Andy Robertson was a relatively loose-change purchase at £8m from relegated Hull City, but what an asset. He had the energy to work forwards and backwards, an essential element of Klopp's playing style. And when I left Anfield that August afternoon, I thought Liverpool had found themselves a promising full-back as well as a possible new striker. In fact, with man of the match Robertson and Salah, Klopp now had both of those modern essentials on his books.

I don't know what we all expected from the new 25-year-old Egyptian striker, and what is it that our men at Anfield spotted that those at Chelsea hadn't?

But Mo Salah was *the* sensation of 2017/18 season – a phenomenal 44 goals in 52 appearances, including 32 in the Premier League alone. He won the PFA Players' Player of the Year, the FWA Footballer of the Year and the Premier League Golden Boot. He also finished third in the 2018 Best FIFA Men's Player, and was African Player of the Year in both 2017 and 2018.

Between them, Salah, Roberto Firmino and Sadio Mané made 150 first-team appearances, with only a handful of those as substitutes. They were the hottest strike force in world football, and a perfect element of Jürgen Klopp's 'gegenpressing' style of play. It was 'full-throttle' football with the emphasis of winning back possession of the ball as quickly as possible after losing it, and as far up the field as could be achieved. It was a counter-pressing philosophy.

It demanded a huge physical commitment from the players. They had to think and act fast, have incredible stamina, both physical and mental, be technically proficient, have tactical discipline, and the full-backs and wing-backs had to be incredibly fit to manage both their attacking and defensive responsibilities. He expected both from players in those positions. Those were the basic attributes the Liverpool players needed under Klopp. As a fan the results were mind-blowing. It delivered some of the most exciting football *ever* seen at Anfield.

Some great examples were witnessed in that season's UEFA Champions League competition.

Liverpool won their group stage, scoring 23 goals in the six matches, including two 7-0 wins, in Maribor and against Spartak Moscow at Anfield.

Coutinho scored a hat-trick in that game but was off to Barcelona in the January transfer window. A sparkling little magician of a player left Anfield to join Messi and Suárez at the Camp Nou. The money Liverpool received for Coutinho, around £140m, was spent very wisely, buying a world-class defender in Virgil van Dijk in the same transfer window, and a world-class goalkeeper, Alisson, later that summer. More on both later.

The knockout stages of the Champions League saw Liverpool win 5-0 in Porto, and then in the quarter-finals against Manchester City they produced a stunning opening half hour – 3-0 up in 31 minutes. The tie was all but won, and a 2-1 win at the Etihad closed the show.

The Reds did it again in the semi-finals, smashing five past Roma inside 70 minutes in an emphatic first-leg win at Anfield.

The Italians pulled two late goals back to slightly spoil the fun but couldn't turn around the aggregate in the second leg.

Now, as a fan, we've all had one of those occasions when we haven't been able to make a very important match because of an unfortunate clash of dates. So, on the night Liverpool were putting Roma to the sword in the UEFA Champions League semi-final with yet another exhilarating display, I was wriggling in my seat in the Royal Albert Hall watching that talented actress Sheridan Smith, who we all loved in the ITV drama *Cilla*, strutting her stuff at a venue where many of the all-time greats had appeared. It had been a Christmas present from my wife Gerry. And a very thoughtful one too. But she did wonder why my phone pinged five times during the concert. My son Joe was under strict instructions to keep me up to date with affairs at another world-famous venue 200 miles away, in Cilla's birthplace, of course.

Without being morbid, every time Liverpool reach the UEFA Champions League Final – which I occasionally still call the European Cup Final just to wait to be corrected by the person next to me – I always wonder if I'll be around to see the Reds the next time they are in it. In Liverpool's case I would only have to wait a year after our miserable defeat against Real Madrid in Kiev before we were doing a flamenco in Madrid.

I did enjoy the trip to Kiev for various reasons. Firstly, I was going as a fan, not a 'suit'; secondly, I could have a gentle beer with my mates before the game instead of engaging in the small talk attached to attending these games in an official capacity. And thirdly, it was more of an adventure. And, in truth, a lot more fun.

In going over to Kiev, I was likely to miss the Summer Bash, a weekend of matches from the second tier of English rugby league held in one location – Blackpool. Always a lively occasion as you can imagine and one, as chairman of the Rugby Football League, I was expected to attend. I had let my rugby league colleagues down lightly, saying I was expected to be at the European Cup Final. 'You mean the Champions League Final,' said three guys in unison. 'Oh, yeah, that.' But I did have a cunning plan.

My weekend started at Euston Station in London, where I caught a Friday afternoon train to Liverpool. I checked into a hotel before being woken at 3am, had a quick shower and shave, and ordered a taxi to pick up my mate Greg in the suburbs. Off to John Lennon Airport where we checked in and boarded a plane full of excited Reds fans who knew all the words to all the songs. It was 7am. We arrived in Kiev around Saturday lunchtime and were given our instructions about where and when to meet after the game.

The meeting didn't seem to take in the possibility of extra time. I did point that out, and was told, 'Well, then it is every man for himself.' 'In Kiev!?!' I said. And realised these guys were experienced travellers with the Reds and I had become a bit of a softie.

Greg and I found a nice restaurant near the stadium and settled in for the afternoon. We were soon joined by two other mates, Andy and Ross. The afternoon flew by discussing best Liverpool teams, worst Liverpool teams, best home match, worst away match, best player, worst player – all that sort of seminal fans' stuff.

Things were going along nicely until a guy who had been staring at me for some considerable time came over and said, 'I recognise you. I know who you are.' I gave him a rather tiresome look expecting him to regale to me the high points of my extensive career in sport and broadcasting. 'Yeah, I've got it now. You're the guy off *Mrs Brown's Boys*!'

Never has my pomposity been so pomped!!

The match itself was a let-down. We never really got going. Sergio Ramos's 'half-Nelson' on Salah took our main man out of the game. Our goalkeeper Loris Karius had a nightmare (late candidate for worst goalkeeper) and Gareth Bale proved to be a more potent substitute than even David Fairclough had been.

We made it safely back to the bus and were the first plane out of Kiev (fair dos – well done the organisers). We arrived at John Lennon Airport around 6am Sunday morning and a car picked me up and took me straight up to Blackpool, where I grabbed a few hours' sleep before heading to Bloomfield Road to watch the start of day two the Summer Bash.

Some bright spark came over and said, 'Eh … Barwick, I didn't see you here yesterday.'

'No, I was in Kiev.'

'Kiev. Bloody Kiev. What were you doing there? Watching the bloody European Cup Final !?!'

'No, the Champions League Final.' And having corrected him I went off to buy a stick of Blackpool rock.

Kop That – *In October 2017, the Centenary Stand at Anfield was renamed the Kenny Dalglish Stand – later changed to the Sir Kenny Dalglish Stand in August 2018 following the Liverpool great deservedly receiving a knighthood in June 2018.*

2018/19 – A SEASON OF
THE EXTRAORDINARY

LIVERPOOL'S CHAMPIONS League semi-final recovery from a 3-0 first-leg defeat in Barcelona has already taken on legendary status, which I believe will not wither in time.

In the Catalan capital, Liverpool had played reasonably well but Lionel Messi (two) and Luis Suárez scored the goals that looked certain to take their club to the UEFA Champions League Final – a short-haul flight to Madrid, and Atlético's spanking new Estadio Metropolitano. It had been a tough result for the Reds in Barcelona, capped by Messi scoring his 600th goal for the club, a stunning free kick in the game's 82nd minute.

I still believe a turning point in the whole tie came six minutes deep into injury time of this first leg, when Semedo and Messi combined to give Dembélé a gilt-edged chance to score a fourth goal for the home side. He fluffed his lines from eight yards out – Alisson saved his tame effort, and suddenly 3-0 looked a whole lot better than 4-0.

Having been around football a long time I have heard the 'let's take the positives out of the game' mantra when a side has been soundly beaten. Not losing 4-0 was the positive.

Six days later, a packed-to-the-rafters Anfield was ready to roar Liverpool on through 'Mission Impossible'. Although as the game had got closer, the Reds coach Jürgen Klopp had grown in the belief that his players could actually turn the tables on the brilliant Spanish side, and so, increasingly, did his players.

An early goal was an essential it seemed, Divock Origi notching after just seven minutes. The Anfield noise levels went up, and when Andy Robertson ruffled Messi's hair and Suárez faced a chorus of boos every time the ball went near him, you just felt it was possible – perhaps.

Into the second half and substitute Gini Wijnaldum, disappointed not to be a starter, scored twice in the 54th and 56th minutes. He only scored five goals all season. More extraordinary. The tie was now level on aggregate. But only one team's players had the heads and hearts to deliver the killer blow. This was already destined to be one of Anfield's greatest European nights – perhaps its greatest – the crowd driving the Reds forward.

And yet amid the red-hot atmosphere at Anfield, it was the ice-cool thinking of 20-year-old Trent Alexander-Arnold, the Reds' foraging full-back, who provided the coup de grâce. It was a corner kick at the Kop end – a quick-thinking ballboy sent Trent the ball, who noticed the Barcelona players were still getting into position to defend the set piece. In a split second of inspired thinking, Trent played a short pass into the penalty area.

Origi, a scorer of important Liverpool goals, picked up on Trent's vibe, and was calmness personified as he stroked the ball into the net. It was simplicity itself. Simple but genius. Everybody looked at the officials to see whether it was legal – it was. Cue bedlam in the stadium.

Liverpool captain Jordan Henderson recalled the match-clincher:

'It was an amazing goal to score in a game of that magnitude. It was fantastic for a young player to have the awareness to be able to do that, and put in the ball, and for Divock to react to that. It was an amazing goal that summed up an amazing night.'

Barcelona still had time to grab a decisive away goal, but they were shot – mentally destroyed.

Liverpool had delivered, and never has 'You'll Never Walk Alone' been sung louder and with such feeling. Jürgen Klopp summed it up. 'It is a night to remember forever.' The Red Army would be on the march again, for their ninth European Cup/Champions League Final.

To Atlético Madrid's Estadio Metropolitano, the 31st venue for European football's show-stopping event. And their opponents would be old European adversaries Ajax ... no, hold that headline ... it's going to be English rivals Tottenham Hotspur.

Spurs had lost their semi-final home first leg to Ajax 1-0, and were trailing 2-0 in the second leg, before staging an astonishing comeback themselves, with their Brazilian striker Lucas Moura scoring a second-half hat-trick, his tie-clinching goal coming in the sixth minute of added time.

Tottenham Hotspur FC v Liverpool FC would be the UEFA Champions League Final on 1 June 2019 – an all-English affair on a sultry summer's evening in the heart of Spain.

This would be the season that probably disproved Bill Shankly's mantra about 'First is first, second is nowhere', because Liverpool's record in the Premier League that season was simply staggering and worthy of much, much more.

They collected 97 points, the third-highest total in the history of the English top division, the highest total for a team not winning the title. They remained unbeaten at home for the second season in a row and matched the club record of 30 wins in a season. They led the Premier League frequently during the season, including being on top on New Year's Day.

In the summer window, Klopp had brought in a world-class goalkeeper Alisson for £55.5m. He proved to be a phenomenally successful purchase, his save against Napoli in the Champions League worth its weight in gold alone. Also coming on board at Anfield were Naby Keïta, Xherdan Shaqiri and Brazilian Fabinho.

The Reds' end-of-season Premier League stats take some believing: P:38, W:30, D:7, L:1 PTS:97. Liverpool had to settle for second place, a massive 25 points ahead of Chelsea in third position. They also scored 89 goals, conceding only 22 during the league season. Manchester City pipped the Reds to the title by a single point, having lost three more games than their Merseyside rivals. Critically, Pep Guardiola's men took four points off the Reds in the two matches against each other.

I was invited as a guest by Liverpool Football Club to their first match-up at Anfield in October. And LFC CEO Peter Moores took me down pitchside to watch the team in their prematch warm-up. I wished Jürgen Klopp good luck on the way back up the tunnel and settled into my seat in the stand.

The match itself fell flat. 0-0. Mind you it could have been worse – Riyad Mahrez putting a late-game penalty high over the bar. That particular penalty 'conversion' would have been more appropriate the following month when I had the privilege of bringing rugby league's England and New Zealand teams to Anfield to play the second match of a three-match Test series. England had won the first match at the KC Stadium in Hull.

All the stars were aligned for me on that early November Sunday afternoon – as a proud Scouser I was chuffed to bring international rugby league to Anfield. England won the match to clinch the series and St Helens's Tommy Makinson scored a hat-trick of spectacular tries. And a crowd of over 26,000 enjoyed the action.

In 2019, when I stepped down from my role as the sport's chairman, I was presented with a huge framed photographic montage of that day – a fantastic memento of my favourite afternoon in that job.

The second match between Manchester City and Liverpool fell on 3 January and the Reds went down to their only defeat of the season – 2-1. Liverpool would go one better in terms of league position the following season, but make no mistake on this occasion finishing second was 'somewhere special', not 'nowhere' as previously quoted. It was an extraordinary performance by Jürgen Klopp's men, week in, week out. But they didn't end the season without a marvellous finale of their own.

As the plane took off from Heathrow Airport to take my son Joe and I to Madrid for the UEFA Champions League Final, I couldn't help but reminisce. This was Liverpool's ninth European Cup Final/Champions League Final and I'd been at them all.

The five victories were each unique in their own way. In 1977 I was just 22 when I set off by train from Lime Street to Rome, an adventure and a massive football match all rolled into five short days. Now at 64 I was working out whether to have the beef or chicken and what to wash it down with as we flew across the continent.

Liverpool's win at Wembley against Bruges in 1978 was a bit of an anticlimax as this time the journey had taken just two and a half hours – easy peasy ... mind you, there must have been 50,000 Liverpool fans travelling in the same direction at the same time.

1981 – a couple of pleasant evenings in Paris, and the Kennedys securing the Reds victory over Real Madrid. Three years later, it was back to Rome combining TV work for the BBC with the pleasure of taking my wife Gerry with me, as Bruce Grobbelaar's 'wobbly legs' spooked the Roma penalty takers.

And 2005, the unforgettable night in Istanbul. Me, properly suited and booted representing the FA, but supporting Liverpool, as became perfectly clear to the assembled dignitaries as the Reds came from behind to lift that magnificent trophy in another European night never to be forgotten. All great memories.

Madrid was full of Liverpool and Tottenham Hotspur fans mixing amicably. Their respective fan parks were absolutely buzzing. It seemed Liverpool fans had come to see their team put the previous year's defeat to Real Madrid behind them, by winning this all-English affair.

Without being disrespectful it seemed to me that the Spurs fans couldn't quite get their heads around the fact they were actually in the Champions League Final. The last European trophy they had won was the UEFA Cup back in 1984, the same season Liverpool were winning their fourth European Cup.

The game was almost won and lost in the first couple of minutes – Sissoko was penalised for a harsh handball and the resulting penalty was dispatched by Mr Reliable, Mo Salah. To be fair the rest of the game was pretty turgid until in the 87th minute Divock Origi picked up a loose end from a corner and drilled the ball home. Origi – the scorer of important goals. That will be his Anfield legacy.

Like all Liverpudlians I enjoyed the moment enormously, and when the final whistle went, I was as excited as I had been back in 1977. 64 or 22. Once a football fan, always a football fan.

As we left the stadium our Joe was on the mobile, sorting us out an Uber in a foreign capital to get us back to the hotel on the outskirts of town. I realised I was falling behind the times. Mind you, when we got back to the hotel, we sat in their garden, ordered two pints of lager (the first two of many) and two large pizzas and relived the game. I felt like a king. Happy days.

Kop That – *Divock Origi has scored five European goals for Liverpool, all in memorable games – the 1-1 draw and 4-3 defeat of Dortmund in 2016 and then two against Barcelona in the 2019 semi-final and one in the subsequent final.*

2019/20 – CHAMPIONS!!!!

THE ORDER had been taken over the phone. 'A portion of crispy duck and some prawn crackers for starters, sweet and sour pork as a main course with egg fried rice on the side, please.' Right, that's the Chinese takeaway all sorted out.

A decent bottle of supermarket plonk was chilling away in the fridge … with a bottle of champagne nestling beside it. The former would get rapidly consumed over the next two hours, the latter hopefully popped open after that. Dependent on the result.

Venue – our house. Activity – watching live coverage of the Premier League match between Chelsea and Manchester City on BT Sport. And we'd be watching the version with the phoney sound effects.

This was how all of us were watching our Premier League football from June 2020 after Covid-19 had invaded our bodies, vastly disrupted our personal lives and turned the whole world upside down.

Horrendous death tolls across the globe, and, at that moment in time, seemingly no way of halting the virus's pernicious progress. It had stopped the daily life of the UK in its tracks since March 2020 – lockdown having kicked in – and, like many other occupations and pastimes, the nation's favourite sport had been mothballed.

Great supporters like my friends Andy and Ross, home and away Liverpool fans for decades, were housebound, and like every Reds supporter frustrated beyond belief, because this season our club was on course to win their first title in 30 years. And very convincingly too.

Jürgen Klopp's men had been denied by a single point in the previous season. This time they were leading from the front (they led the league every day from 17 August), and when the shutters temporarily had to come down on the season, they had already garnered a fantastic haul of 82 points from only 29 games. Manchester City were their closest rival but were trailing the Reds by a massive 25 points.

On the last weekend of Premier League action before the season was brought to a halt Liverpool beat Bournemouth 2-1, whilst Manchester City lost 2-0 to neighbours Manchester United. That left the Reds just six points short of winning the title with still nine games left to play. The potential injustice of not being allowed to finish the season or it even being ruled null and void were played out in the media. All types of theories abounded.

Given the scale of Liverpool's dominance of the season thus far, every fair-minded person could see how unjust Liverpool not being awarded the title would be. But the Reds hadn't crossed the finishing line yet. They wanted to win it on the pitch. They didn't want the record books to name them as champions, but with an asterisk alongside their achievement.

When the country came out of lockdown, some sport was encouraged to get underway. Premier League football, with its massive broadcast contracts to fulfil, was in the vanguard of the return of something familiar to a beaten-up public. After allowing time for teams to prepare properly, and playing behind closed doors, Premier League football got underway. Every game would be televised live.

The first game for Liverpool was a derby match against Everton at Goodison Park on 21 June – my 66th birthday. 0-0. Three days later the Reds beat Crystal Palace 4-0 at Anfield – great efforts had been made to 'dress' the stadium with all the marvellous flags and banners tracing Liverpool's unique history and heroes. Fantastic folk art, and a genuinely special part of the Reds identity. Inventive, amusing, poignant. Like all the songs we sing. Something we are justly proud of.

That win against former Reds boss Roy Hodgson's men meant if Manchester City lost at Stamford Bridge the following night, Liverpool would be named league champions for the first time since 1990.

Liverpool's season thus far had been sensational. They added the UEFA Super Cup to their Champions League triumph. Their penalty shoot-out win over Chelsea in Istanbul, after Mané had notched a double in their 2-2 draw, was the fourth time they had won this trophy.

I headed up to Turf Moor to see the Reds' early-season game against Burnley, who were brushed aside 3-0. This was the game when Sadio Mané publicly showed his frustration at what he perceived to be Mo Salah's selfishness in front of goal. As it was, Roberto Firmino's goal in that game made him the first Brazilian to score 50 goals in English football's top flight.

The Reds were blowing away the other members of the supposed 'Big Six' – Arsenal 3-1, Chelsea 2-1, Tottenham 2-1, Manchester City 3-1, but perhaps it was their gutsy 1-1 draw at Old Trafford, with a late leveller from Adam Lallana, that underlined the Anfield men's determination not to be blown off course in their title tilt.

In the first week of December, neighbours Everton were put to the sword with a thumping-big 5-2 win for the Reds at Anfield. Divock Origi scored twice, adding 2019 derby goals to those he had scored in 2016, 2017 and 2018. Mané's goal that evening was also very special. 'Wonderful goals, sensational passes, super pieces of football. I loved it a lot.'

That was Jürgen Klopp's view of his 100th victory in the Premier League, and 15 games into the season, the Reds had won 14 and drawn one, and already had 43 points on the scoreboard. Liverpool's five Premier League wins in December kept Klopp's men way ahead of their rivals, and the month also marked the club's first win in FIFA's Club World Cup.

Staged in the Khalifa International Stadium in Doha, Qatar, Liverpool beat Brazilians Flamengo to lift their third trophy in six months. Having beaten Monterrey in the semi-final, Roberto Firmino's goal was enough to clinch the title of 'world champions' for Liverpool Football Club. Whatever the merits of this particular competition, anything that allows you to call yourselves 'world champions' sounds okay to me!

Liverpool's Club World Cup trek meant they had to play their youngsters in their League Cup tie at Aston Villa. The home side were just too good, winning easily 5-0.

The Reds had got to that point in the competition by winning another penalty shoot-out, their third of the season, after drawing 5-5 (yes, five-five!) with Arsenal at Anfield. Curtis Jones scored the winning spot kick – he would also score the only goal in a third-round FA Cup tie with Everton.

At the halfway point of the Premier League season Liverpool were top of the league with 18 wins and a draw from their 19 games – a quite extraordinary record. And still the wins kept coming – Sheffield United, Tottenham Hotspur, Manchester United, West Ham (twice), Southampton, Wolves, Norwich City. They finally lost their first league game on 29 February at Watford, but this leap year would be remembered more widely for the savage intrusion into everyday life by Covid-19 – the world over.

The Reds' final match before football was suspended was a home defeat by Atlético Madrid in the Champions League round of 16, which knocked the holders out of the competition. There was heavy criticism that the match had actually been allowed to take place, especially with a sizeable number of fans travelling over from Spain.

Football, like everything we all loved in life, was put on hold, as over-busy hospitals up and down the country fought to save the lives of increasing numbers of people fighting the wilful effects of the pandemic.

Fast forward to June: the Chinese takeaway had arrived, the bottle of white wine had already been under heavy attack and the TV tuned into affairs at Stamford Bridge. 'Come on, Chelsea!'

And I wasn't alone in those sentiments. My phone had buzzed all day with Liverpool-supporting mates telling me how they were willing Chelsea on to do the business that night.

And, gratifyingly, I took a lot of calls from other friends – some football nuts, some not – wishing me luck. Just knowing how much Liverpool winning the league title meant to me (and tens of thousands of other people).

The result of the match was never really in doubt – Chelsea were chasing points themselves and went into the lead through their American Christian Pulisic after 36 minutes. Kevin de Bruyne levelled for City, but Willian smashed home a penalty to give Chelsea three points … And at the final whistle, Liverpool had won the Premier League title.

Cue pandemonium on Merseyside, and all points north, south, east and west! And, yes, those champagne corks were popping in the Barwick household.

After a long 30 years, Liverpool were back, where many believed they belonged – top dogs in English football's elite division.

Perhaps it was the oddest of their 19 title wins, but in many ways one of their best, certainly in terms of the manner they had won it. They had created all sorts of records. Here are just some:

- For the first time in their history Liverpool beat every team in a league season.
- They set a new club record of 13 league 'doubles' in a season.
- They set a new club best of 14 away wins in a league campaign.
- They set a new club record of 99 points in a season.
- They remained unbeaten at Anfield for a third consecutive season.
- They won the latest-ever league title – confirmed on 25 June.
- They set a new club record of eight away wins in a row.
- They set a new club record by scoring in the opening 27 games of a league season.
- And they became the first British team to hold the European Cup, European Super Cup, FIFA Club World Cup and league titles simultaneously.

On 22 July 2020, Liverpool entertained Chelsea, and then those two teams entertained everybody else with a frantic, fabulous, end-of-season tussle which ended with a 5-3 win for the new Premier League champions.

Once the match was complete, the scene was reset inside an empty Anfield. Under floodlights and spotlights, and after a total of 1,156 league games, club captain Jordan Henderson lifted the trophy that symbolised that Liverpool were champions of England. Again. At last. The celebrations went on for days ... and days.

Kop That – *Dejan Lovren (Croatia), Mo Salah (Egypt), Naby Keïta (Guinea) and Sadio Mané (Senegal) became the first players from their respective countries to win a Premier League winners medal.*

2020/21 – ALISSON IN WONDERLAND

THERE MAY have been better goals scored among the 68 netted by the reigning Premier League champions Liverpool in the season that followed their great title triumph – maybe.

But for sheer chutzpah, impact, devilment and importance, goalkeeper Alisson's brilliantly headed goal takes the biscuit for me and many others. Normally, goalkeepers go up into the opposing team's penalty area, for a last-minute corner, as the last throw of the dice if their team is behind. They go really to cause confusion, not to jump and direct a header perfectly into the opposite corner of the net.

The Brazilian's unlikely intervention five minutes into injury time turned a late-season mediocre 1-1 draw at already-relegated West Bromwich Albion into a vital 2-1 win which gave Jürgen Klopp's squad the psychological boost to go on and take maximum points from their final two games and clinch a surprise third place in the league table, and a slot in the next season's UEFA Champions League.

Alisson had suffered a personal tragedy earlier in the year when his father drowned in a lake back in his home country. A hugely popular figure at Anfield, Alisson was unable to go back to Brazil to mourn his father's passing due to Covid travel restrictions. But after a short break, he returned to first-team duty and starred at both ends of the pitch. A very accomplished human being.

This season was very much 'after the Lord Mayor's show' for the Anfield men. The Premier League season started just seven weeks after the end of the Reds' glorious campaign. A penalty shoot-out defeat to Arsenal in the FA Community Shield was followed up with three league wins on the run – Leeds United, Chelsea and Arsenal the casualties.

Then on the first weekend of October Liverpool suffered an astonishing 7-2 defeat at the hands of Aston Villa. Ollie Watkins, a £30m purchase from Brentford, scored a first-half hat-trick and Villa led 4-1 at the break. At one point Liverpool trailed 6-1, and former Everton man Ross Barkley was on target and the talented Jack Grealish got a brace.

Watching the match on TV with me was my son Joe, an avid Aston Villa fan. The previous day, the amateur team he captains, Wandsworth Borough, had won a cup final which had been held over from the previous season, and now his favourite team were trouncing his dad's lot.

It was his happiest weekend in football! Not mine.

Worst was to come. In the following weekend's derby match, Everton goalkeeper Jordan Pickford's reckless challenge on Virgil van Dijk ended the Dutchman's season, just five matches into the new campaign. Also injured that day was another world-class player, Liverpool's close-season signing Thiago, again the victim of a tough hit. Injuries, and especially those at centre-back, became a recurring theme for Jürgen Klopp's team. At times, the German coach sounded like a cracked record as he listed those injured, and the particular problems they had in central defence. But he was right to point out that he was having to put together makeshift pairings at the back, especially as Joe Gomez and Joël Matip also suffered season-ending injuries.

Inspirational captain Jordan Henderson filled in on occasions, and the brilliant Fabinho, and over the season Klopp tried some of his younger squad players at the back, and used the winter transfer window to help ease the problem. Rhys Williams, Nat Phillips and loan star Ozan Kabak were three more recruits to Liverpool's back line, with Phillips, especially, making a series of promising performances.

But this was also a season when goals dried up at the other end of the pitch – 85 scored in their title-winning season, but just 68 in the campaign that followed. Mo Salah still chimed in with his share, narrowly missing out on winning the Premier League's Golden Boot with 22 goals, but his partners in crime, Mané and Firmino, only scored 20 between them.

Thankfully, the Reds' summer signing Diogo Jota from Wolves started brightly, until he too became another on Anfield's casualty list.

Despite the injury problems, and the odd hammering (Villa Park), the first half of the season, which included a 7-0 red blitz at Crystal Palace, was respectable – with too many draws – but following the frolics at Selhurst Park they went five league matches without a win.

After 68 matches without a league defeat at Anfield, Liverpool's famed invincibility at Anfield totally collapsed when following two home league draws, the Reds went on a bizarre run of *six* home defeats on the run. Burnley, Brighton, Manchester City, Everton, Chelsea and Fulham all took maximum points from their matches at a ground previously recognised as a footballing fortress.

If anything underlined the unique value of that special Anfield atmosphere, it was that set of results – two of the sides that beat them were relegated, and two more of the clubs were in the bottom six. What's more, in those six consecutive home defeats, Liverpool only scored one goal.

Playing behind closed doors seemed to affect the Reds more than other teams – they certainly missed the sense of encouragement and urgency they would have got from a packed stadium willing their team on. In time-honoured fashion, the Kop would have tried to suck the ball into the net for their heroes, but also would have given them a sharp collective verbal kick up the backside when needed as well.

Some people questioned whether Jürgen Klopp's gegenpressing expected too much of his players season after season, that they were just plain knackered. Whatever, Klopp's men found a second wind in the closing three months of the season – having won one league game in seven, the Reds went on a run of eight wins and two draws in the last ten games of the season.

And on the final day of the season their 2-0 win over Crystal Palace, and other results around them, left Liverpool in a very credible third place, in what had been a pretty incredible season.

Champions League football secured. Still the world game's top club competition. And, that will continue to be the case, despite the forlorn attempt by six of our biggest clubs, including Liverpool, and some of the rest of European football's most famous clubs, wanting to start a new competition – the European Super League.

No need to add phoney sound effects as a reaction to this proposal. It was resoundingly and deafeningly derided. English football fans rose as one and the men behind the idea summarily lined up to apologise. Including Liverpool's owner John W. Henry. The idea was killed off as quickly as it was leaked to the media.

Football might have had to be played in silent stadiums in recent times, but the fans were certainly in good voice when one of their special birthrights seemed to be about to be undermined. What it underlined was just how precious the famed football pyramid is in this country. I have just spent six years as chairman of the National League, the fifth and sixth tiers of English football.

And to be at Sutton United on the day they were crowned as our champions with a direct pass to the EFL told you everything that's good about a sport based on meritocracy, not sheer wealth.

And, in their 129 years of existence, Liverpool Football Club have enjoyed the spoils of that meritocracy many times over, with fans like me having enjoyed memorable times, unforgettable moments, life-affirming experiences.

And I have enjoyed 60 seasons of following my home-town club, from 'the most talked about city in Europe'. We have seen our team reign as league champions, FA Cup winners, European Cup winners – even world champions.

And we have watched a club grow into a world-famous, world-class sporting institution – revered across the globe. Unique, special but still 'our own'. And we've shared in the glory of it all.

And the sadness too – during the season just past we lost four very special personalities who served the club superbly in their own different ways – the brilliant goalkeeping of Ray Clemence, the ebullient forward play of Ian St John, the cultured football brain of manager Gérard Houllier, and the singer who gave us the anthem that defines the club – Gerry Marsden.

And in late July 2021, Liverpool fan, Andrew Devine, became the 97th victim of the Hillsborough disaster when he sadly passed away 32 years after that fateful day. Much-loved by family, friends and his team of dedicated carers, Andrew suffered life-changing injuries on that April afternoon, and, as with the other 96 victims, was deemed to have been unlawfully killed as a result of the tragedy.

Liverpool players and supporters paid an emotional tribute to him at their first home match of the new season against Burnley. And the fight for justice for the 97 victims continues.

* * *

Although I have had the privilege of watching Liverpool Football Club develop from many different perspectives over the last six decades, I still get a buzz when somebody asks me which team I support.

Firstly, I tell them it is Liverpool. And I then very quickly follow it up by saying I saw them first play when they were in the Second Division.

For me, being a supporter of Liverpool Football Club has indeed been a lifetime's passion.

Sixty years … and counting.

Kop That – *By playing in the European Championship Final in 2021, Jordan Henderson has now appeared in the Finals of the FA Cup, League Cup, European Super Cup, World Club and Champions League. He also played in the Community Shield and was an unused substitute in the Europa League in 2016.*

ONE FOR THE ROAD

AFTER MANY months faithfully writing this book I decided it was only right to set you, the reader, a challenge – the same one I have just set myself.

Having looked back over the past 60 years of the life and times of Liverpool Football Club I decided to give myself the task of selecting two different Liverpool teams from that period – one consisting of players from the Home Nations and Ireland and the other from the multitude of gifted foreign stars (and some less gifted) who have graced Anfield in more recent times.

I also wanted to properly reflect the complete six decades I have concentrated on in the previous pages.

Some will agree with my two line-ups (I've also allowed myself three substitutes per team) but many won't- and that's fine. If nothing else it is a good pub argument, or something with which to while away the time driving to the next match.

So here goes:

Liverpool (Home)	Liverpool (Away)
Ray Clemence	Alisson
Phil Neal	Markus Babbel
Alan Hansen	Virgil van Dijk ©
Jamie Carragher	Sami Hyypiä
Emlyn Hughes	John Arne Riise

Steven Gerrard ©   Philippe Coutinho
Graeme Souness   Xabi Alonso
John Barnes   Sadio Mané
Roger Hunt   Mo Salah
Ian Rush   Fernando Torres
Kenny Dalglish   Luis Suárez
Subs: Ian Callaghan   Subs: Gini Wijnaldum
      Robbie Fowler   Roberto Firmino
      Mark Lawrenson   Dietmar Hamann
Manager: Bill Shankly   Manager: Jürgen Klopp

Yes I know you will all have your own take on those selections – but the quality of those players and the two managers I've chosen shows how far our favourite football club have come in the past sixty years.

And the result of this fantasy match. Well, in October 1961, my first visit to Anfield ended in a 3-3 draw between Liverpool and Leyton Orient. So that's what I'm sticking to with this match ... 3-3 ... and an absolute classic it was too!